"Theology's engagement with popular music is growing apace. This diverse and highly readable collection provokes all the important questions in a vitally important field."

> — Jeremy Begbie
> Duke University
> Author of *Resounding Truth: Christian Wisdom in the World of Music*

"Scholars finally have a book that seriously engages theology and popular music through a variety of methodologies and musical genres. This is a must read for scholars of religion and popular culture and has definite classroom appeal. *Secular Music and Sacred Theology* teaches us that everyday popular music is an entry point into discussions of the serious contemporary theological issues."

> — Michelle A. Gonzalez
> University of Miami
> Author of *Shopping: Christian Explorations of Daily Living*

Secular Music
and
Sacred Theology

Edited by Tom Beaudoin

A Michael Glazier Book

LITURGICAL PRESS
Collegeville, Minnesota

www.litpress.org

A Michael Glazier Book published by Liturgical Press

Cover design by Jodi Hendrickson. Cover images: Thinkstock.

1	2	3	4	5	6	7	8	9

Library of Congress Cataloging-in-Publication Data

Secular music and sacred theology / edited by Tom Beaudoin.
    p.   cm.
    "A Michael Glazier book."
    Includes bibliographical references.
    ISBN 978-0-8146-8024-7 — ISBN 978-0-8146-8025-4 (ebook)
    1. Music—Religious aspects.   I. Beaudoin, Tom, 1969– editor of compilation.

ML3921.S43   2013
782.4—dc23

                        2012045237

Contents

Acknowledgments   vii

Introduction
Theology of Popular Music as a Theological Exercise   ix
Tom Beaudoin

PART ONE
Theology through Artistry

Chapter 1
**To the Void: Karl Barth, Yves Klein, and
Lou Reed's *Metal Machine Music*   3**
David Dault

Chapter 2
**Musical Space: Living "In Between" the Christian and the
Artistic Callings   16**
Maeve Louise Heaney

PART TWO
Theology through Community

Chapter 3
**More Than Music: Notes on "Staying Punk" in the Church
and in Theology   35**
Michael J. Iafrate

Chapter 4

On the Road to the Promised Land: How the NAACP, the Black Church, and Rock Music Helped the Civil Rights Movement   59

Mary McDonough

Chapter 5

Is God Absent on "Grey Street"?: Theodicy, Domestic Violence, and the Dave Matthews Band   75

Gina Messina-Dysert

PART THREE
Theology through Song

Chapter 6

Secular Music and Sacramental Theology   93

Christian Scharen

Chapter 7

Erase This from the Blackboard: Pearl Jam, John Howard Yoder, and the Overcoming of Trauma   108

Myles Werntz

Chapter 8

Baptized in Dirty Water: Locating the Gospel of Tupac Amaru Shakur in the Post-Soul Context   126

Daniel White Hodge

Chapter 9

Tom Waits, Nick Cave, and Martin Heidegger: On Singing of the God Who Will Not Be Named   149

Jeffrey F. Keuss

List of Contributors   167

Acknowledgments

"Bring water out of the rock; let justice roll."
(Num 20:8, Amos 5:24)

I hope that this book will prove a welcome introduction to theological explorations of popular music and that it will prompt the sorts of agreements, disagreements, and questions that help readers further their own journeys in theologizing about contemporary culture.

This book grew out of the community of scholars connected to the Rock and Theology blog that has been generously supported for several years by Liturgical Press. I am grateful for the energetic, collegial, and patient editorial support of Peter Dwyer and Hans Christoffersen at Liturgical Press. Thank you, too, to the many writers and readers at Rock and Theology, whose contributions encouraged the thinking taking place in these pages. Fordham University graciously provided a research leave in the 2011 spring semester that substantially aided the generation of this book. And I am in debt to the fine copyediting skills of Lauren L. Murphy at Liturgical Press.

To my bandmates in The Raina and in The Particulars, praise for the continued pleasures of the rock and roll life—and blame for my continued hearing loss.

I offer and owe the deepest gratitude to my family: to my spouse Martina and our daughter Mimi, who inspire this work by making our family life an irreverent mix of music and theology.

Tom Beaudoin
New York City, August 2012

Introduction

Theology of Popular Music as a Theological Exercise

Tom Beaudoin

Sculpting the Self through Music and Theology

Most people spend a lot of time enjoying music but very little time asking why we care about it so much. In the United States, many people easily and passionately state that they like this or that song, band, or genre, but there are few occasions for asking how these choices connect with what we think our lives are all about. This is perhaps easiest to see among young people. More than one teacher has observed that students today "live inside music. Their musical lives may well be their spiritual lives." They (and their elders) find something "vital, vigorous, intense" in music. But they (and we) lack ways of integrating that pleasure into our larger lives, of thinking about how music relates to the bigger picture of our lives.[1]

The authors in this book, in writing theology, care about "big picture" questions. Theological research focuses on what religious traditions have to do and say concerning the beings, books, and beliefs that people call holy or sacred. Certainly there are fields of inquiry, philosophy or psychology, for example, in which music as part of life's "big picture" can be explored. Theologians and religion scholars are not the only ones who pursue what people call divine. Theologians do, however, make this pursuit central to our work. As a result, everything the authors have to

---

[1] Mark Edmundson, "Can Music Save Your Life?" *The Chronicle Review*, June 8, 2012, B6–9.

say in this book about "popular music" or "secular music"—in short, the music that a lot of people in everyday life find themselves enjoying a lot of the time—is going to be connected to God or to things that are related to God, like "religious" or "spiritual" ideas, texts, or practices. For the authors in this book, making sense of popular music means making a case about how music is more or less related to spiritual things.

The explorations in this book are part of a larger movement among scholars who think that something sacred is at stake in appreciating music in everyday life. The literature on this topic has mushroomed in the last fifteen years, well beyond any one person's ability to track it all.[2] These scholars try to make sense of what happens to religious experience in a world heavily influenced by popular media culture, a world in which songs, movies, musicians, actors, and celebrities influence our individual and collective imaginations about how we might live. Theologian Kelton Cobb, for example, argues that theology cannot remain unchanged when "whole generations in the West have had their basic conceptions of the world formed by popular culture." Out of this newly influential experiential palette, people "invest life with meaning and find a justification for their lives"[3]—or as I mentioned above, people are aided in coming to a sense of the "big picture."

Music has a unique place in the sea of popular culture. It has achieved a position of cultural dominance compared to other forms of cultural expression. With the assistance of several decades of technological breakthroughs, and because of a deep affinity between contemporary social change and popular musical expression, music has come ever more intimately into nearly every aspect of everyday experience, adding to music's traditional place in religious and social rituals. Music is every-

---

[2] Very helpful starting places into the wider literature include Kelton Cobb, *The Blackwell Guide to Theology and Popular Culture* (Malden, MA: Blackwell, 2005); Gordon Lynch, *Understanding Theology and Popular Culture* (Malden, MA: Blackwell, 2005); Anthony B. Pinn and Benjamín Valentín, eds., *Creating Ourselves: African Americans and Hispanic Americans on Popular Culture and Religious Expression* (Durham, NC: Duke University Press, 2009); Christian Scharen, *Broken Hallelujahs: Why Popular Music Matters to Those Seeking God* (Grand Rapids, MI: Brazos, 2011); Jeffrey F. Keuss, *Your Neighbor's Hymnal: What Popular Music Teaches Us about Faith, Hope, and Love* (Eugene, OR: Cascade, 2011). David Nantais, *Rock-a My Soul: An Invitation to Rock Your Religion* (Collegeville, MN: Liturgical Press, 2011) is an accessible meditation on the relationship between rock and roll and the spirituality of Ignatius of Loyola.

[3] Cobb, *The Blackwell Guide to Theology and Popular Culture*, 7.

where.[4] Music, it is now thought, may even have been of particular significance in human evolution, facilitating sexual selection, social cohesion, and even basic cognition. It is no wonder that music has been called a "human obsession."[5]

What I am really talking about here is the way that music has a powerful way of putting together human identity for individuals and groups. Music is a kind of glue that helps different aspects of identity stick together and endure. Many dimensions of experience are tutored and shaped by popular music cultures: who we are racially and ethnically, what we take ourselves to be in terms of gender and sexuality, where we belong generationally, spiritually, and more. One way of talking about this powerful role of music is to use the notion of "subjectification," which means "subject-making," where the "subject" is the human being. In other words, when we talk in philosophy and theology about subjectification, we are pointing to the ways in which who—and whose—we take ourselves to be are deeply influenced by, and substantially implanted in, the ways that we are persuaded to count certain things as being "real" and mattering more than other things. This persuasion happens through the "hidden curriculum" of our families, schools, religious institutions, and larger social environment, including our media, and especially including the music that influences and/or comes from "the people"—"popular music."[6]

Some of this subjectification works through what we choose given the options before us, but a lot of it happens through what is taken as normal, appropriate, worthy, decent, or desirable in the cultures in which we are shaped. Culture makes constant subtle interventions in what we take to count as ourselves and our communities. This influence is not neutral; it is saturated with the history of forces beyond what we can comprehend, forces that are part of the history of our culture, powerful dynamics that carry legacies of being silenced as well as inclinations to speak, all tangled with overt and subtle acts of violence. These forces have resulted

---

[4] T.C.W. Blanning, *The Triumph of Music: The Rise of Composers, Musicians, and Their Art* (Cambridge, MA: Harvard University Press, 2008).

[5] Daniel Levitin, *This Is Your Brain on Music: The Science of a Human Obsession* (New York: Dutton, 2006).

[6] I borrow the term "subjectification" from the philosophy of Michel Foucault. For an introduction to this term and its significance for theology, see Tom Beaudoin, "Engaging Foucault with Rahner: Sketching an Asymptotic Relationship," *Philosophy and Theology* 20, no. 1–2 (2008): 307–29.

in our profoundly unequal, stratified society, with uneven access to social goods—and in which music is created, distributed, and taken in. Popular music is far from simple entertainment. Music is a force that can be a way of being trained to succumb to the history of exploitation and/or of being able to invent new forms of freedom. These popular music practices can run the gamut from listening to music at a live show alone or with others, or while traveling or daydreaming, to creating, performing, and distributing one's own music, to watching music videos and performances on a screen, to analyzing music in everyday conversation or academic discourse, and more. These are just some ways that music becomes a part of our way of dealing with and creating an effective sense of self and other.

Even though the word "subjectification" is not often used in popular music research, music as a force for subjectification—inducing configurations of individuals and communities that accede to or resist the damages our history gives us—has been an important theme of research. The power of the blues for the expression and crafting of African American lives has been well-argued,[7] and rock and roll by African American artists has served to create communities of conversation and activism regarding racial justice and interracial solidarity.[8] Popular music teaches ethical codes by the pleasure it gives, providing listeners a story about how to hold life together and what people can hope for.[9] Women artists and fans have found in popular music a school for self-assertion and gender creativity.[10] Exploring and negotiating models of political participation outside of Latin America through the reworking of Mexican culture have been facilitated by Latino rock "in diaspora."[11] And rock and roll has been a way for young Muslims to craft a pluralistically-informed identity

[7] A classic work is James Cone, *The Spirituals and the Blues: An Interpretation* (New York: Seabury, 1972). This motif also occurs throughout Cornel West, *The Cornel West Reader* (New York: Basic Civitas Books, 1999).

[8] Maureen Mahon, *Right to Rock: The Black Rock Coalition and the Cultural Politics of Race* (Durham, NC: Duke University Press, 2004).

[9] Simon Frith is a singular student of popular music. A good place to start is *Performing Rites: On the Value of Popular Music* (Cambridge, MA: Harvard University Press, 1996).

[10] Gillian Gaar, *She's a Rebel: The History of Women in Rock & Roll*, 2nd ed. (New York: Seal Press, 2002).

[11] Roberto Avant-Mier, *Rock the Nation: Latin/o Identities and the Latin Rock Diaspora* (New York: Continuum, 2010).

within Islam.[12] These examples show that music is frequently a force for pulling together or tugging apart the threads of identity, weaving the ambiguous threads of the society in which popular music comes to be known.

In taking account of the role of subjectification through music, we have not moved very far from theological concerns. Indeed, the more curious we are about what music means for the core of human life, the more that theology can and should be invested, because theological traditions have commonly understood God as both the architect and the goal of life. Theology is the concern for the "place" of divinity in subjectification, for the sake of making human life, and the life of the world, more worthy of its mysterious and sacred "essence." This is one fundamental reason that theologians and religionists argue about what music means. We want to know where that special relation to "something more" is (or is asserted to be) "taking place."

Three Definitions of Popular Music and Their Theological Significance

Thus far, I have been making "popular music" seem more simple a thing than it actually is. But I did allude above to the range of things people do with music, and getting specific about that range is important for theological work on music. Pop music scholar Simon Frith, working from a long career interpreting the role of music in contemporary society, has argued that popular culture can be understood in three basic ways. Because popular music is not only a part of popular culture more generally, but helped to "found" pop culture, these three definitions are of particular importance for understanding how music works in contemporary culture.[13]

Borrowing from the language of democracy, Frith argues that popular culture can be understood as cultural "products" made "for the people," "of the people," and "by the people." First, as something made "for the people," we can think of music as an industrially-produced commodity aimed at a particular social group. This definition directs our attention to the ways that music becomes popular through the way it is planned

[12] Mark LeVine, *Heavy Metal Islam: Rock, Resistance, and the Struggle for the Soul of Islam* (New York: Three Rivers Press, 2008).

[13] Simon Frith, "Popular Culture," in *A Dictionary of Cultural and Critical Theory*, ed. Michael Payne and Jessica Rae Barbera (Malden, MA: Wiley-Blackwell, 2010), 553–55.

and branded for the consumption of a specific social demographic. There is an important insight here: all music is created and made available to certain publics with a more or less sophisticated (perhaps manipulative) attempt to be placed into people's lives. Of course, I also want to know what this definition means for theology. It means that theology can look for the meaning of music by what its makers "design" into it. Theology then asks how God and God-related spiritual texts, ideas, and practices relate to a series of governing intentions: what the artist means to convey, what the record company is trying to sell, how the larger social ideology benefits from its propagation. This definition focuses on music's meaning in the intentions, influences, and intervention of powerful forces behind it.

The second definition Frith presents is that pop culture is the culture "of the people." Here, pop music becomes popular because it so well characterizes a social group's values, behaviors, or identity. The music seems to "fit" or "depict" what people are like, and that is what makes it "popular." For example, there is music that seems to speak particularly to teenage life, to racial-ethnic realities, to religious affiliation, to local or regional tastes, to gender dynamics, or to specific levels of formal education or status or social privilege. Insofar as a musical artist, lyric, song, album, video, concert, or the like symbolizes a quality of a social group, popular music is the music or culture "of the people." Popular music is frequently experienced by fans as "my music" or "our music" precisely for these reasons. For theological research, this means that we may look to the sensibilities of the social group that are "embedded" in the music when we want to understand how to relate spiritual things to popular music. Our interest becomes how the music is symbolizing "where people are," acting like a seismograph for contemporary life.

The third definition Frith offers is popular culture as culture "by the people." This is close to what is sometimes called "folk culture," because here we focus on a specific social group's practices. What people do creatively musically, on their own terms, is "popular music." Though this definition tends to prioritize inventive local artistry, it can conceivably include the creative things people do with the commodities they receive. So popular music as culture "by the people" can include street raps, busking, and home recordings (and how those circulate in use in local communities), but can also include appreciation for what people really do with commercially produced music, such as how they treat lyrics, what they do with musical celebrity, how they construct their own playlists, how they share music, and how they put music into the particularities of their lives for myriad purposes that always have to be studied in context. Theology that wants to work with popular music understood in this way looks to how groups, through music, put their lives together, through both consent and dissent about how to get things done. Theologians look to relate their spiritual materials to the creative and tensive places of music from the "ground up." Music's involvement in negotiations of power and everyday reiterations of identity become of great interest theologically.

Were we to take an ordinary example of pop music, like a song from a mainstream pop, rock, or hip hop album, and ask how it is "popular music" according to these definitions, and how we make theological sense of it, it would look something like this: We might begin by asking who wrote this song, what do we know about their life, and what were they trying to communicate? Who paid for this music to be recorded and marketed, and what are their motivations to have it sell, and to whom? What are the deep social dynamics of the society in which this music is made and sold, and how are those social dynamics being legitimated or interrupted in the sound, the words, the images of this music? We would also want to know what this song tells us about the people who like it, and about the culture in which it came to be—how and why it speaks to these people in this moment. And we should be curious about how this song fits into larger patterns of life on the ground for its fans: when they listen to it, how important the lyrics are and what they mean to people, how the song informs their thoughts, dreams, conversations, perceptions, self-perceptions, and how it opens or closes people to other music, feelings, relationships, politics. That is admittedly a lot to find out, and few scholars can tackle all of that. We are necessarily selective.

Then we would ask (although we are and should be asking all along) more explicitly theological questions. How does religious tradition address itself to these messages, values, and ideological practices? But for good contemporary theological research, especially with a public topic like popular music, we do not merely assert. We have to have good reasons and justly persuasive rhetoric for theological work. By "good reasons," I mean reasons that stand up to scrutiny as good argument among those committed to it inside and outside of theology. By "justly persuasive rhetoric," I mean to recognize that we are persuaded not only by "good reasons" but by persuasive, poetic, even beautiful writing and other forms of theological presentation, and that this persuasive rhetoric ought to ultimately serve justice toward ourselves and all others in our (local and global) society. "Good reasons" can never be separated cleanly from "justly persuasive rhetoric." But good theological researchers keep this sort of thing in mind when they try to talk about culture, or about any theological work for that matter. And so we have to ask ourselves if there are good reasons and justly persuasive rhetoric for having this engagement between theology and music happen? Why do we think our theological traditions might have something significant to say here, and how do we convey that with care, style, and beauty? No less important is the moment in theological work where we ask why this theological engagement with music matters for us and for those affected by this conversation. Do we see that we or others might become different, gain knowledge, insight, wisdom, or virtue, might simply grow or change, as a result? And will this engagement, which is both ever new and ever rooted in our past, make us reconsider both this music and our theological tradition?

The point is that despite theology's historical tendencies to see itself as the protector of the divine property known as "revelation," it is simply the case that neither music nor theology can stay the same in this kind of engagement. We will either reaffirm what we thought and felt about religion and music, or we will not. And we may only later come up with reasons for that reiteration or reconsideration. This is something like the dynamic, explicit or implicit, that most scholars of theology and popular culture undertake, even if we do not undertake every step consciously every time we do our work.[14] To study theology and popular music is to find ways of bringing together musical culture and theological culture and to find how why and how it matters that that happens, and to use that knowledge to make even wiser discernments in the future. These discernments are not ultimately for producing specialized knowledge alone, but for learning how to live with a spiritual sense, more fully and responsibly, in our particular social habitat. Theological research must conform to the best standards of research and, at the same time, realize theology is also for living wisely and well.

---

[14] Among many strong recent works on the changing relationship between theology and culture that the explicit turn to cultural analysis entails, see Sheila Greeve Davaney, "Theology and the Turn to Cultural Analysis," in *Converging on Culture: Theologians in Dialogue with Cultural Analysis and Criticism*, ed. Delwin Brown, Sheila Greeve Davaney, and Kathryn Tanner (New York: Oxford University Press, 2001), 3–16.

Constraints on Theologizing about Music

There are so many ways of putting music and theology in relationship with each other that the possibilities can seem daunting, but it also means that there is a great deal of room for specific engagements and pushing out new frontiers. You might get the impression that one way is as good as another, that because there are so many ways to make theological sense of popular music, that one choice is as "good" as another and that in the end, it does not really matter how one enters the conversation or carries it forward.

However, theology is, and should be, "constrained" by two forces that are beyond its control: history and culture. When we do theology, we have to think carefully about our historical situation and try to name the contingency of our past and the prospects that appear to us as possible avenues forward. We also have to think well about our cultural place-ment, because the basic stuff of theology—practices, ideas, texts—are always testaments to a particular past cultural situation that are used in new present cultural situations. So we have to speak in a "public" way when we do theology, taking responsibility for the way that history and culture have put us where we are with respect to our understanding of God and religion. We have to realize that every theological exploration is a way of dealing with the history we have inherited, and is a way of addressing the multiple cultures actually present as our "publics."

Working creatively with these "constraints" can turn them into new possibilities, new realms of freedom for theologians. Many different areas of theology are coming to terms with these constraints and pos-sibilities. For example, theologian Don Browning argues that a theo-logical encounter with marriage has to be carried out under particular exigencies today. A theology of marriage needs to be a kind of "public philosophy," one that should not be argued by resting on privileged (and increasingly hoary) theological ideas like "orders of creation, covenant, and sacrament." At the same time, theology is part of Western histories of marriage, and so we must "understand our society's indebtedness to what these concepts did to form Western marriage."[15] Something similar is true of theologizing about rock and roll or all popular music: No single theological system is going to be able to make persuasive sense of

---

[15] Don S. Browning, "Can Marriage Be Defined?," *Equality and the Family: A Funda-mental, Practical Theology of Children, Mothers and Fathers in Contemporary Societies* (Grand Rapids, MI: Eerdmans, 2007), 207–19.

popular music today, but due to rock and roll's roots in gospel music, the churches, and different kinds of Christian experience, theology is also part of the history of rock and roll. This makes theological work on rock and roll a complicated venture, one beset by limits and possibilities on all sides. It is hard to integrate these constraints into theological work, but theologians are under particular obligations to think about the constraints on our work, because theology is always a constrained discourse while at the same time being a discourse committed to freedom through the relating of "sacred" (cultural) material to "other" (cultural) material. In this work of relating, we constantly run up against the need to think through the ultimate "force" beyond theology's control that also limits and frees theology: God, or whatever sacred power theology can imagine. Integrating an awareness of these constraints and open-ended-nesses of history and culture can be a way of beginning to acknowledge the more profound, perhaps limitless, limit that divine revelation poses for theological work.

The Shape of This Book

While there are now a fair number of edited books with multiple authors that engage religion and popular culture, a focus on popular music is less common. Although some serious theological inquiries into popular music have appeared in recent years, there are no edited collections that I know of that focus on theology and popular music.[16] This book aims to contribute to the conversation by not only showing different ways in which different authors take different theological approaches to different forms of rock and roll (broadly construed), but also by taking cultural studies of music seriously as a partner for theological engagement. You will notice chapters that take account of "non-theological" vantage points on music, from religious studies literature, cultural studies of music, histories and biographies, interviews with musicians, accounts of live performance, fan perspectives, and more. This new approach emerges from a generation of scholars who live in both academic/religious/theological and pop music contexts, retaining their passion for all domains while disagreeing on how those realms do and should relate to each other. Many of the authors in this book are musicians, all

---

[16] One theologically rich collection that focuses on hip hop is Anthony B. Pinn, ed., *Noise and Spirit: The Religious and Spiritual Sensibilities of Rap Music* (New York: New York University Press, 2003).

are fans, and each believes that the conjoint study of theology and popular music is important and mutually enriching.

The chapters are divided into three sections, characterizing three distinct (but overlapping) ways that theological work proceeds in relation to popular music. The headings direct our attention to how scholars find theologically meaningful material in the world of popular music.

In the first section, "Theology through Artistry," the authors situate the theological significance of music in relationship to the creative process of artistic invention. David Dault juxtaposes the music of Lou Reed with the theology of Karl Barth and the art of Yves Klein, so as to show how all three artists create works that try to name what exceeds naming. The ancient theological question of whether God can be comprehended in human terms is turned by Dault, in his chapter "To the Void: Karl Barth, Yves Klein, and Lou Reed's *Metal Machine Music*," into a triptych of rock and roll, theology, and visual art, all trying to let that which is profoundly "other" appear through their respective mediums. In the process, we are sensitized to the analogies among these forms of artistry, and while theology is not assimilated to music and art, Dault locates it on an evocative map of family resemblances across genres for experiencing what cannot be grasped. Maeve Heaney, in "Musical Space: Living 'In-Between' the Christian and the Artistic Callings," also finds juxtapositions to be a productive site for theological exploration. For her, the life and work of the artist houses a key tension in music culture that is theologically significant: the calling to be a Christian and the calling to be a musician. Heaney works with statements from musicians about their art and their faith, weaves in her own experience as a Christian musician, and finds in contemporary theology resources for making sense of these distinct and yet complementary callings. The deeper one goes, juxtapositions become comparisons, and comparisons become exchanges, or occasions for pursuing places of spiritual convergence and divergence. Through it all, the tensions among callings will be the place for theological work. Thus we have two different takes on why and how one can make musical artistry the center of theologically interested exploration.

The second section of the book, "Theology in Community," investigates ways that music helps create communities of heightened moral consciousness. Michael Iafrate's chapter "More Than Music: Notes on 'Staying Punk' in the Church and in Theology," finds punk rock, and especially the ethics of punk culture, to be a robust place for theological appreciation and criticism. This is so especially because the personal and social commitments of punk and theology frequently coincide, and a theologically aware punk ethic can even help ground everyday adult life and the practice of academic theology. The ways that musical experience changes people in theologically substantial ways also interests Mary McDonough. Her chapter, "On the Road to the Promised Land: How the NAACP, the Black Church, and Rock Music Helped the Civil Rights Movement," puts interracial early rock concerts in the historical context of the civil rights movement, and argues that rock and roll shows are much more than entertainment. They have been crucibles for the American moral imagination about race. Theological analysis of popular music's role in fomenting morally conscious community should take deep account of the politics of the culture in which the music takes place, as well as the contending imaginations of the communities that resist the destructive dimensions of those politics. Misogynistic cultural mores, and the failures of theologies to integrate subjective experiences of suffering into their concepts of God, are at the heart of the chapter by Gina Messina-Dysert. In "Is God Absent on 'Grey Street'? Theodicy, Domestic Violence, and the Dave Matthews Band," she argues that in the experiences and questions of victims-survivors of domestic violence, theology finds itself in need of an alliance with the power of music to enable a more suitable presence to the depth of theological questions in suffering. For this work, she turns to the music of the Dave Matthews Band, arguing that from this band comes a music that can, in telling the truth about suffering and the theological crisis it induces, deepen solidarity on behalf of justice for women. Each of these chapters finds theology's work to be in appreciating, criticizing, and drawing out the implications of music's role in making more ethically responsible communities.

In the final section, "Theology through Song," the authors take songs as the core of theological insight and access other contextual material (such as interviews, concerts, biographies) that help to elucidate the theological significance of songs. Christian Scharen finds the presence of "the festive" in contemporary song in a way that speaks directly to a revived sacramental theology that can draw from popular music. His chapter, "Secular Music and Sacramental Theology," focuses on performances by Arcade Fire, Lady Gaga, and Esperanza Spalding. Scharen finds music creating the occasion for theology to join philosopher Charles Taylor in recovering the notion of festivity in the service of a more rigorous show of embodiment that can inform theological work on the worldly experience of the divine. Myles Werntz, in "Erase This from the Blackboard: Pearl Jam, John Howard Yoder, and the Overcoming of Trauma," sees an entire album posing a theological question that theology should take seriously and can help to answer. Working from a close reading of Pearl Jam's *Ten*, Werntz identifies its pressing theological themes to include trauma and apocalypse, and ultimately hope. Werntz turns to theologian John Howard Yoder to respond, thereby arguing that Pearl Jam's songs are of theological significance, and that Yoder's theology addresses an important theological matter at stake in a widely influential rock record. Daniel White Hodge presents songs as theological innovations in their own right, challenging mainstream theology to revise its assumptions about race, secularity, and salvation. His chapter, "Baptized in Dirty Water: Locating the Gospel of Tupac Amaru Shakur in the Post-Soul Context," argues that Shakur was a theologian from and for his milieu, bringing the life lessons, language, and loves from the streets to discourse about God, Jesus, and religion, and creating a new possibility for theology in the process. Close readings of Shakur's songs show a searching theological sensibility at work that can help theology take itself further into its own deepest commitments and contemporary social relevance. For Jeff Keuss, the songs of Tom Waits and Nick Cave are sources of theological insight, bringing theology poetically into the complex space of the experience and assertion of God's presence and absence already foreseen by the philosophy of Martin Heidegger. In his chapter, "Tom Waits, Nick Cave, and Martin Heidegger: On Singing of the God Who Will Not Be Named," Keuss shows how careful attention to songs can surface deeply theological conundrums. The way that songs navigate theologically can have an integrity of their own and can also be enriched by finding analogues in academic discourse, such as philosophy of religion. Songs turn out to be a way that philosophy of religion happens melodically, and elite philosophy of religion is a way that a popular song's intellectual content can get registered and deepened. For this section of the book, the work of the theologian is in learning how to read and hear songs productively, all the while searching for the existing theological discourse from the tradition to affirm, reject, or complicate.

Theological Engagement with Culture: Capitulation, Interpretation, or Liberation?

These chapters, taken as a whole, teach us about method in theological engagements with popular culture. Academic theology engages culture when theologians read cognate disciplines for material they consider relevant for theological analysis. Through such inclusion of "nontheological" material, the items to count as theologically relevant get rhetorically placed. This display of specific cultural material, disaggregated from its larger context, is a theological maneuver, regardless of whether that material gets an explicitly named theological appreciation, criticism, or mere comment. Theology says through the forms of its narratives, "the holy story can be told in this way," and one thing to notice about theologians' engagements with culture is that this very form becomes as much the content of our theological arguments as any other identifiable "contents."

Now that this dynamic of theological production—the necessary interaction between "theological" and "non-theological" material—is getting noticed more and more in contemporary theology, different reactions have followed. Some argue that such a dynamic is a sad capitulation on the part of theology, because it is an essentially anti-theological submission to non-theological outsiders. Why, they ask, should "cultural" material "spoil" theology and violate its special revelatory privilege?[17] Other theologians see this dynamic as a hermeneutical necessity. Interpretation, they argue, is essential to living faith. We must always interpretively connect a religious tradition to a particular social-cultural situation.[18] Still other theologians argue that this dynamic is valid insofar as it represents a liberative intervention. This is because theology must figure out how to stand critically for freedom in cultural contexts of suffering.[19] These three theological characterizations of the deep placement of theological work amidst cultural investigation can be summarized as: capitulation, interpretation, liberation.

I am writing generally, of course, about theological trajectories today, but each of these generalizations contains some truth. If theology uncritically repeats cultural forms, it is capitulation. Just so, no theology can avoid interpreting cultural situations and interpreting itself along the way. No theology sees itself or its culture "purely," and the skill of prudential judgment is one of the most prized of theological skills. And if that judgment does not issue in the service of justice, we can accuse our hermeneutics of decadence. All three characterizations thus make essential claims. But they carry their own violence as well. All three characterizations of the theology-culture dynamic (capitulation, interpretation, liberation) tend toward a violent special pleading. By this, I mean that they impose theological restrictions on reality by force of a vindication

---

[17] This is typically the response of "radical orthodox" or neo-orthodox theologies.

[18] Correlational or liberal theologies typically make this response.

[19] This response is common to theologies of liberation.

of a certain selective enforcement of ideas and practices that make one Christian. This is what Daniel Boyarin calls "christianicity"—Christianity as a kind of display of identity in a certain time and place, as an experience of being trained to recognize one's essential Christian-ness as resident in beliefs and practices in an over-against relationship with Christianity's "others."[20] The "capitulation" defense is an ancient kind of theological imposition: a failure to learn from what gives others (in contemporary culture) their wholeness, peace, integrity, sense. The "interpretation" response treats religion as a privileged dialogue partner for unlocking cultural meaning, presuming religion's privilege and coherence. The "liberation" strategy prescribes that the freedom to be fostered by theology will necessarily be assimilable to Christianity, instead of potentially transcending Christianity, or standing indifferent to it.

Are there any other ways of understanding this theology-culture dynamic? I propose that we can understand theological work on culture as a pragmatic rehearsal. A notion of pragmatic rehearsal does not aim to put to rest all these conundrums, but places itself within and across the lines of rhetorical force already at work in the other approaches. By pragmatic rehearsal, I am suggesting a theory of the performance of academic theological knowledge: that theological work is a kind of dynamic, performed knowing, and to enact it is to operate intellectually and materially, with situational tools, on a cultural nexus of significance, and from an awareness contingently denominated "theological," for the sake—and with the effect—of a conscious and unconscious intervention in practice.

Theological work is "pragmatic" in the sense of conscious deliberation about what needs to be done in this historical-cultural moment with these specific ways of construing the moment and of specifying what can be done; it is also "pragmatic" as personal-cultural unconscious "deliberation," built out of the personal psychology and cultural genealogy of the theologian and her history, about what this moment is and what can and must be done.

It is a "rehearsal" in the sense that it repeats and reconstructs personal and cultural history. "Rehearsal" is a paradoxical term; it means to do something you have already proven you can do, and it means to do

[20] Daniel Boyarin, *Border Lines: The Partition of Judeao-Christianity* (Philadelphia, PA: University of Pennsylvania Press, 2004), 17.

something that you have not yet fully proven you can do. It means to go through an ensemble of moves that you have already learned as part of a set piece, but it also means to go through that ensemble of moves in order to prepare for a special display, an extraordinary performance. Theological work is a rehearsal in both senses. Theology is a way of dealing with oneself, others, and culture. That dealing is provisional. It is also direct and indirect. This is why practice-based theologies are playing and should play an increasingly important role in contemporary theological research. In these approaches, theologians can come closer to recognizing the practice-character of all theology. All theology studies and enacts practices. Another way of saying this is that all theology involves itself with orchestrations of identity with respect to a claiming power. But this should not lull us into thinking that just because a theology has to do with practical or cultural matters that it is proceeding with full awareness and criticality as a practice-intensive theology. Many practical, pastoral, and praxis theologies can operate just as other theologies, with a reluctance to foreground the problem of the moves and cultural-spiritual interventions it is making, often enough in the name of a renewed, liberating, faithful, or transformed practice.

On this interpretation, theology of popular culture, as a model for and exemplification of theological work "as such," is practice-based, practice-intensive, and practice-effective. On this reading, theologians are engaged in pragmatic rehearsals, enacting the ways of analysis they have inherited, operating on a scene of significance, and confirming and/or challenging an arrangement in view of (a) claiming power(s). This reading potentially holds the diversity of approaches outlined above and in this book, while suggesting their importance for the definition of academic theological labor in the twenty-first century, particularly in "secular" Western contexts. Such reflections also indicate that theological engagements with popular culture harbor something far from being theologically ephemeral and culturally transient; they are ways of approaching difficult problems with which the larger theological community struggles. Or stated differently, such reflections show that the larger theological community's analyses are no less theologically ephemeral and culturally transient than what "theology and popular culture" research discovers.

PART ONE

Theology through Artistry

Chapter 1

To the Void: Karl Barth, Yves Klein, and Lou Reed's *Metal Machine Music*

David Dault

"Some experiences are best left unexplained."

Bob Mould[1]

I remember visiting a museum in Atlanta to see a traveling exhibit, and part of the collection was this huge painting that took up most of one wall. It was a seascape, a stormscape full of roaring, crashing, angry waves. The foam caps on the swells were above my head, and the troughs of these monstrous walls of water met to form a murderous valley at my feet. This was one of the largest paintings I have ever seen, and it was all screaming water.

There in the middle, totally at the mercy of this frozen power, careening toward the depths of wreckage, to death, was a tiny boat.

I don't now recall the name of the artist or the name of the painting. What left an impression, however, was the enormity of this image and the hopelessness and grandeur it conveyed. Staring into that raging sea, I felt small. I felt insignificant. I felt that I was in the presence of power much beyond my comprehension, let alone my control.

That, of course, was the point.

The Romantics—not only the painters, but the poets, too—were preoccupied with this feeling. Their work helped provide us with a technical vocabulary for exploring the heights and depths of human meaning and the mortal questions of awe: Was this the incomprehensible majesty of

---

[1] "Beaster (1993): A Note from Bob Mould." http://www.granarymusic.com /archive/last-dog-and-pony-show/discography/sugar/beaster.html.

the natural world? Was this the overwhelming wrath of an inscrutable God? Yes, and more. In the grandeur of the Romantic gesture, the assured calculations of the Enlightenment—with its world fully described by rationality—find both their fruition and their challenge. Logical descriptions of the divine attributes are retained in Romanticism, but are now coupled with an acute loss of God's domesticity, the beauty of the classical understanding now paired with the terror and absoluteness of the sublime. As Wordsworth put it:

> Tumult and peace, the darkness and the light
> Were all like workings of one mind, the features
> Of the same face, blossoms upon one tree,
> Characters of the great Apocalypse,
> The types and symbols of Eternity,
> Of first and last, and midst, and without end.[2]

These Romantic "characters of Apocalypse"—among them the Sublime, the Void, and the Abyss—invoke the "gulf separating expectation from reality,"[3] that "inner place, which is not a place," to borrow Augustine's phrase, that separates the apprehension we possess in imaginative memory from our ability to positively name that apprehension.[4]

It is this problem of naming that infects the twentieth century (especially so, with the Shoah's dark specter interrupting all delimitations of apprehension, and, following Adorno, even the possibility of poetry itself). Moreover, as with all centuries, when speaking of God, we risk both over-familiarity and domestication or run aground upon the limits of language and terror of the divine. For several of the church fathers, the way forward was apophasis, the path of negative theology, by which we speak only with assurance of what God is not. God cannot be contained and, therefore, God cannot be contained in language.

The response of the Romantic however is not an apophatic response; neither is it a positive one. Rather, in a *tertium quid* to the positivism of scientific modernism and the *via negativa* of the ancients, Romanticism

---

[2] William Wordsworth, *The Prelude; or, Growth of a Poet's Mind* (4.635–40), quoted in M.H. Abrams, *Natural Supernaturalism: Tradition and Revolution in Romantic Literature* (New York: W.W. Norton, 1971), 107.

[3] Abrams, *Natural Supernaturalism*, 451.

[4] St. Augustine, *Confessions* 10.9, in Philip Schaff, *A Select Library of the Nicene and Post-Nicene Fathers of the Christian Church; Volume I: The Confessions and Letters of St. Augustine, with a Sketch of his Life and Work* (Grand Rapids, MI: Eerdmans, 2001), 146.

bequeaths us a vocabulary of gestures. In contrast to both positivism and apophaticism, the gestural vocabulary of Romanticism points to the Abyss, noting it without naming, locating it without logic. Like the fictive crew of the boat tossed by huge swells, Romanticism apprehends from within the overwhelming immensity of the Sublime. This is not a conventional form of logical naming. Instead, falling down the crest of the wave into the unknown below, one may there sing "Of Truth, of Grandeur, Beauty, Love and Hope / and melancholy Fear subdued by Faith,"[5] not because one knows these things, but because in that moment the one so singing is consumed by them.

When one is caught in the crest of the overwhelming wave, it is hard to discern the provenance. Standing far away, one might be able to name the source, but we never meet the Sublime at such a distance. From the middle of the storm, all we know is that there is some power that holds us, be that the power of God or of the devil. We are beholden to this power, and as such, are in no position to properly speak or name the power. If we had any means to properly measure the nature of the wave of the Sublime, the wave of the Abyss, to which we are presently and constantly in thrall, we would have to be somewhere other than the boat in which we presently find ourselves. "The human plight consists fundamentally of enslavement to supra-human powers; and God's redemptive act is his deed of liberation," as J. Louis Martyn put it.[6] What this implies, however, is that God's liberating action might itself be every bit as overwhelming, ineffable, and terrifying as that from which we are liberated. Arthur A. Cohen's description of the attempts of contemporary theology to grapple with the horror of the Shoah is symmetrical to this inbreaking of God unto human salvation: "clearly thinking the *enormous event* is one thing, comprehending and expressing its meaning quite another."[7] Indeed, as Cohen continues, "The thinker has no choice but to stand precariously within his own limitation when he tries to speak . . . about the nature of God."[8]

Is there hope, then, for a gesture that does not consist in "trying to speak?"

[5] Wordsworth, "Prospectus to *The Recluse,*" quoted in Abrams, *Natural Supernaturalism,* 466 passim.

[6] J. Louis Martyn, *Galatians: A New Translation with Introduction and Commentary,* The Anchor Bible Series, vol. 33A (New York: Doubleday, 1997), 97.

[7] Arthur A. Cohen, *The Tremendum: A Theological Interpretation of the Holocaust* (New York: Crossroad, 1988), 3.

[8] Cohen, *Tremendum,* 84.

In what follows I will consider the works of Karl Barth, Yves Klein, and Lou Reed. They are each unrelated, and also unrelated to (at least in the direct sense of being descended from) the earlier Romantic gestures I have mentioned above. Barth offers the incomprehensibility of grace; Klein gives us color without form; Reed creates a rock and roll without structure: what they share in common, however, is their attempt to communicate in this *tertium quid*, without the strictures of positivity or apophasis. I classify such gestures, from Romanticism forward, as serious attempts to address the problem of naming the unspeakable. I will argue that each is a discrete and familial attempt to inhabit subjectivity in the face of the Sublime, the Abyss, the Void.

Barth

In Barth's *The Epistle to the Romans* he makes the enigmatic statement that "only when grace is recognized to be incomprehensible is it grace."[9] In Barth's reading of Paul, the event of Jesus Christ and his resurrection is both historical and meta-historical; it is an event that exists within the world and beyond the world (and, therefore, beyond the world's language). As Barth explains:

> The Resurrection is the revelation: the disclosing of Jesus as the Christ, the appearing of God, and the apprehending of God in Jesus. The Resurrection is the emergence of the necessity of giving glory to God: the reckoning with what is unknown and unobservable in Jesus, the recognition of Him as Paradox, Victor and Primal History. In the Resurrection the new world of the Holy Spirit touches the old world of the flesh, but touches it as a tangent touches a circle, that is, without touching it. And, precisely because it does not touch it, it touches it as a frontier—as the new world.[10]

In this claim, Barth sets out a precise limitation. Our ability to apprehend "the power of God" is suspended between the positive and the apophatic. For Barth, there is no home in the "real world" of common sense and certainty for the Christian community. Inhabiting solely its location in Christ, the Christian community experiences a "krisis" of the power

---

[9] Karl Barth, *The Epistle to the Romans*, trans. Edwyn C. Hoskins (London: Oxford University Press, 1968), 31.

[10] Ibid., 30.

to name, and indeed of all earthly power.[11] (Barth retains the Greek word "krisis," without translation, in his text, thereby maintaining its layers of meaning, which include the concepts of separation, trial, and judgment.) "The assumption that Jesus is the Christ," Barth asserts, "is, in the strictest sense of the word, an assumption, void of any content that can be comprehended by us."[12]

Under "normal" circumstances, of course, recognition and comprehension operate in tandem, however Barth insists that the circumstances within any Christian community must always be far from normal: "The activity of the community is related to the Gospel only in so far as it is no more than a crater formed by the explosion of a shell and seeks to be no more than a void in which the Gospel reveals itself."[13]

Within the void of the crater, there is nothing to be "named," properly. The "presence" of the void is not a formal presence, and therefore does not offer itself positively. However, precisely to the degree the cratering can be comprehended as void, it can be "named" as such. The "absence" within the void is not an apophatic absence; it does not confound our language. Instead, what Barth seems to be suggesting here is the *tertium quid*, between positive naming and the refusal to name. For Barth, the crater in question is not (as commentators often fail to emphasize) simply the crater of a bombshell; rather, it is the crater ripped in our cosmos by the tangential intersection of the Holy Spirit with our reality. The absence that marks this crater is not merely a void in an earthly sense. Rather it is the Void: a "frontier," an alien "new world" unto its own, indecipherable in its presence, yet undeniably present in the event of Christ's Resurrection.

This Gospel, Barth claims, "sets a question-mark against all truths."[14] Indeed, Barth asserts that there is no truth of the Gospel within us that we might claim as our own. "Therefore the power of God can be detected neither in the world of nature, nor in the souls of men," Barth insists.[15] To follow Christ, therefore, consists in recognizing the total lack of Gospel within us, recognizing this lack (and therefore the Gospel-shaped hole itself) as the Void, the infinite and terrifying frontier of otherness. As with the figure of Grünewald's John the Baptist, so esteemed by Barth,

---

[11] Ibid., 36.
[12] Ibid.
[13] Ibid.
[14] Ibid., 35.
[15] Ibid., 36.

our only hope is in pointing, a gesture toward the Void, and in allowing the contours of that Void, as with the contours of a crater, to suggest for us the shape of grace not that we possess, but that possesses us. Here we recognize only the terrifying incomprehensibility of the Sublime, the Abyss, the Void, the lack of truth within us. In these circumstances, then, where recognition and comprehension are so radically decoupled, Barth is certainly demonstrating for us the limitations of language, in particular, to express the divine truth and grace of the Gospel.

Klein

Klaus Ottman sums up succinctly the effect Yves Klein's work has had on the world of art. Indeed, as Ottman puts it, "to talk about Yves Klein one must talk about the wound caused by the effects of his art and ideas inflicted upon the French artistic tradition."[16] (Barth, it should be noted, also uses this language of wounding, as when he announces that the name of Jesus "marks the point where the unknown world *cuts* the known world."[17]) Kerry Brougher and Phillipe Vergne, the curators of a major Klein retrospective held at the Walker Art Center and Hirshorn Museum in 2010–11, tell us that

> Klein's goal was no less than radically to reinvent what art could be in the postwar world. Through a diverse practice, which included painting, sculpture, performance, photography, music, architecture, and writing as well as plans for works in theater, dance, and cinema, the artist shifted the focus of art from the material object to the 'immaterial sensibility'; he levitated art above the weariness induced by the Second World War, resurrecting its avant-garde tendencies, injecting a new sense of spirituality, and opening doors for much to follow in the 1960s and beyond, including Pop, conceptual art, Minimalism, monochromatic painting, perceptual experimentation, and performance. Thus, Klein is important to consider not only for his own art and times, but also as a crucial figure in the evolution of contemporary art in general. The self-proclaimed 'painter of space,' Klein artistically and literally leapt into the void and there discovered the full potential of his vision. As Albert Camus so memorably

---

[16] Klaus Ottman, "Introduction," in Yves Klein, *Overcoming the Problematics of Art: The Writings of Yves Klein*, Klaus Ottman, trans. (Putnam, CT: Spring Publications, 2007), ix.

[17] Barth, *Romans*, 29, my emphasis.

wrote in the visitor book to Klein's 1958 'Void' exhibition at Iris
Clert's gallery, *'Avec la vide, les pleins pouvoir'* [With the void, full
powers], encapsulating succinctly both the artist's agenda and his
legacy.[18]

As you can see, Klein was a master provocateur across the range of the
visual arts. Pablo Picasso had a "blue period" (a body of work, produced
between 1900 and 1904, which was preoccupied with meditations on
twilight shades and blue-green hues), for example, and many artists
have followed Picasso's lead into the monochromatic world. Few, however, have taken it to the radical lengths Klein did, for whom blue became
a trademark (and trademarked) shade. Beginning in 1956 and continuing
until his untimely death from a heart attack in the summer of 1962, Klein
made the decision to paint exclusively in one shade of deep ultramarine
blue. Critics have noted the "religiously transcendent language with
which Klein spoke of the color"[19]—even going so far as to trademark his
own personal shade, International Klein Blue (IKB), described as an
"ordinary ultramarine with polymer binder to preserve its intensity."[20]
Klein's audacity led him to exhibitions that featured repetitious canvases,
all covered in the same nonrepresentational hue, and at least once to an
exhibition in a major gallery consisting of a completely empty room.
This exhibition, entitled "The Void" by Klein, as mentioned above, was
at the Galerie Iris Clert in Paris.

Klein has been most often compared to another artist-provocateur of
the early twentieth century, Marcel Duchamp. Though the comparison
is apt, the mention of Duchamp does little to categorize Klein's work or
motivations. Such gestures as repetitive, monochromatic canvases and
the proffering of empty space as a content could be classified as "abstract
art," of course, but Klein adamantly resisted this label, insisting that he
was "not an abstract painter but, on the contrary, a figurative artist, and
a realist."[21]

Klein pursued this "realism" by profoundly unorthodox means, which
he elaborated upon in the several short philosophical manifestoes he

[18] Kerry Brougher and Philippe Vergne, "Acknowledgments," in Kerry Brougher,
et al., *Yves Klein: With the Void, Full Powers* (Washington and Minneapolis: Hirshorn
Museum and Walker Art Center, 2011), 13.

[19] Leo J. O'Donovan, "Blue Streak: Review of 'Yves Klein: With the Void, Full
Powers,'" *Commonweal* (September 2010): 28.

[20] Ibid.

[21] Ibid.

wrote concerning his work. In "My Position in the Battle between Line and Color," for example, Klein unequivocally rejects the conventions of line and form in painting, dismissing them as a "prison window" of psychological limitation. "Lines concretize our mortality," Klein writes. "Color, on the other hand, is the natural and human measure; it bathes in a cosmic sensibility. The sensibility of a painter is not encumbered by mysterious nooks and crannies. Contrary to what the line tends to lead us to believe . . . color is sensibility become matter—matter in its first, primal state."[22] Klein's monochromes were not abstract; rather, they were absolutely factual representations of reality. Klein was often asked, "what does this [painting] represent?" He responded, in the beginning, "This simply represents blue," and eventually ceased responding altogether.[23]

Klein insisted throughout his career that such literal representations were neither jokes nor clichéd provocations. When he proffered a canvas painted entirely in blue (or, at other times, entirely in an orange hue, which he also referred to as "blue"), he was deadly serious. "When there are two colors in a painting," he writes, "a struggle is engaged; the viewer may extract a refined pleasure from the permanent spectacle of this struggle between two colors in the psychological or emotional realm . . . but it is one that is no less morbid from a pure philosophical and human vantage point."[24] This principled refusal to enter into the conflict of colors, to provide observers with the base pleasure of the struggle of strong against the weak, elevates Klein's project above the aesthetic realm. His monochromes at their core are moral statements.[25]

Klein's intention in all of these gestures—his monochromes, his later "flame paintings" (created with fire, as you would expect), and even with the empty gallery of "the Void"—is simply to present, and represent, reality itself. Through his gestures Klein awakens our senses to the space around us as a valued world; that is, a world of ordinary things made precious through extraordinary and invisible relationships: "The painter

---

[22] Klein, *Problematics of Art*, 19.

[23] Ibid., 138.

[24] Ibid., 140.

[25] Indeed, much of Klein's "The Monochrome Adventure" strikes this sort of idealistic and moral tone, as summed up by the following quotation: "The role of the painter in the society of the future will be to live 'externally,' to live *in* a collectivity in which he will refine, through his presence, the best, the purest, and the most delicate states of sensibility and its atmosphere so that these, quite simply, may be healthful, gay and good!" Ibid., 149.

is the one who knows how to specify that real value, that sensibility that is born out of the belief and the knowledge that there is poetry if matter consists of concentrated energy, as science has concluded in its latest analysis."[26] Klein's faith in these invisible relationships is not a faith in positivist expression. Klein explicitly rejects the conventional tools of line, shape, form, and structure. For Klein, true art is alchemy, not photography. "The canvas beholds, in an instant, the 'indefinable,' which stands between a truly and poetically free person and itself."[27]

This insistence, that the Void actually functions as a representation, helps to elucidate this notion of the avant-garde gesture in light of Barth's epistemic challenge. Throughout each, ever increasingly serious, action, Klein managed to maintain and indeed heighten his reputation as a central and vital artist. In other words, far from excluding him from the artistic milieu, these gestures, though incomprehensible in terms of classification, were nonetheless recognized in their incomprehensibility. In short, these gestures were communicative and effective, for if they were not, Klein would not have long remained accepted as a serious artist. Far from being rejected, however, *Paris Match* once referred to Klein as "the greatest painter in the world."[28]

Reed

In the thirty-five years since its initial release, it is unclear how best to understand Lou Reed's uncanny *Metal Machine Music.* The work consists of four LP album sides of meticulously recorded, stereo-separated, multiple-guitar feedback. The result is a screaming wall of undulating, shimmering noise. The tonal register is reminiscent of standing in the middle of a busy factory floor without earplugs. Long, siren-like drones swirl, punctuated by machine gun-like bursts of treble. The mixture grows insistent, whistling and humming, and then ebbs to a growling calm. It is a room full of radios all tuned to static, the volume pegged at eleven. It is the whine of the telephone at the end of the movie *Fail Safe.* In its uncompromising sonic landscape, *Metal Machine Music* is all of this and much, much more.

[26] Ibid., 146–47.
[27] Ibid., 156.
[28] O'Donovan, "Blue Streak," 28.

Dismissed by some as a joke intended to get Reed out of a contract with his record company,[29] others have heralded the work as the inspiration and anticipation of punk rock and avant-noise groups like Sonic Youth, Hüsker Dü and Germany's Einsteurzende Neubauten. David Fricke, writing the liner notes for the 2000 reissue of the album, explains that moreover

> *Metal Machine Music* now enjoys a second life as Art. It is considered a pivotal work of ambient music and was recently used as the soundtrack for a museum installation in Germany. But *Metal Machine Music* was made with rock & roll tools, built from the base elements of electric teenage revolution: rage, joy, sabotage, righteousness. *Metal Machine Music* was not a new kind of rock; it was every kind of rock, boiled down to its molten essence.[30]

In this assertion that *Metal Machine Music* represents the "molten essence" of rock we hear an echo of Klein's assertion that his blue monochromatic paintings "simply represent blue." Like Klein's work, Reed's album is troubling to those who seek clear boundaries of style and genre; where Klein's detractors may have demanded he add a line or a dot of contrast to his monochromes to render them "acceptable," one also hears in the early critical reception of *Metal Machine Music* the condemnation of Reed for his refusal to offer any semblance of structure. "In its droning, shapeless indifference, Metal Machine Music is hopelessly old-fashioned," James Wolcott wrote in his 1975 *Rolling Stone* review of the work, giving the album no stars. "Lou Reed is disdainfully unveiling the black hole in his personal universe, but the question is, who's supposed to flinch?"[31]

I flinched, for one. I have made several forays into listening to the entire four side wall of sound that careens from the first second of the recording to the last, lingering, locked-groove instant of the thing. The process is always uncomfortable and very jarring—at least at first. I would not say it is possible to enjoy the piece, but I can say without reservation that I appreciate it. The sound is not simply white noise or

---

[29] Amanda Petrusich, "Interview with Lou Reed," Pitchfork Media Online, http://pitchfork.com/features/interviews/6690-lou-reed.

[30] David Fricke, "Most of You Won't Like This, and I Don't Blame You at All," liner notes to reissue of Lou Reed, *Metal Machine Music: An Electronic Musical Composition, * The Amine ß Ring*, compact disc, Buddha Records/BMG 74465 99752 2.

[31] James Wolcott, "Review of Lou Reed, *Metal Machine Music*" (original review appeared August 14, 1975), *Rolling Stone* online, http://www.rollingstone.com/music/albumreviews/metal-machine-music-19750814.

feedback. It offers an overwhelming amount of information for the ears to take in, particularly when listening through headphones. With such over-stimulation, the mind begins to hear layers and patterns within the sound. Fricke agrees, "If you go back through the rest of *Metal Machine Music*, you start to hear a certain oblique cohesion, patterns and effects that surge in and out of the chaos: shrill pipe-organ-like chords; treble-y shivers of demented surf guitar."[32] I can attest to this phenomenon. There are, however, no pipe organs in the recording, and neither are there surf guitars. Instead, what the listener experiences through continued exposure to the sounds is an alchemy similar to the one Klein described. In the fray of the noise, Reed's world of sound becomes invisibly valued. As a gesture of "music," Reed's *Metal Machine Music* is, like Klein's canvasses, an event that is "indefinable," but nevertheless communicative.

Fricke writes that "to truly love *Metal Machine Music*, you have to learn to laugh with it." At times Reed may laugh, too, as he has in later interviews, but there is a gravitas to the work upon which Reed has always insisted. His own self-assessment, from the original liner notes of the album, strongly resonates with Klein's attestations about the moral nature of art: "passion—REALISM—realism was the key . . . this [record] is what I meant by 'real' rock, about 'real' things," Reed proclaims.

Even if you are clear in your expectations when you begin listening, however, *Metal Machine Music* is likely to thwart them and take you somewhere else entirely. Because it is a decisively non-"rock and roll" record from a quintessential "rock and roll" musician, the work remains an enigma. When critics approach it, they often must do so at the most basic, architectural level, giving description instead of interpretation: "The harsh feedback sounds are, of course, tones; some of them have a drone-like character, others swarm chaotically," writes Torbin Sanglid. "There is no structure, but there is a *texture* with the drones as temporary points of orientation between traditional opposites—the expressionistic scream and the meditative mantra."[33]

Despite the difficulties we may have in deciphering the message, Reed himself is adamant that the work is meant to be a gesture of communication, even in its incomprehensibility. "If *Metal Machine* is anything, it's energy and physicality, and you should be able to physically feel it,"

---

[32] Fricke, liner notes to *Metal Machine Music*.

[33] Torben Sangild, "Noise: Three Musical Gestures; Expressionist, Introvert and Minimal Noise," *JMM—The Journal of Music and Meaning* 2 (2004), printout, accessed at http://www.musicandmeaning.net/issues/showArticle.php?artID=2.4.

Reed explains, adding, "the myth is sort of better than the truth. The myth is that I made it to get out of a recording contract. OK, but the truth is I wouldn't do that, because I wouldn't want you to buy a record that I didn't really like. . . . The truth is that I really, really, really loved it."[34]

It's clear that other listeners have loved it, too, despite its difficulty. Steve Albini and Lester Bangs have both written appreciative commentaries of the piece, with Bangs going so far (with tongue in cheek, one imagines) as to insist that it was "the greatest album ever made." "If you ever thought feedback was the best thing that ever happened to the guitar," Bangs writes, "well, Lou just got rid of the guitars."[35]

When I think of that painting I saw in the museum—the tiny boat, the enormous wave engulfing them, pulling them down down into the Sublime, the Abyss, the Void—I have no doubt whatsoever that *Metal Machine Music* would be the soundtrack for that terrifying moment.

To the Void

Starting with the Romantic poets, we have briefly attempted here to understand the "characters of the great Apocalypse," the specters of the awe-filled silence that hold us in thrall as we confront the Void. Barth names the silence as the "frontier" where the event of Christ robs us of solidity, as a bombshell opens a crater and where "By faith we are what we are not."[36] Klein insists upon the simplicity and moral shape of this emptiness, the Void that presents and represents the world in its truth, offering the world its value. Similarly, in the molten essence of *Metal Machine Music*, Reed also seeks to present and represent truth, to offer us "real" rock about "real" things. Reed makes the gesture as a wholly gratuitous act, calling the album "the only recorded work I know of seriously done as well as possible as a gift."[37]

The avant-garde gesture, the *tertium quid*, is the gift of truth, of "real" things. But it is a gift only given on the deck of the ship, in the heart of the storm, as the waves are crashing. It marks a communicative action

---

[34] Lou Reed, "Interview with Lou Reed," Amanda Petrusich, Pitchfork Media Online, http://pitchfork.com/features/interviews/6690-lou-reed.

[35] Lester Bangs, "The Greatest Album Ever Made," *Creem* (March 1976), reprinted with permission by Matt Carmichael at http://www.rocknroll.net/loureed/articles/mmmbangs.html.

[36] Barth, *Romans*, 149.

[37] Reed, liner notes to *Metal Machine Music*.

taken in desperation of being understood, in the face of the radical limitations of language. To return to Wordsworth's poem, with which we began this reflection, the gesture functions "as if it had a voice," despite (or indeed because of) the impossibility of giving words to the "real" things with which it is consumed—the Abyss, the Sublime, the Void.

As such, the avant-garde gesture offers a third possibility, suspended beyond the apophatic gesture of the negative theologian and the positivity of the scientist. Though it may be misunderstood as an empty refusal to communicate, the avant-garde gesture is instead simply empty communication. Like Grünewald's John the Baptist, the gesture names all that words cannot. It points to the Void, and, in pointing, invokes a nameless name for the Beauty of that terrifying frontier. Echoing Reed, it is the pure molten essence of "energy and physicality," confronting the recipient in the vastness of the wave and the vacuousness of the crater, in the blue that is simply blue itself, beyond language but not beyond communication.

Chapter 2

_____

Musical Space:
Living "In Between" the Christian
and the Artistic Callings

Maeve Louise Heaney

*An essential pre-requisite for the salvaging of the truly real from
among its surrounding confusion is that the individual existence
should know about both the reality and the confusion.
Accordingly, poetic activity can only occur in a frontier position.*

Ladislaus Boros, SJ[1]

The boundary is the best place to acquire information.

Paul Tillich[2]

I read somewhere that when asked about their move away from explicit Christian music in the early stages of U2's existence, Bono quipped
that now they were doing the same but without looking like they were.
When a band can stand before thousands in a rock concert and invite
them to "turn this song into a prayer, if you are the praying kind," round-
ing off an impassioned plea for peace with a song/prayer to Jesus,[3]
I guess one can at least say that the path taken was a fruitful one. There
are many ways to describe the position they and many other musicians
have chosen: the boundary between the "sacred" and the "secular" (if

---

[1] Quoted in Rosemary Haughton, *The Passionate God* (London: Darton, Longman
and Todd, 1981), 85.

[2] Paul Tillich, *Sulla linea del confine: schizzo autobiografico* (Brescia: Queriniana, 1969),
29. Translation mine.

[3] See http://www.youtube.com/watch?v=tw3GuCUKJAM.

such a clear-cut line even exists); the frontier between music explicitly born of and meant to transmit the Christian experience, and music born (simply) in and of life experience, an honest expression of human living; or the space "in between" one's identity as a Christian and one's identity as a musician.

In the complex world we live in, in which rock concerts can look and sound like major worship sessions and seem to feed the experience of "spirituality" of those who attend, this chapter explores that space: the frontier which is not only (or even) external, but that runs right through anyone who has faith and, therefore, knows doubt; who inhabits the world as a Christian, and is, therefore, "in this world, but not of this world" (John 17:16); who discovers in contemporary, secular (rock, pop, or indie) music a space or a place in which their Christian existence breathes, moves, dances and even thrives, precisely because it *is* "in between," on the boundary and frontier of the various dimensions of their lives.

I contend that there is a need to inhabit and explore this "space," precisely because it is not an external one, but rather one which any Christian artist feels in their flesh, blood, and bones. David Tracy describes the triple audience of theology as being the Church, Culture, and the Academy, and Lonergan identifies its role as one of mediating between lived religion and the cultural matrix it inhabits.[4] But the first "space" in which that mediation takes place is inside oneself—where church, culture, and thought overlap, intersect, and sometimes disagree or argue! These are the "in-between" places in and through which the Spirit blows where she wills (John 3:8), and bridges worlds, as well as opposite sides that are perhaps not meant to be resolved one way or the other, but precisely to be held together. A bridge is a bridge, not a campground; a frontier is a place that marks a line, a relationship. It marks a point of union and of separation, in dialogue, or in tension, and could it not be that the tension needs to be held so that the resulting sound is what it should be? (A guitar string relies on the right tension to be played.) Life is rich and complex, and from the surplus of meaning our refraining to resolve all things allows, new and fruitful insights could be born. It is in inhabiting that space inside ourselves between these

---

[4] See Bernard Lonergan, *Method in Theology* (New York: The Seabury Press, 1972), xi.

diverse "worlds" that we will think, play, and express ourselves in such a way that we can be a bridge for others.

I think the above invitation applies to all theology, but for the realm of music and theology, it is indispensable. There is an "in-between" space in the life of a Christian musician and/or composer that is a place of creative tension, which this chapter seeks to identify, reflect upon, and offer as a *locus* in need of attention and thought. In doing so, I will draw from a few different sources: the first is the work of Italian theologian and musician Pierangelo Sequeri on the thought of Hans Urs von Balthasar, which highlights the similarities and differences between the artistic and Christian callings.[5] It is on art in its various forms, rather than only music, and highlights the similarities and differences of two "vocations" or "callings": the artistic and the Christian. The second is an amazing prayer-article of Karl Rahner called "Prayer for Creative Thinkers,"[6] which reads like a plea from the heart for "thinkers" who dare to write unashamedly from the core of human experience. He is not only calling for creative writing in theology (which would also be nice!), but for creative "thinkers" for the world at large, who explore and offer poetic "primordial words"[7] capable of enlivening and renewing not only our language but also our perception of reality. These theologians point

---

[5] Pierangelo Sequeri, *Anti-Prometeo. Il Musicale nell'Estetica Teologica di Hans Urs von Balthasar* (Milano: Glossa, 1995), 71–77. Balthasar was an Austrian theologian, and although it is probably fair to say he would never have written on rock music, to him we need to attribute the return of beauty and the arts to the center of theological discourse in western theology. Pierangelo Sequeri, although little known in the English-speaking world, is one of the most well-known and respected contemporary Italian theologians who is an expert on Balthasar's thought. Born in Milan, a son of two musicians and himself a composer and musician, he writes in the area of fundamental theology and theological aesthetics, as well as pioneering pastoral initiatives such as *Esagramma*: a "music-therapy" initiative with children and young people with learning difficulties. He is one of the few authors who insightfully analyses Hans Urs von Balthasar's scarce writings on music, and as such is an invaluable source for theology on and about music.

[6] Karl Rahner, "Prayer for Creative Thinkers," in *Theological Investigations* 8, trans. D. Bourke (London: Darton, Longman and Todd, 1971), 130–32. Unless otherwise stated, quotations from Rahner are from this short two-page writing. The translation I use is directly from the English edition, albeit adapted with inclusive language.

[7] See another beautiful writing called "Priest and Poet" in which he talks of the difference between primordial words and "utility" words and the need for Christian expression to be spoken afresh through the former. Karl Rahner, "Priest and Poet," in *Theological Investigations* 3 (London: Darton, Longman and Todd, 1974).

toward the "holding together of tensions" that inhabiting the world of music and theology implies. As will become clear, my conviction is that this is unmarked ground, and there is no clear-cut formula to explain the way forward. If, however, we understand that there are, in fact, tensions or even oppositions that have to be held in creative tension, then we are better equipped for that path. Doing so implies listening to the experience of artists, composers, and performers about how they live that calling, so I include in this chapter some reflections drawn from a personal and helpfully introspective book of interviews with Bono,[8] as well as some other musicians or composers. And finally, since this is not a thought process I can stand neutrally outside of, it is colored by my own experiences of composing and making music, as well as the theological insights gained over the last few years from seeking to understand what happens there.

Two Callings in One

Invoke your Holy Spirit upon them!
Raise up among us people endowed with creative powers,
thinkers, poets, artists [musicians]. We have need of them.[9]

Perhaps this is our best starting point: a prayer to God to call forth and grace us with people "called" to be musicians, composers, creative presences in the world and the Church. And although the point may seem obvious, it is important: the humble recognition that it is indeed a vocation, a calling, a gift and giftedness written in the genes, and which comes from another. And even where all musicians may not express themselves in the same terms as a theologian such as Rahner would, is it not true that artistic creativity is experienced as vocation, as the necessary and unique response to one's existence in the world, nearly a "command" on which one's meaning and role in life depends? Melodramatic, perhaps, but not uncommon, as the artistic experience goes: American composer Aaron Copland, when writing on the dynamic he experiences in composing music, starts by asking the question, not about the "how" of composing, but rather about the "why":

---

[8] *Bono on Bono: Conversations with Michka Assayas* (London: Hodder and Stoughton, 2005).

[9] Karl Rahner, "Prayer for Creative Thinkers," 130.

[W]hy is it so important to my own psyche that I compose music? What makes it seem so absolutely necessary, that every other daily activity, by comparison, is of lesser significance? Why is the creative impulse never satisfied; why must one always begin anew?[10]

This echoes the eloquent advice of poet Rainer Maria Rilke to a young poet upon being asked for an opinion about his work. Rilke, in his answer, went to the very foundation of the artistic calling and advised the young poet:

Above all, in the most silent hour of your night, ask yourself this: *must* I write? Dig deep into yourself for a true answer. And if this answer rings out in assent, if you can confidently meet this serious question with a simple, "I must", then build your life in accordance with this necessity.[11]

If not, Rilke says, then serenely, and without regret, do something else.

Some would say this position of Rilke is excessively demanding and that good art or poetry need not be felt quite so acutely in order to be valid. And yet, there is something profound and urgent about the creative call and process which affects the very depths of who we are, and therein lies its importance. It is not something one does with little personal involvement or cost, and therefore must have an important place in our overall understanding of our Christian calling to share in God's own life, and in some way to minister or mission in the Church and the world. But that general Christian calling to the following of Christ unfolds in each and every person's individual life and particular ministry, which is unique, personal, and nontransferable. I would contend that uniqueness and particularity have a rather intense color of their own in the artistic realm, and necessarily so, although within Christian consciousness this is sometimes lived as a battle of opposites, or a stumbling block, instead of as a source of creative and fertile faithfulness.

Since a useful posing of the problem is formulated by Balthasar and transmitted by Sequeri, let us continue there. Talking about how music fits into Balthasar's theological aesthetics, Sequeri explains how, according to the Swiss theologian, both Christians and artists share the sense of a calling and the fact that both are incapable of inscribing "the absolute in the singular," although the call to do so underlies both. The difference

---

[10] Aaron Copland, *Music and Imagination* (Cambridge: Harvard University Press, 1952), 40.

[11] Rainer Marie Rilke, "The First Letter," in *Letters to a Young Poet 1*, trans. J.M. Burnham (Novato, CA: New World Library, 2000), 11.

lies in the fact that that the religious person receives his or her call in total obedience, whereas the artist, in the most perfect autonomy:

> The religious person and the artistic one present . . . peculiar points of contact and outright opposition. Although both are depositories of a "command" that in some way comes from outside oneself, as an "inspiration" and a "grace," they are, however, separated by the form of the required obedience to that vocation. The person who is consecrated religiously receives his or her command in absolute detachment through ecclesiastical obedience; the artist, instead, carries it out in the most perfect creative freedom. *Their respective spiritual realms are radically separate from the point of view of the involvement of the subject*: so much so that *it remains impossible to think that one would automatically develop through the complete involvement of the spirit implicated in the other.*[12]

The dilemma is clear. Despite the fact that religion and art are both lived as "callings," they pull against one another. And yet, are these two callings really destined to pull against each other? Are they incompatible? Or would identifying these "points of contact and outright opposites" help us to hold them together and play them out? I believe it would, and that not only are they unavoidable but also something of a condition of possibility for a fruitful outcome of the artistic endeavour, without which we could not be present to the world nor prophetic. In the following reflections, I reflect upon a few such traits, in the hope that recognition may at least ease felt tensions and open further reflection.

Obedience and Autonomy

Artists are selfish People.[13]

> *Those men and women who are engaged in constantly producing new expressions of their own nature and spirit, [are] people who are the architects of themselves. You love the sort of person who realizes her own being in what she achieves and produces, who discovers and expresses that nature which is an image and likeness of your own glory.*[14]

Rahner's description of what a creative thinker is doing is an audacious one. It surely implies a noteworthy sense of self, of what one feels

---

[12] Pierangelo Sequeri, *Anti-Prometeo. Il Musicale nell'Estetica Teologica di Hans Urs von Balthasar* (Milano: Glossa, 1995), 72. Translation and emphasis mine.

[13] *Bono on Bono*, 25.

[14] Rahner, "Prayer for Creative Thinkers," 130.

and wants, an awareness of the surrounding world as well as one's reaction to it, to "constantly engage in producing new expressions of one's own nature and spirit." We could debate how even this self-understanding of an artistic or musical person is a product of modernity's coronation of self at the center of the universe, but postmodernity, as its offspring, still carries some of that heritage. However mature and humble a musician or an artist may be, there is a huge amount of self and individual expression in any good music or other artistic form. This, I would say, beyond any superficial quest for limelight or fame, is why we are so fascinated by the lives behind those whose music or art we admire. We ask: Where did it come from? Who is the person who from whom this piece of music emerged? What were they living at the time?

George Steiner, in his beautiful book on art as a "real presence" of the divine in the world, seeking to understand the artistic phenomenon, suggests that the impulse behind its creation is a type of envy: "I believe that the making into being by the poet, artist and . . . composer, is *counter*-creation."[15] Picasso talks of the "other craftsman" who worked in six days! The question underlying artistic work, albeit implicit, would be something akin to: "Why was I not at the beginning, why is not mine the organizing deed of form coming into meaning?"[16] So is it obedience versus autonomy, imitation versus creation, self versus the supreme Other? Or is it both?

Sequeri talks about another common trait between a Christian and an artist: devotion (commitment, dedication, surrender—*hingabe* in German; *dedizione* in Italian):

> [A]ccording to Balthasar . . . the motivating nucleus of every religious and artistic experience is also always one of devotion. . . . Dedication to the impossible possibility of saying the unsayable is rooted in a vocation which in both cases presents profound affinity.[17]

Here lies another in-between space: an attitude of devotion and surrender to God, from which Christian musicianship is born, and the absolute dedication of any composer or band writing and mixing their music in

---

[15] Steiner, *Real Presences*, 203.

[16] Steiner, *Real Presences*, 205. He qualifies this statement with an observation on the difference between men and women in this dynamic, which I would agree with in part. As an intuition, I think it holds some truth.

[17] Pierangelo Sequeri, *Anti-Prometeo. Il Musicale nell'Estetica Teologica di Hans Urs von Balthasar* (Milano: Glossa, 1995), 75.

order to make what one intuits musically sound *exactly right* when it is performed or recorded. Listening to God and listening to self as something is birthed can be difficult. John Paul II talks about the *pathos* of the artist as a participation in God's own pathos:

> None can sense more deeply than you artists, ingenious creators of beauty that you are, something of the pathos with which God at the dawn of creation looked upon the work of his hands . . . you have admired the work of your inspiration, sensing in it some echo of the mystery of creation with which God, the sole creator of all things, has wished in some way to associate you.[18]

This pathos is not without tension or pain. In the words of Irish poet Patrick Kavanagh, in a poem ironically called "Sanctity":

> *To be a poet and not to know the trade,*
> *To be a lover and repel all women;*
> *Twin ironies by which great saints are made,*
> *The agonising pincer-jaws of Heaven.*[19]

Sensibility and the Understanding of Faith

> *In words and in images, in their whole attitude and presentation they express what is in [humans] because they proclaim what they themselves experience. And in expressing this let them express everything!*[20]

A Christian is called to live by faith, not by appearances, or by feelings that can come and go. Yet the musician's call is to compose and play from a place of honest feeling and experience. "And . . . let them express everything!" Should musicians express things that seem to challenge the serene conviction of their faith? Should temptation be played out? Should songwriters write something that is born of anger with the world or with God, or despair in the face of evil, or hopelessness that things will ever change? And even more profoundly, perhaps the real question is: should they feel it? I think of the profound honesty of Damien Rice's prayer-song "Cold Water,"[21] which to my mind crystalizes (perhaps even without attempting it) how the Irish people *feel* faith at the present time. Or the

---

[18] John Paul II, *Letter to Artists,* 1999, number 1.
[19] Patrick Kavanagh, "Sanctity," in *Collected Poems* (London: Allen Lane, 2004), 17.
[20] Karl Rahner, "Prayer for Creative Thinkers," 130.
[21] Damien Rice, "Cold Water," *O,* Vector Recordings, 2002.

understated and "oh so English" (dis)interest in faith expressed in The Streets' poignant "Never Went to Church."[22] Or the implicit idolatry in the cry for healing mercy from another human being in Coldplay's "Fix You"[23] (organ and polyphony included). In honest, felt, and expressed human experience something happens. Something is transmitted. And that something implies an artist "behind" the song who is not afraid, not only to express love, laughter, deep happiness, pain, and suffering, and yet believe in and through it all, but also to *feel* it. Contemporary sensibility describes the effect of this kind of honesty as somehow "salvific." There is a great scene in the film *Walk the Line* about Johnny Cash, marking his move from singing explicit songs on faith to singing about life, in all its crudeness, that expresses precisely what I am trying to say. After singing a "typical" faith-inspired song about the peace God gives, a producer challenges him with the following words:

> If you was hit by a truck, and you was lying outside that gutter dying, and you had time to sing one song, one song that people would remember before you're dirt . . . One song that would let God know what you felt about your time here on earth, . . . you telling me that's the song you would sing . . . about peace within and how you're gonna shout it? Or would you sing something different, something real, something you felt? Cause I'm telling you right now, that's the kinda song that people wanna hear; that's the kinda song that truly saves people.[24]

Whether or not this reflects how he made that shift, the point is clear and it is one that various chapters of this book seek to illustrate with regard to diverse human experiences in need of salvation, such as trauma, abuse, or racism—honest expression can be liberating and salvific. The way to experiencing God's grace is not avoiding the harshness of human existence and paying more attention to the potential (or future?) goodness of life in God, but rather to follow God's gaze, and the direction of his loving action, through the incarnation, to human life and history, and find God there, or rather, here. Our images of God sometimes underestimate God's passion, as if the depth of our feelings (especially the negative ones) were too much for God to handle! Sequeri, in an excep-

---

[22] The Streets, "Never Went to Church," *The Hardest Way to Make an Easy Living*, Locked on Records, 2006 [Accessed June 28, 2012]. http://www.virginmedia.com/music/musicvideos/thestreets_neverwenttochurch_hi.php

[23] Coldplay, "Fix You," *X&Y*, Parlophone, 2005.

[24] *Walk the Line*, 2005, directed by James Mangold. [Transcription mine.]

tional book called *The Fear of God*[25] unfolds a biblical narrative sketching the Abba of Jesus and challenging our feeble images of God's love. In the God of Jesus there is the "depth of an affection that sweeps away the impassive marmoreal profile of the dignity of God" and the staidness of our expressions evoking "senile tolerance we dare to call mercy."[26] God is not offended by human feeling and pain. Indeed, the passionate and tender God of Jesus is the very root of our human capacity to feel. This is the backbone of the contemporary theological approach which names human experience as the first stage of knowledge, theological included. And coming back to our point about musical expression, naming experience and allowing people to find themselves in that mirror can be the first stage to being found there by grace.

Bernard Lonergan wrote little on art or music, but what he does say is eloquent. In the dynamic of human knowing, he situates art and music on the level of experience (the first step in all human knowledge), as an enrichment of our concrete living:

> Art is relevant to concrete living, that is, it is an exploration of the potentialities of concrete living. That exploration is extremely important in our age, when philosophers for at least two centuries, through doctrines on politics, economics, education, and through even further doctrines, have been trying to remake [humanity], and have done not a little to make life unliveable. The great task that is demanded if we are to make it liveable again is the re-creation of the liberty of the subject, the recognition of the freedom of consciousness.[27]

Music, therefore, is not a privilege of the elite who have certain interests, or theologians who have time to delve into enjoyable pastimes, but an important means of renewing the way we experience and live out our concrete life, because it aids in freeing our awareness, our consciousness, the way we apprehend the world we inhabit and ourselves in the midst of it. In the words of Steiner, "The exceptional artist or thinker reads being anew."[28] Instead of accepting how the meaning of things is given to us, a creative musician reads the world anew, differently, and helps us experience life in a richer and deeper way. Copland answers his own

---

[25] Pierangelo Sequeri, *Il Timore di Dio* (Milan: Vita e Pensiero, 1993).
[26] Ibid., 75.
[27] Lonergan, "Art," 232.
[28] Steiner, *Real Presences*, 195.

question on the experience and role of composing by underlining this bond between art and experience:

> [E]ach new and significant work of art is a unique formulation of experience; an experience that would be utterly lost if it were not captured and set down by the artist.[29]

Of course, not only artists have this capacity or privilege. God graces the world with creative thinkers in many ways, but is it not precisely how music makes us feel about the world and ourselves that draws us to it? As a consequence, having music that enriches how we feel and experience life implies musicians who embrace and live *through* their sensibility, in both its strength and fragility: looking at the world in all its beauty and ugliness; trusting in God's strength even when it is nowhere to be seen; risking new experiments although the old stuff still "kind of" works.

To do so suggests a dynamic of hope while not withdrawing one's gaze from the darkness seen outside or felt within; trust and risk, Christian artists.

> *Give them the courage to attain to the light and to the joy in the darkness of this age and in all the hunger and poverty of our hearts.*[30]

This is a priceless and costly business. Life in Jesus is a promise of full life,[31] and if Jesus' life is anything to go by, then fullness of life is painfully beautiful, life in the realm of love's call, where one will laugh with all one's laughter and weep with all one's tears.[32] Jesus assumed humanity in all that it is, and therefore God can be found "in all things," in the depths of our human living and loving, trusting, doubting, celebrating, and mourning. Living at depth is for all Christians. Understanding it, intuiting it, finding meaning and expressing that in ways that open rich spaces to appreciate it is the artist's task. In Lonergan's terms:

> Meaning lies within the consciousness of the artist but, at first, it is only implicit, folded up, veiled, unrevealed, unobjectified. Aware of it, the artist has to get a hold of it; he is impelled to behold, inspect,

---

[29] Copland, *Music and Imagination*, 41.

[30] Rahner, "Prayer for Creative Thinkers," 131.

[31] See John 10:10.

[32] See Kahlil Gibran, "Speak to us of Love," in *The Prophet* (Middlesex: The Echo Library, 2006), 4.

> dissect, enjoy, repeat it; and this means objectifying, unfolding, making explicit, unveiling, revealing.[33]

Lonergan's language tends to be quite technical, but if we keep in mind that the experiences a composer is called "to behold, inspect, dissect, enjoy, repeat," may well be ones of love, pain, anger, or prayer, then one can intuit just how central and developed the musician's sensibility is called to be. I wonder that Christian churches and communities are still so unaware of the preparation, training, and even spiritual wisdom implied in such a vocation. Sandra Schneiders, from the perspective of Catholic religious life and Christian spirituality, has stated that the maturity of a Christian community can be noted in the capacity they have to integrate their artists.[34] Instead of complaining about an "over-developed artistic sensitivity," or fearing personality clashes, if we allow spontaneity free reign, understanding the role and importance of sensibility in art and growing in wisdom and knowledge about how it works would open paths more easily and serenely.

But this pertains especially to the explicitly Christian domain, which needs both to grow in its understanding of music itself and to face up to the implicit (and often unconscious) assumptions that colour its positions before it will ever solve the "worship wars" that plague our celebrations. Let us return to the "in between" space of our theme and look at one final area of creative opposites in need of being held together.

From Implicit to Explicit and Back Again

> *And therefore, whether we realise it or not, every creative activity of the human spirit has become an element in the personal history of your Word, because everything has come to belong to this world, the world into which he came in order to share with it in its living experiences, to suffer with it and to glorify it with himself.*[35]

Rahner's theology of "Anonymous Christianity" is famous, and at this stage is, I believe, part of our shared *sensus fidelium*, whether because it has filtered down into lived religion, or because he was ahead of his time

---

[33] Lonergan, *Method in Theology*, 63–64.

[34] I am grateful to Prof. Schneiders for confirming this statement with me as part of her conviction, although she has not (yet) written explicitly on the theme. December 5, 2011.

[35] Rahner, "Prayer for Creative Thinkers," 131–32.

in understanding how God's grace works. For those readers who may be unfamiliar with this aspect of his thought, it proposes that, in God's universal desire to reach out and save all humanity, grace is readily offered to all, be it explicitly, through the teaching and message of the Church, or in a hidden way, implicitly, through God's love poured out in the world, silently and constantly.[36] Rahner calls this grace the "supernatural existential." He says that, in every option of knowledge and freedom that we make, we either open up to and receive that grace, implicitly welcoming God's love into our lives, and as such becoming channels of that grace to the world, or we close off and "say no" to love's grace. Those who are receptive he called (although the term was very contested and has its own pitfalls) "anonymous Christians": people who, although they do not identify themselves as Christians or belong to any institutional church, live in God's saving grace as they are open to it in the existential options of their daily life. Despite the obvious problems the concepts he uses may provoke in us (such as seeming patronizing to those who do not identify with Christian faith, and the apparent danger of relativizing the role of the Church and the need to belong to it), this theological perspective sketches a plausible explanation of how we experience God in our lives and in the lives of those we interact with: present, powerful, graced. This is the understanding underlying his prayer for those of us working in the creative field:

> For this kingdom does not only come from without as the end and the final judgment of this present world. It emerges as the hidden grace which has been present in the midst of this earthly reality ever since your own Word descended into creation and became the heart of all things.[37]

And "every creative act of the human spirit" is implicated in the history of God's action in the world through the Word, whose grace works efficaciously in the hearts of all those open to it "in a manner known only to God."[38]

This Rahnerian teaching opens an "in between" space for music and theology to share and create in. Grace dances in and moves between the worlds of explicit and implicit faith, human and divine love, and know-

---

[36] For an accessible and fuller account of Rahner's theology on this point, see Michael Paul Gallagher, *Faith Maps: Ten Religious Explorers from Newman to Benedict XVI* (London and New York: Darton, Longman and Todd / Paulist Press, 2010), 36–49, especially 40–42.

[37] Rahner, "Prayer for Creative Thinkers," 132.

[38] See *Gaudium et Spes* 22.

ing that does not in any way imply relativizing our beliefs, but rather celebrating the generosity and wisdom of God, who freely gives. It can help us hear Sting's honest definition of himself as a "devout musician," and his fear of [organized] religion as potentially dangerous,[39] without defensiveness or cynicism, at the same time as lamenting whatever it is that scandalizes him about our attempts at lived faith. It allows us to listen to and make music without having to delineate ever so clearly the secular-sacred divide, since God passes through that wall effortlessly. It allows us to compose songs which speak of God in new ways, perhaps not quite so obviously, free of the fear of not saying everything that needs to be said. Maybe God doesn't need that much help. Maybe the ineffable can transmit itself without so many of our words to point the way. I would go further and ask why ambiguity is such a problem in certain theological circles. Were Jesus' parables not ambiguous at times? Do we not need to learn to be at peace with not being able to express or explain it all?[40]

> *They do not need to be constantly bringing you into everything they say. They must make mention of you by name only when they are filled with the spirit of the purest happiness or the deepest pain. For the rest let them honor you with their silence. For the rest let them praise the earth and humanity.*[41]

Implicit and explicit are not only external spheres. There is another implicit/explicit boundary that musicians invite us to explore: from within to expression. Any musician or composer knows that there is a place from where music emerges which is before or beyond our conceptual grasp of things, and which does not even "submit" to words once it has actually emerged.

In explaining his process of writing music, Bono describes "finding his voice," as opposed to "figuring out his thoughts," "instinct" over "intellect." "Instinct," he suggests, "is what you always knew; intellect

---

[39] "It's not a frivolous answer. I'm essentially agnostic. I don't have a problem with God. I have a problem with religion. I've chosen to live my life without the certain ties of religious faith. I think they're dangerous. Music is something that gives my life value and spiritual solace." Belinda Luscombe, "Ten Questions for Sting," *Time* (November 21, 2011): 64.

[40] To my mind the emerging area of Theopoetics has a lot to offer theology in learning to find new ways to express that which cannot be fully expressed. See http://theopoetics.net.

[41] Rahner, "Prayer for Creative Thinkers," 131.

is what you figured out."[42] Copland, in different terms, eloquently explains how hard it is to allow musical intuition, or inspiration, as he calls it, freedom:

> The inspired moment may sometimes be described as a kind of hallucinatory state of mind: one half of the personality emotes and dictates while the other half listens and notates. The half that listens had better look the other way, had better simulate a half attention only, for the half that dictates is easily disgruntled and avenges itself for too close inspection by fading entirely away.[43]

James MacMillan speaks of the "pre-creative silence."[44] I describe the process as one of allowing the body to express its music. It may sound strange, but when I am in a creative space, either on my own or with other musicians, the impression I have is that my center of gravity shifts from my mind to what can be best described as my "gut," which is not only physical but which does help me sense when the music emerging feels right or not. The embodied nature of musical symbolism is well witnessed to in musicological and ethnomusicological writings. So allowing music to come into being implies inhabiting, or at least being receptive to, the implicit and unknown parts of our mind and our bodies. Grace can be at work. Of course, this also implies getting over centuries of the dualistic anti-corporeal inclinations of western philosophy and theology, but music has been pushing that frontier relentlessly in recent years.[45]

There are many other creative opposites we could mention, such as the relationship between solitude and others, vulnerability and publicness, inspiration and hard work, but this is enough to start the conversa-

---

[42] *Bono on Bono*, 116.

[43] Copland, *Music and Imagination*, 43.

[44] The expression is used by MacMillan in a piece in *The Guardian* on July 18, 2003, called "Divine Accompaniment," addressing the role of music in our "post-religious" times. The full quotation is: "And as musicians and lovers of music we know that music itself grows out of silence. Every composer knows that the pre-creative silence is not empty but pregnant with possibility."

http://www.guardian.co.uk/music/2003/jul/19/classicalmusicandopera.arts features.

[45] Many authors have underlined embodiment as a central aspect of musical semiotics, and it is at the heart of my book, *Music and Theology: What Music Has to Say about the Word* (Eugene, OR: Wipf and Stock, 2012).

tion. I hope what has come through in this chapter is just how enriching it could be to explore the places where contemporary music is born, and how it touches and speaks to and into human living. There is a graced place that music-makers know and enter into the moment they pick up the guitar, sit down at the keyboard, or stand before a microphone and begin to count the beat. Something happens, something is shared. The space you're in becomes charged with . . . something. It brings to mind a phrase from Wuthering Heights which haunts me from time to time. Catherine says of her love for Heathcliff: "I have dreamt in my life dreams that have . . . gone through and through me, like wine through water, and altered the colour of my mind."[46] As for me, I have heard music that has run through and through me like sap through stone, and altered the shape of the world I live in, evoking in me a prayer:

> *Raise up among us, Lord, women and men endowed with creative powers: thinkers, poets, musicians. We have need of them.*[47]

---

[46] Emily Brontë, *Wuthering Heights* (Rockville, MD: Arc Manor, 2008), 62.
[47] Rahner, "Prayer for Creative Thinkers," 130.

PART TWO
Theology through Community

Chapter 3

More Than Music:
Notes on "Staying Punk"
in the Church and in Theology

Michael J. Iafrate

"[P]unk is a story of a community that has persisted, imperfectly but
powerfully, to raise a vision of a better world that might still be."

Mark Andersen and Mark Jenkins[1]

A growing number of theologians and cultural theorists have noted the
various ways that popular culture fulfills a "religious" function in people's
lives,[2] particularly in the way(s) that it serves as a source of personal and
communal identity.[3] Contrary to earlier predictions, the West is not becoming more secular, but religious belief and practice is shifting from
traditional forms of religion to new religiosities that have been obscured
by the dominant modern view of religion.[4] The breakdown of the modern

---

[1] Mark Andersen and Mark Jenkins, *Dance of Days: Two Decades of Punk in the
Nation's Capital* (New York: Akashic Books, 2003), 397.

[2] Gordon Lynch, *Understanding Theology and Popular Culture* (Oxford: Blackwell,
2005), 27–33.

[3] Theodore Gracyk, *I Wanna Be Me: Rock Music and the Politics of Identity* (Philadelphia: Temple University Press, 2001); Thomas Turino, *Music as Social Life: The Politics
of Participation* (Chicago: The University of Chicago Press, 2008).

[4] Gavin Langmuir has described "religiosity" as "the dominant pattern or structur-
ing of nonrational thinking—and the conduct correlated with it—which the individual
trusts to establish, extend, and preserve consciousness of his or her identity." Gavin
Langmuir, *History, Religion, and Antisemitism* (Berkeley: University of California Press,
1990), 162, cited in Linell E. Cady, "Loosening the Category That Binds: Modern
'Religion' and the Promise of Cultural Studies," in *Converging on Culture: Theologians*

35

view of religion has implications for theology because, as Linell Cady argues, "[i]f theology remains ensnared in the conceptual grid of the modern religions discourse, it will be unable to attend to new forms of religiosity emerging in contemporary life."[5] When the category of "religion" is rethought in radical ways and popular culture phenomena are recognized for their religious character, it becomes interesting and essential to probe these new forms of religiosity in theological reflection,[6] and theology may be reconceived as "the interpretation, critique, and reconstruction of the major religiosities of a culture, which may or may not correlate with its traditional forms."[7] And for people who identify with traditional religions, we begin to see new kinds of syncretism that have in fact always been present as religious people negotiate between their traditional religious beliefs and practices and those of secular (popular) culture(s).

I have for some time been interested in "tracking spirit"[8] in the world of "do-it-yourself" (DIY) punk rock culture, a culture in which I have lived, moved, and had my being, in one way or another, since junior high school. I have been an active musician ever since taking up the guitar at age fourteen, and have participated in a variety of independent music communities over the years by playing in bands, recording and releasing records, booking shows and tours, and supporting other local musicians. My own musical practices, despite my involvement with various genres of music, have been rooted in my early experiences of the DIY music ethic which I will describe below. At the same time, my own experiences of music-making in these communities are not entirely isolable from my experience in Christian communities. I learned guitar,

---

in Dialogue with Cultural Analysis and Criticism, ed. Delwin Brown, Sheila Greeve Davaney, and Kathryn Tanner (Oxford: Oxford University Press, 2001), 36.

[5] Cady, "Loosening the Category That Binds," 35.

[6] Clive Marsh has pointed to the new directions theology must explore if traditional religious texts are not the only or even the most important sources for "narratives of self." See "Theology as 'Soundtrack': Popular Culture and Narratives of the Self," *Expository Times* 118, no. 11 (2007): 536–41. See also Anonymous, "Exploring the Research Agenda for Theology, Religion and Popular Culture: Report of a Panel Discussion at the American Academy of Religion, November 2005," *Journal of Religion and Popular Culture* 12 (Spring 2006), available at http://www.usask.ca/relst/jrpc /report12-AARpanel.html.

[7] Cady, "Loosening the Category That Binds," 36.

[8] Mark McClain Taylor, "Tracking Spirit: Theology as Cultural Critique in America," in *Changing Conversations: Religious Reflection and Cultural Analysis*, ed. Dwight N. Hopkins and Sheila Greeve Davaney (New York/London: Routledge, 1996), 123–44.

for example, largely by strumming along to R.E.M. songs with friends at a Catholic youth group during the week and strumming along to songs by the St. Louis Jesuits at my church's folk Mass on the weekend. The first rock show I played was with a band called Anamnesis, which I formed with a fellow punk rock altar server from my parish. Another band on the bill that night was a "Krishna-core"[9] band made up mostly of young people who lived at a nearby Hare Krishna community. While working on my master's degree in theology, I played in a band that enjoyed some success in the world of hardcore punk,[10] and on one of our tours I recall studying for biblical Hebrew and comprehensive exams while selling CDs and shirts at our "merch" table. My experiences of religious community and musical community have always interpenetrated and informed each other, and indeed many of my formative experiences of community, cultural agency, diversity, social justice, radicalism, and political activism took place through my participation in independent music communities long before they happened in any sort of ecclesial or religious context. Indeed, I often learned what it means to be "church" in contexts typically seen as outside the church.

An exploration of the interaction of these two worlds might be counterintuitive in light of popular perception that punk rock is inherently "anti-religious."[11] While many forms of punk rock are well known for their rejection of organized religion, especially dominant forms of North American Christianity, the relationship between religion and punk rock

---

[9] Krishna-core was a movement within 1980s and 1990s hardcore punk, loosely analogous to Christian rock, in which Hare Krishna devotees formed bands whose lyrics expressed devotion to Krishna and promoted the philosophy and lifestyle of Krishna Consciousness. Very little documentation of this vibrant movement exists. See Erik Davis, "Krishnacore," *Spin* (August 1995): 68–73; James Andrew "Jimi" Wilson, "Punk Rock Puja: (Mis)Appropriation, (Re)Interpretation, and Dissemination of Hindu Religious Traditions in the North American and European Underground Music Scene(s)" (MA thesis, University of Florida, 2008), 74–79; and interviews with Krishna-core bands Shelter and 108 in Brian Peterson, *Burning Fight: The Nineties Hardcore Revolution in Ethics, Politics, Spirit, and Sound* (Huntington Beach, CA: Revelation Books, 2009).

[10] "Hardcore" is a sub-movement of punk which stylistically moved punk into harder and faster territory in the 1980s, often with screamed vocals and unconventional song structures. Hardcore punk is also much more intentionally independent of major labels and traditional rock culture than earlier forms of punk.

[11] Other seemingly counterintuitive explorations of the relationship between theology and various genres of popular music are now appearing, e.g., Anthony B. Pinn, ed., *Noise and Spirit: The Religious and Spiritual Sensibilities of Rap Music* (New York: NYU Press, 2003).

is in fact far more complex. And more than this, participants in DIY punk rock communities often—and increasingly—express the meaning of their participation in religious terms. The DIY approach to music-and-culture-making (forming bands, producing records and labels, and organizing concerts and touring networks) found in various expressions of punk rock spills over into the personal ethics and politics of punks, constituting not only a style of and approach to music but an entire way of life that shapes personal and communal identity and that can be explored theologically. The recognition of this "punk rock religiosity" is but one example of what Tom Beaudoin identifies as a wider "agreement among musicians about the spiritual value of rock music in a way that remains distanced from institutions, and the significant awareness of this too on the part of many fans immersed in rock culture."[12]

Following the understanding of "religiosity" in circulation in discussions of theology and popular culture noted earlier, this chapter probes the religiosity of punk rock culture (including punk commitments and practices beyond a mere style of music), especially its more grassroots, DIY, and directly political expressions. It will then move to a discussion of the ways that the religiosity of punk continues to shape and influence the lives of punks beyond youth and into the changes of life that come with adulthood. It will end with a reflection on what it might mean to "stay punk" as an adult who has made an investment in the world of academia, and especially what it might mean to "stay punk" as a theologian. It includes two types of theological engagement with popular culture according to the typology developed by Gordon Lynch.[13] It begins with a description of the way that punk rock music and culture serve a religious function in the lives of its participants. It then probes DIY punk rock culture as a *source* of theological reflection, namely how it might "provid[e] models and methods for how theologians might conduct their own work"[14] and how the worlds of DIY punk and academic theology are interacting syncretically in my own work.[15]

---

[12] Tom Beaudoin, "Give It Up / for Jesus: *Askeses* of Dispossession in Rock and Christianity," paper presented at the Catholic Theological Society of America Annual Convention (Halifax, Nova Scotia, Canada, 2009).

[13] Lynch, *Understanding Theology and Popular Culture*, chapter 2.

[14] Ibid., 40.

[15] Portions of this essay were previously presented in " 'I'm a Human, not a *Statue*': Saints and Saintliness in the Church of Punk Rock," paper presented at the Catholic Theological Society of America Annual Convention (San Jose, CA, 2011).

The Emergence of DIY Punk

If you want to seize the sound / you don't need a reservation

Fugazi, "Target"[16]

Many genres and subgenres of Western popular music have claimed to be "alternative" or "independent." In general terms, punk rock arose explicitly as an alternative to the dominant musical, cultural, and political ethos of its times. This general observation, however, is about as close as one could get to a description of what punk rock was, or is, about. Those who attempt to narrate the story of punk often end up portraying it in monolithic terms that do not do justice to its complexity and diversity. But any succinct expression of "what punk rock is about," including mine, should be treated with some degree of suspicion. Despite the images that come to mind of spiked hair, body piercings, mosh pits, and audience members and the band spitting on one another, punk rock contains a surprising amount of internal diversity and disruption, not only in terms of musical and clothing styles but in its range of political and ideological commitments, many of which are contradictory and in conflict with one another.[17] And although my account of the emergence of DIY punk largely focuses on the movement's liberating aspects, it is important to admit that the story is far more complex. As Roger Sabin has noted, "most accounts assume that punk was 'liberating' politically, and created a space for disenfranchised voices to be heard—notably women, gays and lesbians, and anti-racists (punk's involvement with Rock Against Racism being a key reference-point). . . . Yet, there is plenty of evidence to counter these claims. [P]unk, far from being liberatory, could in fact be very reactionary, and was riven through with sexism, homophobia and racism."[18] Therefore one cannot settle for the

---

[16] Fugazi, "Target," on *Red Medicine*, Dischord Records, 1995.

[17] On the diversity of punk movements and styles, see Roger Sabin, "Introduction," in *Punk Rock: So What? The Cultural Legacy of Punk*, ed. Roger Sabin (London: Routledge, 1999), 4; as well as Craig O'Hara, *The Philosophy of Punk: More Than Noise!* (Oakland, CA: AK Press, 1999).

[18] Sabin, "Introduction," 4. Indeed, although many if not most punk communities were and are publicly antiracist, most of the participants in the communities in North America are white. Also, even though some of the first punk communities (especially in Britain) were explicitly class conscious, some strains of early British punk were also racist (see Roger Sabin, "'I Won't Let That Dago Go By': Rethinking Punk and Racism," in *Punk Rock*, 199–218), and much of subsequent punk rock has developed

kinds of essentialism that frequently show up in popular narrations of its history. Sabin rightly observes, "At a time when every new account of punk styles itself as 'the last word,' there has never been more to say."[19]

A descendent of a variety of countercultural movements, punk rock developed almost simultaneously in Britain and in the United States in the late 1970s and early 1980s as a set of movements in response to increasing corporate consumerism and the social conservatism of the Thatcher and Reagan administrations.[20] Punk is known for its ethos of rebellion which was expressed in the music's lyrics, loud and abrasive sounds, and shocking clothing styles and imagery, all of which were denounced by clergy, politicians, and parents alike, much like previous incarnations of rock music.[21] Punk rock communities provided safe spaces for marginalized youth who felt that they did not fit the mold of the socially conservative values of society and of right-wing Christianity. But beyond the familiar punk rock icon of the rebellious outcast, it is punk rock's DIY ethic that is widely recognized as the heart of the movement. In addition to wider social and economic trends, these youth detested the increasingly centralized and corporatized music industry that focused on a small elite group of superstar artists. Mainstream rock, they insisted, did not speak to the socio-political conditions in which they found themselves and tended to function as more of a distraction from "real life."[22]

---

a strain of classism, particularly in the way participants in mainstream and depoliticized forms of punk tend to look down on "redneck" culture. Finally, the reality of sexism continues to plague punk and other types of heavy alternative music, even after the rise of the feminist Riot Grrrl movement within punk. On the Riot Grrrl movement, see Sara Marcus, *Girls to the Front: The True Story of the Riot Grrrl Revolution* (New York: Harper Perennial, 2010). On the construction and negotiation of gender in alternative hard rock (including punk), see Mimi Schippers, *Rockin' out of the Box: Gender Maneuvering in Alternative Hard Rock* (New Brunswick, NJ: Rutgers University Press, 2002).

[19] Sabin, "Introduction," 12.

[20] Peter Gartside, "Bypassing Politics? a Critical Look at DiY Culture," in *Young Britain: Politics, Pleasures and Predicaments*, ed. Jonathan Rutherford (London: Lawrence & Wishart, 1998), 59; Ben Holtzman, Craig Hughes, and Kevin Van Meter, "Do It Yourself . . . and the Movement Beyond Capitalism," in *Constituent Imagination: Militant Investigation, Collective Theorization* (Oakland, CA: AK Press, 2007), 47.

[21] Holtzman, Hughes, and Van Meter, "Do It Yourself," 46–47.

[22] Such sentiments are reflected in the song "Panic" by the British post-punk band The Smiths in which lead singer Morrissey sings "Burn down the disco / Hang the blessed D.J. / because the music they constantly play / it says nothing to me about my life" (The Smiths, "Panic," on *Louder Than Bombs*, Sire/Rough Trade, 1987).

In response, new local music scenes emerged in both urban and rural communities. Of course, local music scenes have always existed, but these irruptions of DIY-oriented communities were consciously driven by a rejection of corporate music values and practices, nurturing alternative forms of cultural production and distribution.[23] Outside the confines of the music industry, and without the aid of tools such as the internet, these movements demystified and democratized the music-making process, taking the insider "gnosis" of the production of culture out of the hands of corporate record labels by doing it themselves: forming communities and developing global networks that allowed them to start bands, play shows, tour, create their own record labels and release music outside of the corporate record label and live venue systems. In doing so, punk rock restored a sense of cultural agency by challenging rock culture's hierarchical division between professional musicians and music consumers and by emphasizing the communal and participatory nature of music over its individual and performative aspects, insisting that music is an "uncommodifiable shared experience"[24] and an essential part of human life. As independent musician and writer Mat Callahan notes, "People can make their own music wherever they want to, wherever they are. They don't need to have it provided for them by anyone. They only need to be encouraged and, in the longer term, given better and better music tools."[25]

DIY punk's ideal of an uncommodified and communal experience of music can be seen in the way these communities view recordings and live performance. Although punk music scenes produce countless DIY recordings as "products," they are often seen as more than mere products but as artifacts, often handmade, that document the cultural creativity of their communities. Additionally, recordings are often seen as secondary to the social experience of live music. Whereas many corporate musical acts make records and then tour in order to support (i.e., sell) the record, punk often views live music as primary with the record supporting or documenting the live music experience. Like most traditional forms of music,[26] punk rock often resists rock music's traditional separation of artist and audience, breaking this barrier by denouncing rockstar attitudes, encouraging sing-alongs at shows, doing away with stages and lights, and holding concerts in nontraditional venues such as

---

[23] Holtzman, Hughes, and Van Meter, "Do It Yourself," 46–47.

[24] Mat Callahan, *The Trouble with Music* (Oakland, CA: AK Press, 2005), xxi.

[25] Ibid., xxii–xxiii.

[26] Turino, *Music as Social Life*.

community halls and homes ("house shows"). So despite what the term "do-it-yourself" sounds like and the connotations that it might have today,[27] the DIY punk movement was and is not predominantly rooted in liberal ideas of individual autonomy, self-reliance or refusal of others, but has been much more community-centered, even communitarian, in nature. As Peter Gartside notes, "It would be more accurate to call it a Do-it-*Ourselves* culture, a collective resistance to commodified culture."[28]

Like many countercultural movements, punk rock devolved away from its best impulses when it was co-opted by the music industry, commodified, and repackaged simply as a consumer fashion choice and musical genre rooted in a vague spirit of "nonconformity."[29] But counter-subcultures of punks who remain committed to the DIY ethic and radical politics continue to reemerge as a challenge to the "commodification of dissent"[30] represented by commercialized forms of punk. The hardcore punk scene in Washington, DC, in the early 1980s is one such community in which a scene-within-a-scene developed in resistance to mainstream punk's increasing fascination with stardom, fashion, and reckless lifestyles.[31] One of the central bands of this sub-community was a group of teenagers called Minor Threat who spearheaded (somewhat unwillingly) the straightedge hardcore scene by consciously and publicly refusing alcohol and drugs. The straightedge movement, as well as other communities that retained punk's original DIY ethic, emerged as a rejection of the larger punk scene and what it was becoming, establishing a new scene within the old based on friendships, healthy lifestyle choices, and making music in a supportive community.[32]

---

[27] The phrase "do-it-yourself" often brings to mind the "do-it-yourself" home improvement ethos, rightly questioned by Vincent Miller, which is rooted in the phenomenon of the single-family home as the locus of consumption habits. See *Consuming Religion: Christian Faith and Practice in a Consumer Culture* (New York: Continuum, 2004), 51.

[28] Gartside, "Bypassing Politics?," 59.

[29] Holtzman, Hughes, and Van Meter, "Do It Yourself," 46.

[30] Miller, *Consuming Religion*, 148.

[31] This description of the history of the bands Minor Threat and Fugazi and the label Dischord Records is drawn mostly from Andersen and Jenkins' *Dance of Days*, Jem Cohen's documentary on Fugazi titled *Instrument* (Dischord Records, 1999), as well as various published interviews with Fugazi band member and Dischord co-founder Ian MacKaye.

[32] For a critical review of a recent sociological work on the straightedge movement which gives a good summary of the ambiguities and plurality of straightedge and of hardcore punk in general, see Alan O'Connor, "Review Essay: The Sociology of

Minor Threat's lead singer and lyricist Ian MacKaye became a sort of unofficial spokesperson (again, mostly unwillingly) for both the straight-edge movement and those punks committed to the more political, DIY style of punk, but who had no interest in following the straightedge code. MacKaye describes the times in this way:

> Washington had an underground punk/new wave scene, but it was largely people that were looking to New York or London for fashion sense. It seemed more like people who were interested in copping a look. We were teenagers and we just wanted to play music. We had heard about punk rock, and what we got from punk rock was the idea of being able to create our own thing. Again, not waiting for anyone's permission.[33]

MacKaye and friends' cultural localism prompted them to start a record label to document the DC punk scene and to be a gravitational center for this new "communitarian" punk community. Dischord Records,[34] founded in 1981, was envisioned not so much as a record *company* but as an organization for documenting and preserving the community's musical output. The label has maintained a set of peculiar practices that have made them distinctive even among independent record labels and have inspired the creation of similar labels in other communities. With very few exceptions, Dischord maintains a local focus, releasing only artists from Washington, DC. They do not use the music industry's system of legal contracts but instead forge friendships, and the relationship between the bands and the label is rooted in this friendship. Dischord keeps their CD and record prices low and their only advertising appears exclusively in independent music magazines and

---

Youth Subcultures," *Canadian Journal of Sociology Online* (March–April 2007), available at http://www.cjsonline.ca/reviews/youthsubcultures.html.

[33] Peter Hepburn, "Ian MacKaye (Interview)" (2004), available at http://www.cokemachineglow.com/feature/2314/ian-mackaye. Elsewhere, MacKaye recalls, "In 1980, D.C. was just not thought of as a music town at all. Nobody came to Washington to play music, nobody came to Washington to hear music and in fact, people who lived in Washington told me that if I wanted to be in a punk band I should move to New York. I'm a fifth-generation Washingtonian, so I wasn't about to move to New York. This is my town, I'm of this town. Frustration and anger and creativity and passion—these are not geographic designations. We are who we are, where we are. So we said, 'We're not moving anywhere. We're gonna do it right here. We're gonna create something'" (Matthew Fritch, "Ian MacKaye [Interview]," available at http://www.magnetmagazine.com/interviews/ian.html).

[34] http://www.dischord.com.

fanzines. And they have continually resisted being bought out by the major labels courting countless independent labels ever since Nirvana became popular in the early 1990s.

When Minor Threat broke up in 1983 after a short three-year career, MacKaye continued to run Dischord Records, documenting the ups and downs of DC's music scene. After involvement in a few short-lived music projects, he helped to found the band Fugazi, whose significantly longer career would challenge preconceived notions of punk with their unique post-hardcore sounds (experimental and intricate by punk rock standards) and an equally challenging set of musical practices. Like Dischord, Fugazi is committed to their local community of Washington, DC, not only to the music community but to the city itself, playing many local benefit shows throughout the year and supporting local community justice efforts. They insist through word and action that music is not a product for individual consumption, but a communal practice.

Despite their prominence and ability to draw large audiences, Fugazi has remained committed to DIY music-making practices. They resist rock music's traditional separation between band and audience by allowing audience members to sit or stand with them on the stage and by refusing to use the elaborate and alienating rock lighting systems installed in most venues. The band handles their own booking and management and they prefer to play non-traditional venues such as community halls and school gymnasiums rather than standard rock venues. This frees them from the circuit of money-driven rock establishments, encourages community participation in putting on a show rather than leaving it in the hands of professional promoters, and allows them to keep their shows all-ages. Fugazi also resists rock commercialism by keeping ticket prices extremely low: their ticket price, with few exceptions, has remained five dollars when a band of their stature could easily charge fifteen to thirty dollars a ticket. They have continually turned down major label offers and, unlike most bands, Fugazi does not make and sell band merchandise such as T-shirts, nor do they sell their recordings at shows, in part to emphasize that the shared experience of music is not about buying and selling but the experience itself.[35] Finally, Fugazi has taken an active role in discussions about the politics of punk, shunning many of the destructive aspects of punk culture such as violent "slam dancing" and punk's tendency to alienate women and men who do not embrace punk rock's macho tendencies.

---

[35] Still, many rock merchandisers sell bootleg Fugazi merchandise such as stickers and T-shirts, including a shirt available years ago that ironically proclaimed, "This is Not a Fugazi T-Shirt."

Fugazi and Dischord Records are certainly not the only communities that have attempted to "stay punk" by sticking close to punk's foundational principles and impulses. Examples could be multiplied, and some could even argue that my exclusive focus on Fugazi and Dischord Records neglects less prominent but equally interesting and important scenes and communities in North America and throughout the world. Despite continual (and often successful) attempts to commercialize various types of punk rock, the counter-subculture of DIY punk persists on the margins as a kind of "Radical Reformation" within in the punk world, keeping its music as communal, oppositional, political, and non-commercialized as possible. They continue to encourage new, experimental bands and musical forms and to take communal responsibility for setting up shows in homes, basements, and other alternative venues. Finally, in a popular music climate that increasingly encourages the individualized "iPod-ization" of musical consumption, these communities engage in communitarian practices of post-concert hospitality (show promoters often take responsibility for putting touring bands up for the night and feeding them), communal discernment of how to deal with problems in the scene, and radical political activism around causes such as racism, feminism, homophobia, militarism, capitalism, eco-justice, animal rights, and so on.[36]

More Than Music[37]

It's as if they belong, and they've been here all along
Five corporations / There's a pattern

Fugazi, "Five Corporations"[38]

DIY punk's anarchistic tendencies have had a notable impact on other types of popular music. Part of this is due to the fact that punk rock itself

[36] Common forms of political activity in punk circles include the production of alternative media such as photocopied fanzines, information tabling at shows, benefit concerts, political stage banter between songs during performances, and the inclusion of political spoken word and speeches as bonus material on records and CDs. Other sectors of the punk community, however, have been strongly anti-political to the point of glorifying political apathy. Both tendencies, of course, claim that they represent the "true" spirit of punk. For an excellent history of DIY fanzines, see part one of Amy Spencer, *DIY: The Rise of Lo-Fi Culture* (London: Marion Boyars, 2008).

[37] This phrase, used also in the title of this chapter, is inspired by a popular punk/hardcore music festival that took place for several years in the 1990s in Columbus, Ohio called the "More Than Music Fest."

[38] Fugazi, "Five Corporations," on *End Hits*, Dischord Records, 1998.

has never stood still and has continually evolved and generated count-less offshoot genres. Post-punk, college rock, hardcore, post-hardcore, alternative rock, grunge, alt-country, etc.—all have their roots in punk rock and often took cues from the DIY ethic. Punk artists also tend to branch out beyond any perceivable genre connection to punk rock, embracing such musical forms as folk, electronic, and dance music, taking the values of DIY punk along with them. DIY punk's influence has not been limited to music, however. Its influence as a socio-political movement is particularly notable. The real political significance of punk rock lies less in the radical political content often contained in punk rock songs and more in the inherent politics and ethics contained within DIY practices themselves. With its emphasis on direct action, bypassing the given-ness of culture industries, DIY has had an impact on how its participants think about and engage in politics,[39] inspiring movements such as Reclaim the Streets, Critical Mass, Food Not Bombs, and "hacktivism"; media projects such as Independent Media Centers (IMCs) and AK Press; and community centers/infoshops such as ABC No Rio in New York City.[40] Such projects embody a type of politics that rejects the established state-centered "politics of demand" in favor of a "politics of the act."[41] That is, a DIY approach to politics focuses less on making demands on political leaders to reform the system and more on building alternative social forms that prefigure the types of communities punks want to see in the world, making them present in the here-and-now. This approach to politics intends to render traditional political structures and strategies irrelevant and it is in such a way, punks hope, that oppressive structures will be destroyed rather than through revolution as conceived by tradi-tional Marxist and other state-centered approaches.[42]

Finally, DIY punk continues to inform the lives of its participants as they age, becoming an entire way of life. Punk rockers who were exposed to the DIY ethic through music communities often speak of the desire to "stay punk" as an adult, realizing that "staying punk" has less and less to do with music as their lives progress.[43] DIY punk influences what

---

[39] Holtzman, Hughes, and Van Meter, "Do It Yourself," 48; Gartside, "Bypassing Politics?," 59. See also Richard J. F. Day, *Gramsci Is Dead: Anarchist Currents in the Newest Social Movements* (Toronto: Between the Lines, 2005), chap. 1.

[40] Day, *Gramsci Is Dead*, chap. 1.

[41] Ibid., 14–15.

[42] Ibid., 34–35.

[43] DC punk historian and activist Mark Andersen is a great example. Though not a musician himself, Andersen has been involved in DC punk for decades, helping

people buy, what careers they choose, what foods they eat, how they parent, and so on.[44] The DIY ethic has fanned the flames of the desire for something beyond the alienations of consumer culture, inspiring punks (and former punks) to develop practices of culture-making, approaches to political action, and lifestyle and career choices that encourage human agency and participatory human community in various dimensions of life.

Punk Rock and/as Religion

> *We love the sound, the sound is what found us*
> *The sound is the blood between me and you*
>
> Wild Flag, "Romance"[45]

As the politico-ethical impulse of DIY punk impacted more and more aspects of life for punks, it was eventually bound to touch on matters religious. While many punks defiantly proclaimed "fuck religion" as part of punk's more general kerygma of "fuck authority," many punks, especially into the 1990s, found in hardcore a context for experimentation with different approaches to religion and spirituality.[46] Although the

---

to found the youth-based punk activist group Positive Force DC (http://www .positiveforcedc.org). Now in his forties, Andersen has brought DIY punk into the broader arena of his life and of the community. While still very connected with the DC music scene and punk activist community, his primary work these days is social justice activism with the homeless and elderly that he says is animated both by his Catholic faith and his punk rock roots, which he says he hopes he will never lose. For Andersen's thoughts on punk as a way of life, see Andersen and Jenkins, *Dance of Days*, 409; Mark Andersen, *All the Power: Revolution without Illusion* (Chicago: Punk Planet Books, 2004). For an account of his linkage of punk and religious faith through youth activism, see Celeste Kennel-Shank, "Green Hair, Gray Hair: What Do You Get When You Mix Punk Rockers with Senior Citizens?," *Sojourners* 35, no. 3 (March 2006): 34–37.

[44] See the handful of "punk rock parenting" guides that have been published in recent years, including Jessica Mills, *My Mother Wears Combat Boots: A Parenting Guide for the Rest of Us* (Oakland, CA: AK Press, 2007).

[45] Wild Flag, "Romance," on *Wild Flag*, Merge Records, 2011.

[46] Craig O'Hara, e.g., claims that the antireligious sentiment is intrinsic to punk (*The Philosophy of Punk*, 148–49). Ibrahim Abraham rightly argues that this common view of punk as inherently antireligious overlooks a complex history of the intersection of religion and punk. Punk rock, he says, is necessarily syncretistic, "an inherently hybridized cultural category of minority and marginalized cultural groups," such that "rendering punk as secular discourse becomes rather problematic" ("Punk Pulpit:

intersection of religion and punk was not new, as bands like Bad Brains and Cro-Mags had sung and spoken openly about religion in earlier waves of punk, the 1990s was a period in which interest in so-called alternative religions exploded in hardcore, resulting in movements like Krishna-core, Christian hardcore (mostly, but not limited to, conservative evangelical expressions) and Muslim hardcore.[47] Punk audiences during this period often could not escape the feeling that concerts were becoming gatherings for interfaith (including atheist) discussion, sharing, and even worship!

But beyond the recognition of the experimental *combination* of punk and religion, or the view that punk served as a mere *context* for spiritual experimentation, is the ever-more frequent claim that punk rock *itself* often functions *as* religion for its participants. This claim about the religiosity of punk culture mirrors wider trends in the analysis of rock culture and religiosity noted earlier.[48] As Brian Peterson writes in a recent collection of reflections on the political, cultural, and spiritual dimensions of 1990s punk, "Every form of music comes from within, but the passion displayed at a hardcore show can be similar to what is seen at a religious ritual. At nearly every hardcore show, bands play their songs with the utmost intensity, singers testify to an issue that is close to their hearts, and fans struggle to reach the stage in an effort to be a part of the experience."[49]

It is becoming increasingly clear that punk rock music and culture, like music and culture generally, "*literally* accompan[y] people in their lives"[50] in a way at least analogous to "traditional" religious and spiritual

---

Religion, Punk Rock, and Counter [Sub]Cultures," *Bulletin of the Council of Societies for the Study of Religion* 37, no. 1 [February 2008]: 4). For additional recent discussion of the complexity of the "punk and religion" question, see the unique zine series *Conversations with Punx: A Spiritual Dialogue* by Bianca Valentino which features interviews with punk rock musicians on religion and spirituality (Michael J. Iafrate, "The Spirit of Punk: An Interview with Zine Author Bianca Valentino," *RockAndTheology.com*, October 19, 2010, available at http://www.rockandtheology.com/?p=2444).

[47] See Abraham, "Punk Pulpit"; Peterson, *Burning Fight*.

[48] For recent expressions of the rock-as-religion view, see Tom Beaudoin, "Ambiguous Liturgy: Rock Music as Religious Experience," *Books & Culture* 6, no. 5 (September 2000): 29; Tom Beaudoin and Brian Robinette, "Stairway to Heaven: Can You Be Saved by Rock 'n' Roll?" *America* 201, no. 11 (26 October 2009): 20–21; Master's thesis of Ian W. Fowles, self-published as *A Sound Salvation: Rock N' Roll as a Religion* (Claremont, CA: Sonic Mystic, 2010); and David Nantais, *Rock-a My Soul: An Invitation to Rock Your Religion* (Collegeville, MN: Liturgical Press, 2011).

[49] Peterson, *Burning Fight*, 109.

[50] Marsh, "Theology as 'Soundtrack,'" 537.

traditions.[51] And this is true even for persons who are connected to the various traditional religions and who consider those traditions the primary sources of their individual and communal identities because even the dominant forms of religion are always "entangled with multiple other frameworks"[52] such as popular culture. Syncretism, therefore, is not automatically a lamentable phenomenon in which established religious traditions are compromised through mixture with culture or with other traditions but a permanent feature and dynamic of all religiosities.[53] As Clive Marsh argues, "Bible-reading, participation in worship, prayer, social and political action all happen alongside the consumption and use of art, media and popular culture, and the multiple influences of one activity on another is not always easy to grasp. Nevertheless, theologians will have to show how theological reflection occurs within lives constructed in this way. Every person is a complex network of cultural influences."[54]

"Staying Punk" and the Negotiation of Adult Identities

I might be an adult, but I'm a minor at heart
We're just a minor threat

Minor Threat, "Minor Threat"[55]

Whether conceived as a form of religiosity or not, punk rock music, culture, and commitments often continue to inform the lives of its participants as they age. Joanna Davis' research on punk rock ideologies and processes of aging tunes into how punk identity is continually renegotiated and reintegrated into life as punks age.[56] Her ethnography points to nurses and teachers who grew up punk and who have integrated the commitments of DIY punk into their careers as examples of successful negotiations of punk and adult identities. Other scholars in a variety

---

[51] See also Beaudoin and Robinette, "Stairway to Heaven."

[52] Marsh, "Theology as 'Soundtrack,' " 539.

[53] For a helpful description of several different types of syncretism, see chapter 7 of Leonardo Boff, *Church: Charism and Power: Liberation Theology and the Institutional Church*, trans. John W. Diercksmeier (New York: Crossroad, 1985), 89–107.

[54] Marsh, "Theology as 'Soundtrack,' " 540.

[55] Minor Threat, "Minor Threat," on *Minor Threat* EP (Dischord Records, 1981).

[56] Joanna R. Davis, "The Scene Is Dead, Long Live the Scene: Music, Identity, and the Transition to Adulthood" (PhD diss., University of California, Santa Barbara, 2006); Joanna R. Davis, "Growing up Punk: Negotiating Aging Identity in a Local Music Scene," *Symbolic Interaction* 29, no. 1 (2006): 63–69.

of disciplines have discussed what it might mean to "stay punk" in academia. Seth Kahn-Egan, for example, has outlined a "punk pedagogy" inspired by punk's DIY ethic as well as its characteristic anger and passion.[57] For Kahn-Egan, the classroom should be a place

> where students learn the passion, commitment, and energy that are available from and in writing; where they learn to be critical of themselves, their cultures, and their government—that is, of institutions in general; and, most importantly, where they learn to go beyond finding out what's wrong with the world and begin making it better. The punk classroom helps them move from being passive consumers of ideology to active participants in their cultures. Along the way, they may have to deconstruct the realities they've brought with them, but the focus of the pedagogy is on constructing new realities of their own design.[58]

Likewise, Kevin Dunn has reflected on what attention to punk rock might bring to his field of international relations (IR).[59] Punk's DIY ethic is central to his argument, as is the necessity of producing committed, "angry" scholarship as opposed to scholarship that is objective and detached.

> I am increasingly convinced that anger and passion are exactly what are needed when discussing world affairs. As a punk, I had those things in spades. But my education, graduate training, and professional career have all been instrumental in stamping those elements out of me and out of my detached scholarly writing. In order to communicate to the people I want to communicate with, I need to get those emotions and passions back. As the Clash taught me many years ago: "Let fury have the hour, anger can be power / You know that you can use it." I need to be able to communicate with anger and emotion. The scholarly discipline of IR doesn't provide me the tools to do that, but punk rock does.[60]

---

[57] Seth Kahn-Egan, "Pedagogy of the Pissed: Punk Pedagy in the First-Year Writing Classroom," *College Composition and Communication* 49, no. 1 (February 1998): 99–104.

[58] Ibid., 100.

[59] Kevin C. Dunn, "Never Mind the Bollocks: The Punk Rock Politics of Global Communication," *Review of International Studies* 34 (2008): 193–210.

[60] Ibid., 210.

"Staying Punk" as a Theologian

The reflections of Kahn-Egan and Dunn have inspired me as a musician-theologian to reflect on what it might mean to "stay punk" as a theologian, taking into account my own identity formation as shaped by ecclesial and theological cultures as well as by DIY music and political cultures. There are, of course, a number of recent North American and European ecclesial movements that embody a lived theology that incorporates many of the commitments of DIY punk. Movements such as the New Monasticism, various expressions of Christian anarchism, and newer waves of Catholic Worker communities have all been influenced by punk rock culture and live out of what might be called an implicit "punk theology."[61] What follows are notes on what "staying punk" might require of me as an academic theologian with similar commitments.[62]

First, "staying punk" as a theologian will require my theological production to be committed rather than neutral or objective.[63] Practitioners of punk theologies will admit, as does Dunn, that "the punks are right: the world is fucked up, and we need to do something about it,"[64] and we will align ourselves with the various strands of liberation theology, which have challenged theologians to commit to the struggle for justice as the first step in the work that they do.[65] Punk theologians, in the words of Robert Beckford, know that "we achieve nothing unless we change the way things are,"[66] and we will make a methodological option for theological writing as a mode of cultural agency and social change. And

---

[61] A good resource is the Christian anarchist Jesus Radicals project/community which maintains an active website and sponsors an annual conference. See http://www.jesusradicals.com.

[62] As notes, I consider these reflections tentative and open to revision.

[63] Readers will notice that I bounce back and forth between writing in the first person and the third person in this section. My use of the first person expresses my own wrestling with what it means to "stay punk" as a theologian in my own life. The use of the third person acknowledges that I am merely one theological life who has come in contact with various circles of "punks" for whom the questions and concerns raised in this section are of real importance and by whom I have been influenced.

[64] Dunn, "Never Mind the Bollocks," 210.

[65] Gustavo Gutiérrez famously presented this view of praxis-oriented theology in Gustavo Gutiérrez, *A Theology of Liberation: History, Politics and Salvation*, rev. ed., trans. Caridad Inda and John Eagleson (Maryknoll, NY: Orbis Books, 1988). See also Stephen Bevans' description of the "praxis model" of theology in *Models of Contextual Theology*, rev. ed. (Maryknoll, NY: Orbis Books, 2002), 70–87.

[66] Robert Beckford, *Jesus Dub: Theology, Music and Social Change* (London: Routledge, 2006), 149.

this commitment will necessarily be rooted in liberation theologies' option for the poor, oppressed, and excluded, an option that DC punk Mark Andersen argues is part of punk's legacy as well.

> [O]ne thing common to all the meanings [of the word "punk" over time] is: It always refers to somebody who is seen by society as worthless, unimportant or useless. For me, if you claim that title, then you're claiming to be one of those throwaway people, one of the disposable ones, and you're asserting your own value and by implication the value of all of those folks. . . . We're trying to encourage a punk political perspective, which might be seen as solidarity with the folks who are on the losing end of the historical bargain. You know, a standing with and for those folks and looking towards a world or a community or a city where there's a place for everyone and where everyone matters. And for me, that's revolutionary.[67]

Second, the participatory commitments of punk rock—in which boundaries between rock stars/experts and fans/audience are questioned if not broken down and in which postures of passivity and consumption are transformed into stances of cultural agency—also pose a challenge to Western, academic, professional theology. Ian Svenonius, the lead singer of a number of DC punk bands and prominent "prophet" of political DIY punk, captures the spirit of agency and participation of nonprofessionals well when he lifts up the makers of "unimportant" music: "The whole problem with music is that people are thinking of it in this historical, sophisticated way. They're thinking about their place in history. And that's the problem with all this rock history crap. Where all we hear about is the 'innovators.' In actuality, those people are great, but there's thousands of people all making music all the time. That narrative of rock and the importance of these certain people and their place in history, that's bullshit."[68]

Such participatory impulses are mirrored in various strands of contemporary theology. Liberation theologies, for example, have called for participatory theology, or people's theology, in which the people take the lead and the professionals do the reporting. While there is much to

---

[67] Tim Follos, "(Interview with) Mark Andersen," available at http://timfollos.com/2009/08/03/mark-andersen-interview.

[68] Evan Hanlon, "Interview: Ian Svenonius on Sam Cooke, Kanye West, and His New Band, Chain and the Gang," *Village Voice* (April 20, 2009), available at http://blogs.villagevoice.com/music/2009/04/interview_ian_s.php.

discuss about how this type of theology works in practice,[69] this sort of impulse seems called for in an approach to theology that "stays punk." If anything, a punk take on theology must insist that everyone has a theological voice, not only theological experts or magisterial defenders of ecclesial traditions, and that the voices of those on the margins, those often deemed "indecent,"[70] are voices to which we must attend and which we must indeed amplify. This commitment challenges not only ecclesial leaders who imagine themselves as the only spokespersons for their traditions, but also theologians who still tend not to take the voices of average people seriously.[71] Such an approach also has much in common with Vincent Miller's concern with theology's task of promoting religious agency, the active participation in religious cultures and interaction with religious symbols and practices rather than the mere passive consumption of them.[72]

Third, DIY punk's construction of alternative networks of culture making in response to mainstream gatekeepers can offer insights and perhaps even concrete models for alternative practices of theological production and dissemination that make room for the emergence of suppressed theological voices. Theological discourse in many ways remains tightly controlled by its own gatekeepers, i.e., the theological publishing industry, the academic journal system, ecclesiastical disciplinary bodies. Technology, of course, has opened up new opportunities for publishing, both in print and online, and open-source journals have become a particularly important development toward the liberation of knowledge production. A number of open-source theological journals intentionally privilege voices neglected by the theological mainstream, such as the *Journal of World Christianity*, the *Journal of Postcolonial Networks*, and the various journals of Sopher Press,[73] and some theologians

---

[69] Marcella M. Althaus-Reid, "Gustavo Gutiérrez Goes to Disneyland: *Theme Park Theologies* and the Diaspora of the Discourse of the Popular Theologian in Liberation Theology," in *Interpreting Beyond Borders*, ed. Fernando F. Segovia (Sheffield: Sheffield Academic Press, 2000), 36–58.

[70] Marcella M. Althaus-Reid, *Indecent Theology: Theological Perversions in Sex, Gender and Politics* (London: Routledge, 2000).

[71] A great example of a "participatory" (and therefore punk!) approach to theological reflection is Mary Ann Hinsdale, Helen M. Lewis, and S. Maxine Waller, *It Comes from the People: Community Development and Local Theology* (Philadelphia: Temple University Press, 1995).

[72] Miller, *Consuming Religion.*

[73] See http://www.journalofworldchristianity.org; http://www.postcolonialnet works.com; and http://www.sopherpress.com, respectively.

have begun to make theological arguments for a more widespread embrace of open-source theological publication.[74] This bypassing of the traditional gatekeepers of the theological academy makes some theologians uncomfortable, as they fear that theological quality will be sacrificed if the bar is set too low by new technologies. Indeed, some explicitly insist that "not everything that gets published in theology today deserves to be published."[75] From a DIY punk perspective, this view strikes me as profoundly elitist. To make an analogy to the music industry, the possibility of opening up the processes of musical production beyond the gatekeepers of the major label system has certainly unleashed a flood of new musical output, especially today as countless artists take advantage of home recording technology and online methods of releasing music. This has resulted in a massive increase in the amount of music that is available, admittedly music of varying quality. But the ability to release music more easily has not done away with the possibility of thinking critically about music or being concerned with its quality, and discussion and criticism of music has gone on as it always has. The same is true in the world of theological production. Discussion and debate about the relative merits of various theological proposals continue despite the introduction of new technologies for disseminating more and more theological texts, as that is the entire point of theology. The real issue is one of cognitive or epistemological justice, the ability of new, other, and

[74] Mary E. Hess, "Possible New Futures for Our Journal on the World Wide Web," *Religious Education* 100, no. 1 (Winter 2005): 78–88; Kevin L. Smith, "Open Access and Authors' Rights Management: A Possibility for Theology?," *Theological Librarianship: An Online Journal of the American Theological Library Association* 2, no. 1 (June 2009): 45–56. Part of Smith's argument includes the statement that open source publishing offers scholars of the North the ability "to serve the needs of churches and seminaries in the developing world" through easy online access to scholarship. He does not acknowledge the potential for scholars from the "developing" world to publish more easily or the gift that theological voices of the global South might be to the churches of the North. A good example of the potential for "marginalized" voices to be heard on broader scales through digital publishing is the collection published by the Ecumenical Association of Third World Theologians in defense of Jon Sobrino (International Theological Commission of the Ecumenical Association of Third World Theologians, *Getting the Poor Down from the Cross: Christology of Liberation*, 2nd digital ed. [2007], available at http://www.eatwot.org/TheologicalCommission/Books).

[75] James K. A. Smith, "(Unsolicited) Advice for Young (Theological) Authors," http://forsclavigera.blogspot.com/2011/03/unsolicited-advice-for-young.html.

alternative knowledges to be heard.[76] The exploration and embrace of alternative publishing possibilities, such as the online open access journal movement, in order to amplify neglected voices seems to be a necessary practice of a theology that "stays punk."

And yet, this understandable concern for theological quality is itself open to scrutiny. So a fourth point to consider is the challenge presented to contemporary theology by punk rock's aesthetic embraces of messiness, and de-professionalized edginess, versus autotuned and overly produced corporate rock. To suggest another analogy: to what extent are our theologies autotuned or over-produced? Are we willing to let our theology be raw, messy, and unpolished?[77] Again, Ian Svenonius' take on punk rock's raw and garbage-like characteristics might inspire an entirely new approach to the task of theology:

> I'm not into quality. I'm into trash. I think trash is appealing. I think the exciting thing about American pop music from the sixties or whatever is the garbage quality of it. Like soul music, gospel music. Not that it sounds like garbage, it's really well done, but it has a tossed off quality to it. The problem with music is the "importance" of it. Who wants to hear Radiohead, or Pink Floyd, or Kanye West, or someone who's so important? "Oh, the record is seventy minutes long, and it's so *important*, it's such an event." And it's like, "No, good music is not an event." It feels organic. And when it's important, it's because of the narcissism of the star.[78]

I do not mean to suggest that punk theologians should make theological garbage or that we should not strive to produce quality work. But the "tossed off quality" that Svenonius points to might reorient how we conceive of the very notion of theological quality. In the spirit of Svenonius, one might say that just as punk rebelled against the godlike importance of stadium rock, a punk theology would necessarily reject as mere pretension the continuing temptation toward grand system-building

[76] Lee Cormie, "Toward an Epistemology of the Spirit: Academic Freedom and the Struggles for Cognitive Justice," Faculty Forum on Academic Freedom, Faculty of Theology, University of St. Michael's College (Toronto, Ontario, 2010).

[77] Anthony B. Pinn, "In the Raw: African American Cultural Memory and Theological Reflection," in *Converging on Culture: Theologians in Dialogue with Cultural Analysis and Criticism*, ed. Delwin Brown, Sheila Greeve Davaney, and Kathryn Tanner (Oxford: Oxford University Press, 2001), 106–21.

[78] Hanlon, "Interview: Ian Svenonius."

reflected in official Roman Catholic theology and many academic systematic theologies. Or that, in being more humble about theology's importance, a punk approach to theology should be significantly more occasional and less concerned with being all-encompassing or systematic, a theology expressed, we could say, in the spirit of the seven-inch single rather than the epic seventy-minute important album or career-spanning box set.

This type of occasional, tossed-off theology is reflected in some ways in the emerging practice of theological blogging which is increasingly becoming a standard way young theologians connect with one another. While some "theo-bloggers" write in a way very similar to their more formal, traditionally published output, others are explicitly tailoring their writing to the spirit of the medium, using blogs as a way to test out ideas or "think out loud" and to interact in a more relaxed, immediate way. Analysis of the impact blogging is having in the world of theology, and blogging's potential contributions to theological discussion, is lacking. It seems to me, however, that there is something of the DIY punk spirit present in the theo-blogging phenomenon and that it is bringing some refreshing—if ambiguous— changes to the world of academic theology.

Fifth, in our resistance to the tendency to build airtight and permanently valid theological systems, punk theologians will not concern ourselves primarily with continuity but will be open to and even encourage rupture/interruption. Just as Guy Piccioto of the band Fugazi insists that punk rock, at its heart, is "unsettling," "dangerous," and "constantly moving,"[79] a theology informed by punk commitments will say with Marcella Althaus-Reid that "in theology it is not stability but a sense of discontinuity which is most valuable. The continuousness of the hermeneutical circle of suspicion and the permanent questioning of the explanatory narratives of reality implies, precisely, a process of theological discontinuity."[80] Or, in the language of Johann Baptist Metz, punk theologies will commit to being the bearers of "dangerous memories" that "interrupt" the narratives of the powerful, the mainstream, the familiar, and the "normal."[81]

Sixth, this stance of permanent questioning suggests a commitment to ongoing internal critique and revision. Despite its sectarian tendencies,

---

[79] Piccioto's comments can be heard in the Fugazi documentary *Instrument*.

[80] Althaus-Reid, *Indecent Theology*, 4.

[81] Johann Baptist Metz, *Faith in History and Society: Toward a Practical Fundamental Theology*, new ed., trans. J. Matthew Ashley (New York: Herder & Herder, 2007).

punk was not only critical of the world outside of punk but continually internally critical of punk itself, producing the irruption of new "scenes" such as DC hardcore and various "irruptions within the irruptions" (e.g., Riot Grrrl and queer-core). This persistent self-criticism of punk rock finds parallels in the irruption of and dialogues between liberation, black, feminist, womanist, critical, political, and postcolonial theologies over the last several decades. Constant rethinking, renegotiating, and argument-making is part of punk communities and is also an important part of postmodern theology. "Staying punk" as a theologian will require an embrace of this postmodern tendency in theology, even looking to those who have rejected the church (such as punks who have rejected religion) as sources of theological insight, as Beaudoin has argued.[82]

Seventh, just as DIY punk communities resist the commodification of music, a theology that "stays punk" will resist the commodification of theology, theological texts, movements, religious symbols, etc. that tends to take place under the influence of global consumer capitalism. Such commitments find resonance with the views of writers like Michael Budde and Vincent Miller who analyze the effects of global capitalism and culture industries on the beliefs and practices of religious communities (including the Roman Catholic Church)[83] and postcolonial theologians like Marcella Althaus-Reid and R. S. Sugirtharajah who have noted the commodification even of liberation theologies and theologies of the marginalized.[84] The processes by which countercultural phenomena like punk rock have been scooped up and sold back through the corporate culture industries can point to similar processes in the appropriation and commodification of "progressive" movements in the church and in theology. Liberal appropriations of liberation theologies within mainstream Catholic theology and the appropriation of the *language* of liberation theology in magisterial teaching without attention to its *methodological commitments* are perhaps two concrete examples of such

---

[82] Tom Beaudoin, "Faith and Apocalypse," in *Witness to Dispossession: The Vocation of a Post-Modern Theologian* (Maryknoll, NY: Orbis Books, 2008), 136–42.

[83] Michael L. Budde, *The (Magic) Kingdom of God: Christianity and the Culture Industries* (Boulder, CO: Westview Press, 1997); Michael L. Budde and Robert W. Brimlow, *Christianity Incorporated: How Big Business Is Buying the Church* (Grand Rapids, MI: Brazos Press, 2002); Miller, *Consuming Religion*.

[84] Althaus-Reid, "Gustavo Gutiérrez Goes to Disneyland"; R. S. Sugirtharajah, "Textual Takeaways: Third World Texts in Western Metropolitan Centres," in *Postcolonial Reconfigurations: An Alternative Way of Reading the Bible and Doing Theology* (London: SCM Press, 2003), 162–75.

tendencies. Punk rock and radical theologies have both, in their own ways, been domesticated within dominant systems by taking on the role of the "official" marginalized "other."[85]

Finally, a commitment to "staying punk" as a theologian will affect not only how I do theology in general but how I engage in theologies of popular culture. Radical expressions of DIY punk rock have served as a challenge not only to traditional forms of religiosity, but also to traditional forms of *rock* religiosity, consistently and relentlessly deconstructing the system of stars, hits, and rock celebrity "gods" represented by the mainstream popular music industry in North America and Europe. This should lead to a certain skepticism about claims regarding the religiosity of rock music, enthusiastically expressed in the recent theologies of popular culture. This of course is not the standard skepticism that often comes from a traditional Christian stance that wants to protect ecclesial tradition and identities at all costs, but a skepticism which lies at the very heart of the punk rock impulse. Attention to the "religious" function that rock music plays in people's lives is important and necessary but risks reproducing many of the alienating tendencies of religion in the excitement over viewing rock stars as saints[86] (or even as "gods"!), rock albums as "scripture," concerts as "liturgies," and so on. Punk rock's deconstruction of the alienating tendencies of the mainstream popular music industry's system of stars and hits may have much to teach us about the alienating tendencies of traditional religion—and even of new forms of religiosity like popular culture—in an age when popes tour the globe to strut across stadium stages in front of thousands of adoring fans.[87]

---

[85] Sugirtharajah, "Textual Takeaways," 173.

[86] My reflections on mainstream versus punk rock "saints" and the relevance of this distinction for Roman Catholic "saint-making" practices were presented in "I'm a Human, not a *Statue.*"

[87] I thank Brian McCord, Jeff Miller, Vanessa Miller, and Eddie Sloane for insightful comments on this chapter, as well as A. K. M. Adam, Mark Andersen, Vincent Miller, and Brian Walsh for comments on earlier versions of some of the ideas presented here.

Chapter 4

On the Road to the Promised Land: How the NAACP, the Black Church, and Rock Music Helped the Civil Rights Movement

Mary McDonough

In the spring of 2010, I rented the *Tami* show, a concert DVD recorded at the Santa Monica California Civic Auditorium in the fall of 1964.[1] The concert featured a large group of gifted performers including Chuck Berry, The Rolling Stones, James Brown, The Supremes, The Beach Boys, Smokey Robinson and the Miracles, Gerry and the Pacemakers, and Marvin Gaye. Aside from the wonderful music, I was struck by the racially integrated composition of the performers, including a large group of dancers, because the *Tami* concert took place when the battle for civil rights was still raging.

In fact, for over a decade, the country had been embroiled in legal struggles, protests, boycotts, marches, and race-related violence. Only months before the concert, three civil rights workers, Michael Schwerner, Andrew Goodman, and James Chaney, in Mississippi to conduct a voter registration drive, disappeared after being stopped for speeding. Six weeks later the FBI found their bodies buried under an earthen dam.

Yet the mostly white audience at the *Tami* concert had no qualms about attending a desegregated concert and enthusiastically cheering for black entertainers. James Brown's electric performance brought the entire audience to their feet, applause almost drowning out his strong voice.

---

[1] Steve Binder, *The Tami Show* (US: American International Pictures, 1964).

Since I have a law degree and a Ph.D. in ethics, I was aware of the roles that the courts and the black church played in the civil rights movement. However, although I am a long-time rock music fan and guitar player, until I watched the concert I had never considered what role, if any, rock music played in the civil rights movement. So I began to review the NAACP's (National Association for the Advancement of Colored People) involvement in the civil rights movement, the role of the black church in the movement and the early roots of rock and roll. What I discovered is that each of these institutions represented an alternative moral culture which challenged perceptions about African Americans and helped propel the civil rights movement.

As a Catholic academic with a specialty in moral theology (sometimes called Christian ethics), I am interested in the interplay between character ethics, a specific approach to moral theology, and the various communities to which we belong. For a long time Catholic moral theology focused primarily on act-analysis—whether or not a person's actions were sinful. Today, however, the discipline has broadened its focus to include human agency because actions express a person's internal belief system. Morality, therefore, stems from an individual's character and not from an individual's actions or consequences. Our character includes the beliefs we live by and the habits we practice. Catholic moral theologian Richard Gula argues that many of our decisions are not based on rational principles or logical procedures. Instead, we make choices based on our underlying vision, our perception about situations. Gula puts it this way: "In fact, most of what appears in our decisions and actions is the result of what we see going on, rather than the result of conscious rational choices. For example, if we look on our children as a burden, we refuse to carry them; if we look on our colleagues as competitors, we refuse to cooperate with them."[2]

Moral visions are closely linked to communities because we internalize the visions and beliefs held by the communities with which we identify.[3] Sociologist James Davison Hunter calls such communities "moral cultures." Hunter has studied moral cultures and their role in influencing moral behavior and education. He argues that character development is formed in relation to "a normative order or moral culture."[4] Moral

---

[2] Richard M. Gula, *Reason Informed by Faith: Foundations of Catholic Morality* (Mahwah, NJ: Paulist Press, 1989), 140.

[3] Ibid., 142.

[4] James Davison Hunter, *The Death of Moral Character: Moral Education in an Age without Good or Evil* (New York: Basic Books, 2000), 24.

cultures consist of "principles, maxims and habits" that are interwoven into people's consciousness guiding their behavior.[5] In contemporary society, moral cultures are not monolithic. We can belong to several at the same time. Any community with which we identify, a church, sport, hobby, political group, is a moral culture. They can overlap, complement, or even clash with each other.

Most of us are hardly aware of the strong influence of moral cultures. While they do not serve as major ethical systems, they provide a vital mechanism for generating our beliefs and values. More importantly, Hunter argues that, at times, character "is formed *against* the dominant culture by the more powerfully internalized codes of an alternative culture."[6]

In the 1950s, the NAACP, the black church, and rock music each acted as an alternative moral culture, maintaining values that rejected segregation, eventually giving many white people a new underlying vision of African Americans that made them more supportive of the civil rights movement. Both the NAACP, acting as a legal alternative moral culture, and the black church, acting as a theological alternative moral culture, intentionally tried to eradicate segregation. Rock, on the other hand, acted as a musical alternative moral culture which unintentionally aided the movement in that there was no anti-segregation coordination within the rock industry. I will examine these three alternative moral cultures to show how each worked toward what theological ethics considers a universal human good: racial equality. My essay will also demonstrate the power of alternative moral cultures to change the dominant moral culture.

The road leading up to the modern civil rights movement was arduous, to say the least. After the Civil War ended, the states ratified the thirteenth, fourteenth, and fifteenth amendments to the Constitution. While the thirteenth amendment abolished slavery and the fifteenth guaranteed freed slaves the right to vote, it was the last clause in the second sentence of the first section of the fourteenth amendment that eventually played a critical role in ending legalized segregation. Known as the equal protection clause, it states that no state can "deny to any person within its jurisdiction the equal protection of the laws."[7]

[5] Ibid., 25.

[6] Ibid.

[7] See http://www.archives.gov/exhibits/charters/constitution_amendments_11-27.html.

For a short time, freed slaves participated in local, state, and national elections, electing several blacks to office. However, after the contentious presidential election of 1876 and the endorsement of the Hayes Compromise of 1877, which resulted in the withdrawal of the troops from the South, a reign of racial violence began. States enacted Jim Crow laws mandating racial segregation in public facilities. The laws, which represented the dominant moral culture of the time, were endorsed by the US Supreme Court in the 1896 case, *Plessy v Ferguson*. The *Plessy* case upheld a Louisiana law requiring the segregation of blacks and whites on railroad cars on the grounds that as long as segregated facilities were "separate but equal" they were not discriminatory and did not, therefore, violate the equal protection clause. This was the law for the next fifty-eight years.

Racial segregation led to the formation of several alternative moral cultures. Some, like the Ku Klux Klan, formed to maintain the status quo. Others formed based on a different moral vision of American society, where segregation would no longer exist. With specific beliefs, values, and patterns of behavior endorsing racial equality, the NAACP is an example of the latter. Established in 1909 in response to violence against African Americans, the NAACP decided to attempt an all-out legal frontal attack on educational segregation in the summer of 1950.

The most important case challenge came when the NAACP decided to take on segregation in public schools by filing five cases in four states and the District of Columbia. In 1952, the Supreme Court heard the cases consolidated under the Kansas case called *Brown v Board of Education of Topeka, et al*. In this case, the NAACP used a new kind of argument that changed the way the justices viewed segregation. They offered social science data to show the harmful effects of segregation on children.

The innovative argument worked. On May 17, 1954 the Court overturned the "separate but equal" doctrine of the *Plessy* case finding that public school segregation violated the fourteenth amendment because it deprived black children of an equal educational opportunity. In a single sentence Chief Justice Earl Warren summed up the court's new way of seeing segregation: "To separate [schoolchildren] from others of similar age and qualifications solely because of their race generates a feeling of inferiority as to their status in the community that may affect their hearts and minds in a way unlikely ever to be undone."[8] Rather than rely on

---

[8] *Brown v. Board of Education*, 347 U.S. 483, 494 (1954).

traditional constitutional concepts, the Court chose, instead, to use the social science evidence to support its decision. Within the opinion is a famous footnote, number eleven, which cites various writings of contemporary social scientists, psychologists, and sociologists attesting to segregation's psychological and emotional harm on children.

The Court's conclusion that segregation causes psychological harm was based primarily on the research of Dr. Kenneth Clark who performed a study on some African American schoolchildren. He asked them to select among an assortment of black and white dolls. The children preferred the white dolls, describing them as "nicer." Clark concluded that school segregation is psychologically harmful to black children because it lowers their self-esteem.[9] Footnote 11 also cited a study showing that Clark's conclusion was shared by 90 percent of social scientists surveyed in a 1948 study.[10]

This was the first time the US Supreme Court used social science evidence to support its conclusion. The evidence gave the justices a new moral vision that saw segregation as harmful and, therefore, they rejected it. While its use of social sciences has been criticized over time,[11] the implications of the *Brown* case were immense. The decision not only forbade public school segregation but strongly implied that any publicly authorized or publicly permitted racial segregation was unconstitutional. While the *Brown* case made segregated schools illegal, the decision was largely ignored in the South. By the end of 1956, six southern states had not desegregated one single school. Still, with its use of the social science method, the NAACP was able to get the Supreme Court to view segregation differently, eventually leading to the eradication of Jim Crow laws which had been a part of the dominant moral culture for decades.[12]

[9] See generally Kenneth B. Clark, "The Effects of Prejudice and Discrimination on Personality Development," in *Mid-Century White House Conference on Children and Youth* (Washington, DC: Children's Bureau, Federal Security Agency, 1950); Kenneth B. Clark and Mamie P. Clark, "Racial Identification and Preference in Negro Children," *Readings in Social Psychology* 169 (1947).

[10] M. Deutscher and I. Chein, "The Psychological Effects of Enforced Segregation: A Survey of Social Science Opinion," *Journal of Psychology* 26 (1948): 259–87.

[11] See, for example, Michael Heise, "Brown v. Board of Education, Footnote 11, and Multidisciplinarity," *Cornell Law Review* 90 (2004–5): 279–320.

[12] Some people argue, however, that there is a new kind of Jim Crow which is reflected in the US prison system with its massive numbers of incarcerated African Americans. See Michelle Alexander, *The New Jim Crow: Mass Incarceration in the Age of Colorblindness* (New York: The New Press, 2010).

While the NAACP was fighting for civil rights in the courts, the black church was fighting from the pulpit. The church's importance in the movement cannot be downplayed. Rev. Fred Shuttlesworth, one of the movement's leaders, once remarked that what people in the South did not understand was that participants in the protests and marches thought that "God is with me and if God is with me how can you lose?"[13] For any student of Black History, the dominant role the church played in the movement would not have come as a surprise. For generations, the church has served as one of the primary moral cultures for the African American community. Black congregations formed in response to segregation in churches. Ex-slave and Methodist minister, Richard Allen, led a group of blacks out of St. George Methodist Church in Philadelphia in 1787, eventually founding the African Methodist Episcopal Church (AME) in 1816. Other black congregations were eventually established including the African Methodist Episcopal Zion (AMEZ) and several separate Baptist congregations.[14] After the Civil War most black Christians joined Methodist or Baptist congregations led by black ministers.[15]

Severed from the institutional life of the greater society, the black church provided its members with an alternative moral culture encompassing not only religious pursuits but also educational and political activities. It also became the institutional center for the civil rights movement because, as black theology scholar James H. Cone explains: "Unlike white churches, which separated religion and politics when the racial question was involved, black churches have always viewed them as belonging together, *especially* in regard to race."[16]

The power of the black church's alternative moral culture is evidenced during the bus boycott in Montgomery, Alabama. In December 1955, Rosa Parks was arrested for refusing to vacate her seat on a city bus for a white passenger. Recognizing the need for a coordinated response to her arrest and to the racial segregation policies on Montgomery's city buses, several local ministers and other civil rights activists organized the Montgomery Improvement Association (MIA) choosing Dr. Martin Luther King Jr. as its leader.

---

[13] Henry Hampton, "Eyes on the Prize: America's Civil Rights Years: 1954–1965," in *American Experience Series* (US: PBS, 1987), disc 1 of 3.

[14] James H. Cone, *Martin & Malcolm & America: A Dream or a Nightmare* (Maryknoll, NY: Orbis Books, 1991), 6.

[15] Ibid., 7.

[16] Ibid., 143.

The black church was essential to the success of the boycott. Ministers used the pulpit to encourage participation. Churches were also used as centers for an alternative transportation system so blacks could get to their jobs. Forty-eight dispatch and forty-two pickup stations were organized, most at black churches that would open their doors early in the morning, allowing people to wait inside the churches for their rides.[17] After 381 days the boycott finally ended when the US Supreme Court ruled that segregation on Alabama's buses was unconstitutional. Although it took a court decision to end bus segregation, the Montgomery boycott was proof that black churches acting as an alternative moral culture could inspire and mobilize thousands of people into effective collective action.

Theology played a vital role in the black church's ability to act as an alternative moral culture through its use of theological principles to inspire and organize supporters. In researching their book, *Rhetoric, Religion and the Civil Rights Movement, 1954–1965*, David Houck and David Dixon listened to audiotapes, reviewed videos and read texts of hundreds of civil rights meetings, sermons, and speeches. They concluded "that civil rights was fundamentally a religious affair."[18] Among the documents they reviewed, several common theological themes emerged. From the Old Testament, stories about slavery, about the chosen people wandering in desolation and the promise of justice dominated. From the New Testament, congregations were inspired by the Parable of the Good Samaritan, Christ's ministry and suffering, and St. Paul's appeal for unity: "There is neither Jew nor Greek, there is neither slave nor free, there is neither male nor female; for you are all one in Christ Jesus" (Gal 3:28).[19]

The view of religion as a vehicle for social change was part of the moral vision of the social gospel movement that most of the civil rights movement's ministers had studied. One of the primary founders of the social gospel movement was Walter Rauschenbusch, author of *Christianity and the Social Crisis*.[20] Rauschenbusch viewed the Christian ministry as rooted

---

[17] Aldon D. Morris, *The Origins of the Civil Rights Movement: Black Communities Organizing for Change* (New York: The Free Press, 1986), 58.

[18] Davis W. Houck and David E. Dixon, *Rhetoric, Religion and the Civil Rights Movement, 1954–1965* (Waco, TX: Baylor University, 2006), 2.

[19] See ibid., 11–12.

[20] Walter Rauschenbusch, *Christianity and the Social Crisis* (New York: Macmillan, 1907).

in a social ethics where social sins against humanity must be addressed. His book was among the few that Dr. Martin Luther King Jr. actually cited as a primary influence on his theology.[21]

The sheer power and influence of the black church as an alternative moral culture continued to increase throughout the 1950s. By 1957, several minister-led local movements to end segregation were underway in the South. For example, Rev. A.L. Davis, head of the New Orleans Interdenominational Ministerial Alliance, organized a group of black students, mostly from Xavier University, to defy segregation laws on a city bus in New Orleans. Around this same time, three ministers from Alabama, Dr. Martin Luther King Jr. of Montgomery, Rev. Joseph Lowery of Mobile, and Rev. Fred Shuttlesworth of Birmingham met to discuss the possibility of working together on a state level. Other southern ministers were contacted. Discussions ensued about starting an organization to coordinate local protest movements. Eventually, the Southern Christian Leadership Conference (SCLC) was created, whose purpose was "to redeem the soul of America" by ending segregation.[22]

The SCLC expressly emphasized their church roots early on. Statement five of their working paper number one stated: "The campaign is *based on the most stable social institution in Negro culture—the church.*"[23] Ministers who had led various local protest groups became leaders in the SCLC. King was chosen as president, Rev. C.K. Steele as vice-president, and Rev. A.L. Davis as first vice president. In total, the SCLC had thirty-six leadership positions of which all but four were filled by ministers.

For the remainder of the 1950s the SCLC met throughout the South, mostly in churches and at church-related organizations, mobilizing thousands of people. SCLC leaders referred to these organizations as the "invisible hand of God."[24] The creation of the SCLC strengthened the black church's alternative moral culture by increasing the bonds between protestors across the South and also fortifying their internal organizations. Their various marches and protests received a lot of national media attention. The media attention proved to be a valuable tool for changing

---

[21] Taylor Branch, *Parting the Waters: America in the King Years 1954–63* (New York: Simon and Schuster, 1988), 73.

[22] Cone, *Martin & Malcolm & America: A Dream or a Nightmare*, 66.

[23] Aldon D. Morris, "The Black Church in the Civil Rights Movement: The SCLC as the Decentralized, Radical Arm of the Black Church," in *Disruptive Religion: The Force of Faith in Social-Movement Activism*, ed. Christian Smith (New York: Routledge, 1996), 40.

[24] Ibid., 2.

many white people's underlying visions about African Americans by educating them about the horrors of segregation. With these new insights came an increased awareness and concern for the plight of blacks in the South, paving the way for white involvement in the movement in the 1960s through participation in campaigns such as the Freedom Riders and voter registration drives.

While the NAACP and the black churches were trying to change the dominant moral culture's underlying visions and perceptions about African Americans, a new genre of music emerged that would unintentionally help the civil rights movement by acting as an alternative moral culture that changed the way many white people, particularly teenagers, viewed African Americans.

Every generation of teenagers rebels against the dominant culture of its parents in order to find its own identity. What did the dominant moral culture look like in post–World War II America? The country was largely segregated by race. By the early 1950s, Americans found themselves amidst the "Cold War"—an era of intense anxiety marked by unsubstantiated accusations, loyalty oaths, and the McCarthy hearings. Yet it was also a time of general prosperity[25] with a moral culture founded on conservative values. The decade saw record rates of young marriages, births, and white households moving to the suburbs. Low divorce rates were the norm. Premarital sex was considered taboo. Nuclear families, built around traditional roles of fathers who worked and mothers who stayed home, dominated society.[26]

The alternative rock moral culture that formed in the 1950s gave baby boomers a discourse through which they could examine and challenge their parent's values. They questioned, reacted to, and ultimately rejected the dominant cultural values of the decade regarding family, sexuality,

[25] Between 1940 and 1955 the average personal income of Americans rose 293 percent, Landon Y. Jones, *Great Expectations: America and the Baby Boom Generation* (New York: Coward, McCann & Geoghegan, 1980), 20. However, while African Americans earned four times the wages they made in 1940, this was still only 61 percent of the pay earned by whites; Glenn C. Altschuler, *All Shook Up: How Rock 'N' Roll Changed America* (Oxford: Oxford University Press, 2003), 11.

[26] Altschuler, *All Shook Up: How Rock 'N' Roll Changed America*, 9. This was not the case, however, for African Americans. Up until 1950, marriage and divorce rates were fairly similar for blacks and whites. After 1950, marriage rates for African Americans slowly began to drop and the divorce rate began to increase; see census data from J. Mandara and C.B. Murray, "Effects of Parental Marital Status, Income, and Family Functioning on African American Adolescent Self-Esteem," *Journal of Family Psychology* 14 (2000): 475–90.

and most important for the purposes of this essay, race. After eschewing the traditional values of their parents, eventually the baby boomers identified with freedom: Freedom from traditional roles, freedom to do what they wanted, freedom from restraints on what kind of music they listened to, freedom from racial segregation.[27]

While there is debate about which song was the first rock and roll record (Roy Brown's 1947 jump blues classic "Good Rockin' Tonight," Fats Domino's 1949 debut single "The Fat Man," or Jimmy Preston's "Rock the Joint"), there is no dispute that the music originated with African American artists. While rock and roll opened numerous doors, both economic and social, for African Americans, these gains came at the expense of many individual black musicians. Often the music industry did not treat them justly. Many black artists were robbed of royalties, residuals, and copyrights for their songs. Regardless, their influence touched every great rock performer after them. In his autobiography, *Life*, Rolling Stones guitarist Keith Richards describes how he and Mick Jagger bonded over Chuck Berry and Muddy Waters records.[28] When Bob Dylan was inducted into the Rock and Roll Hall of Fame in 1988, he thanked Little Richard saying, "I don't think I would have even started out without listening to Little Richard."[29]

The following summary of rock and roll's complex roots will help us understand how it evolved into an alternative moral culture. When Africans were transported to the United States as slaves, they brought their music with them. Plantation owners tried to eradicate it entirely, so the music adapted. Still, several traits survived: aspects of style incorporating a strong, distinct rhythmic drive; a hoarse vocal quality; call-and-response forms; and, melodies that revolved around blues scales.[30] In the early twentieth century a new type of black secular music emerged called the blues. Record companies began marketing blues

---

[27] Numerous books have been written on the appeal and influence of rock music. See, for example, Altschuler, *All Shook Up: How Rock 'N' Roll Changed America*; James Miller, *Flowers in the Dustbin: The Rise of Rock and Roll 1947–1977* (New York: Fireside, 1999); Rob Roy, "Bias against Rock 'N' Roll Latest Bombshell in Dixie," in *The Pop, Rock, and Soul Reader: Histories and Debates*, ed. David Brackett (New York: Oxford University Press, 2009).

[28] Keith Richards, *Life* (New York: Little, Brown and Company, 2010), 79.

[29] Holly George-Warren, *The Rock and Roll Hall of Fame: The First 25 Years* (New York: Collins Design, 2009), 35.

[30] Robert Palmer, "Rock Begins," in *The Rolling Stone Illustrated History of Rock & Roll*, ed. Anthony DeCurtis, James Henke, and Holly George-Warren (New York: Random House, 1992), 4.

records under the category "race records," with *Billboard* magazine monitoring them on its "Harlem Hit Parade." In 1949, *Billboard* began to use the term "rhythm and blues" (R&B) instead of "race records" for all records by black artists. Around this same time, the 45 rpm single vinyl record was invented, popularizing single songs. Then a new sound emerged within R&B: mixing gospel-styled vocals, R&B rhythms, and often risqué lyrics. This music would eventually be called rock and roll and would change the way many white people saw African Americans, which in turn influenced their attitudes toward segregation.

There are two pivotal years in early rock music history. The first was 1951 when the seeds for an alternative moral culture were planted. Alan Freed, a twenty-eight year old disc jockey at WJW in Cleveland whose parents were Lithuanian Jewish immigrants, was having a drink with Leo Mintz, the owner of one of the largest record stores in Cleveland. Mintz told Freed he had recently noticed an interesting trend at his store. The sales of R&B records had increased dramatically. Wanting to capitalize on this trend, Mintz asked Freed if he could buy several hours of airtime at WJW and have Freed host a radio show featuring R&B music.[31] Mintz's idea was innovative; like much of America, the radio airwaves were essentially segregated.

On July 11, 1951, Freed started playing R&B records on WJW during his radio show "Moondog Symphony." In order to get past the racial stigma the music had, he eventually started calling it rock and roll, a term for sexual intercourse that had been used in R&B for decades. The new name took a few years to catch on, but Freed's show grew in popularity. Within a year or so, other white disc jockeys began playing R&B songs and tapes of Freed's show turned up on New York City radio stations.

With the availability of cheap transistor radios,[32] radio shows became very popular in the 1950s. White listeners started hearing the new R&B music and demanded that white radio stations play it. The radio stations, desiring high ratings, obliged. Jerry Wexler, an Atlantic Records executive and producer during this time, noted in his autobiography: "You could segregate schoolrooms and buses, but not the airwaves."[33] As the

[31] Miller, *Flowers in the Dustbin: The Rise of Rock and Roll 1947–1977*, 60.

[32] By 1959, fifty-six million radios were in working order in the United States, which was three times the number of televisions. Altschuler, *All Shook Up: How Rock 'N' Roll Changed America*, 15.

[33] Jerry Wexler, "Rhythm and the Blues: A Life in American Music," in *The Pop, Rock, and Soul Reader: Histories and Debates*, ed. David Brackett (New York: Oxford Univeristy Press, 2009), 97.

music grew in popularity, whites wanted to buy the records, but record stores were also segregated so they had to go to black neighborhoods to purchase the music. R&B record stores began to see a marked increase in sales to whites. For example, in 1952, Dolphin Record Store, a large music outlet in a Los Angeles African American neighborhood, sold 40 percent of its R&B records to whites.[34] This trend reflected not only the growing popularity of the music but shows that whites were willing to defy the racial barriers endorsed by the dominant moral culture to buy it.

The second pivotal year was 1955 when two major events occurred: the release of the movie *Blackboard Jungle* and the rise of three African American rock stars. Just one year after the Supreme Court announced its landmark decision in the *Brown v Board of Education of Topeka, et al.* case and nine months before the start of the Montgomery bus boycott, MGM studios released a movie called *Blackboard Jungle*. Depicting turmoil in an inner city, inter-racial all male high school, the movie was shocking for its time. The film opens up with a snare drum and Bill Haley & His Comets singing "One, two, three o'clock, four o'clock rock/ five, six, seven o'clock, eight o'clock rock / nine, ten, eleven o'clock, twelve o'clock rock / We're gonna rock around the clock tonight!" The movie's producers deliberately chose "Rock Around the Clock" as a "symbol of youthful mayhem and menace."[35] They also raised the bass and treble levels (the norm in Hollywood had been to lower the volume of soundtracks) so that for many people it was the loudest music they had ever heard.[36] The sheer volume of the music tied the music to power and aggression.

In a critical scene, one of the teachers brings his jazz record collection to play to his class. The students do not like the music. They destroy his records in defiance while the rock soundtrack plays in the background. The reaction to the movie was strong. Violence broke out in movie theaters showing the film. Several cities actually banned the movie, some because of its multi-racial content, others out of fear it would spark violence. The combination of the movie's integrated high school, inner-city violence, teenage delinquency, and loud soundtrack welded rock music to an alternative moral culture rooted in anti-establishment, anti-authoritarian, and anti-segregation values.

---

[34] Altschuler, *All Shook Up: How Rock 'N' Roll Changed America*, 18.
[35] Miller, *Flowers in the Dustbin: The Rise of Rock and Roll 1947–1977*, 92.
[36] Ibid.

That same year, three black artists hit it big with rock music releases. New Orleans native Fats Domino (Antoine Domino) broke through with his 1955 hit "Ain't That a Shame," reaching number one on the R&B charts and number ten on *Billboard*'s best-seller list. The vivacious and flamboyant Little Richard (Richard Penniman) also appeared on the rock scene with his first big hit "Tutti-Frutti." Selling five hundred thousand copies, the record brought him lots of fans, both black and white. Finally, Chuck Berry, who eventually became rock's first superstar, released "Maybellene." Although Chess Records never audited their accounts to determine the song's exact sales numbers, experts claim it sold at least a million copies.[37] "Maybellene" hit number one on the R&B, country/ western and pop charts. Berry was awarded the most promising artist of 1955 by *Cash Box* and *Billboard*. The high demand for the records by these black rockers forced music stores in white neighborhoods, whose inventory did not include records by black artists, to begin selling their music.

Rock's alternative moral culture caught the attention of the dominant American moral culture and the cultures clashed. In February of 1955, *Variety* published an editorial complaining about rock's lewd lyrics, noting that "our teenagers are already setting something of a record in delinquency with this raw musical idiom."[38] In 1956, *The New York Times* reported that "a noted psychiatrist described 'rock 'n' roll' music today as a 'communicable disease' and 'another sign of adolescent rebellion.'"[39] For two years the newspaper printed dozens of articles linking the music to destructive activities. For a time rock concerts were actually banned in several cities including Boston, New Haven, Santa Cruz, and Jersey City.

With the popularity of black rock artists soaring, racially mixed audiences started attending rock concerts, often dancing together. In 1955, Alan Freed put together a New York City concert featuring Fats Domino and other black performers. Much to his astonishment, almost half the audience was white.[40] In September of that same year, Chuck Berry

[37] Robert Christgau, "Chuck Berry," in *The Rolling Stone Illustrated History of Rock & Roll*, eds. Anthony DeCurtis, James Henke, and Holly George-Warren (New York: Random House, 1992), 62.

[38] "A Warning to the Music Business," in *The Pop, Rock, and Soul Reader: Histories and Debates*, 102.

[39] "Rock-and-Roll Called Communicable Disease," in ibid., 127.

[40] Miller, *Flowers in the Dustbin: The Rise of Rock and Roll 1947–1977*, 86.

played at the Brooklyn Paramount Theater before an almost completely white, sold-out audience.

Not everyone, however, was happy with rock's ability to dissolve racial barriers. Segregationists, particularly in the South, had their own alternative moral culture rooted in racism. They targeted the music, contending it was a tool used by the NAACP to further the civil rights movement. Segregationists tried to stop rock music from being played. In 1956, the Louisiana legislature even banned interracial dancing, and Little Rock, Arkansas banned all interracial social functions.

One of the most vocal anti-rock music groups was the Citizens' Council.[41] Established in 1954 in Mississippi to preserve white political power by opposing desegregation, chapters spread throughout the South. Asa Carter, executive secretary of the Birmingham chapter, was a vocal critic of rock music, saying it was a plot by the NAACP to "mongrelize America"[42] and encouraged "for the purpose of undermining the morals of white people."[43]

Carter organized a state-wide petition calling for rock music to be banned from jukeboxes. The North Alabama Citizens' Council began picketing interracial rock concerts featuring entertainers like Bo Diddley, the Platters, and Bill Haley. Birmingham's city commissioners told the local auditorium not to book any interracial shows. Pop music singer Nat King Cole was actually assaulted during one of his concerts in Birmingham. When asked about the incident, Carter, who was at the concert but denied involvement in the attack, said it was "a short step . . . from the sly, nightclub technique vulgarity of Cole, to the openly animalistic obscenity of the horde of Negro rock 'n' rollers."[44]

Others, however, defended rock's ability to transcend race. *Ebony* magazine proclaimed Fats Domino the "King of Rock 'n' Roll" with a photo caption noting his appeal to a racially diverse audience.[45] The *Pittsburgh Courier* wrote that criticism of the music was actually "an indirect attack against Negroes . . . because they invented rock 'n' roll . . . and because it has so captivated the younger generation of whites that they are breaking down dance floors and gutting nightclubs. As

[41] Originally called the White Citizens' Council, the name was changed to Citizens' Council in 1956.

[42] Altschuler, *All Shook Up: How Rock 'N' Roll Changed America*, 38.

[43] Rob Roy, "Bias against Rock 'N' Roll Latest Bombshell in Dixie," 130.

[44] Altschuler, *All Shook Up: How Rock 'N' Roll Changed America*, 39.

[45] Ibid., 43–44.

between rock 'n' roll . . . and the chill austerities of white supremacy, we think the young white Americans will choose the former with all of its implications."[46] *Cash Box* also made a connection between rock music and racial tolerance noting that the music changed people's perceptions: "How better to understand what is known to you than by appreciation of the emotional experience of other people. And how better are the emotions portrayed than by music?"[47]

Even the performers themselves commented on the ability of black rockers to cross traditional racial lines. Herbert Reed of the Platters described how racial barriers dissolved around rock music: "White kids beg us for autographs. . . . [In Austin] a rope was put up to separate Negroes and whites in the audience. When we started singing, the kids broke the rope and started dancing together. That rock 'n' roll beat gets them all."[48]

Regardless of the efforts of the dominant moral culture or other alternative moral culture to control or halt the influence of rock, the music's power could not be stopped. By the end of the 1950s, rock had desegregated the airwaves, record stores, concerts, and the dance floor. By the end of the 1960s, rock's alternative moral cultures would be fully developed, influencing language, fashion, and politics worldwide. The music would eventually become associated with the Free Speech Movement, the anti-war movement and just about every other sit-in and protest that one can imagine. It would move away from its R&B roots, however, to become dominated by white performers, several from Britain.

By the time the *Tami* concert took place in 1964, the civil rights movement had made strides. Some 250,000 people had participated on the March on Washington where Dr. Martin Luther King Jr. gave his "I Have a Dream Speech." Congress had passed the Civil Rights Act of 1964 outlawing all major forms of discrimination. Still, looking back at that audience in the Santa Monica auditorium, I doubt that any of them knew what had transpired over the previous decade or why this transformation had occurred. Three alternative moral cultures, the NAACP, the black church, and rock music, permanently changed the dominant moral culture in the United States. A team of resourceful lawyers using social science evidence; a group of courageous ministers and their congregations rooted in a theology of justice and equality; and a music, featuring

[46] Ibid., 42.
[47] Ibid., 48.
[48] Ibid., 42.

a strong beat, blazing electric guitar, and catchy lyrics which exposed the largest generation in US history to black rhythms and individual black artists, fundamentally changed many white people's underlying moral visions about African Americans, helping propel the civil rights movement.

Chapter 5

Is God Absent on "Grey Street"?: Theodicy, Domestic Violence, and the Dave Matthews Band

Gina Messina-Dysert

Acknowledging the suffering endured in relation to faith by women who are in violent relationships, Carol Winkelmann completed a study that focused on the theodicies expressed by women living in a domestic violence shelter.[1] She noted the numerous theodicy questions and various statements made about why the women believed God allowed them to suffer. Many of the women openly spoke about feeling punished or abandoned by God. Carolyn stated, "My suffering stems from decisions I have made that are incorrect."[2] Dela commented that "I think that is why I am having such a hard time now, because I haven't been going to church or listening to the Word."[3] Lisa reflected, "I prayed over and over every day, asking God to take the burden and the whole situation off my shoulders, that I gave it to him to bear. I felt like God was not listening to me."[4]

---

[1] See Carol Winkelmann, " 'In the Bible, It Can Be So Harsh!' Battered Women, Suffering, and the Problem of Evil," *Christian Faith and the Problem of Evil*, ed. Peter Van Inwagen (Cambridge: Eedermans, 2004), 148–84. In this study, Winkelmann examines the religious language of women who have experienced domestic violence in relation to suffering. The study focused on women who sought safety at a battered women's shelter. The shelter was located in an economically depressed area in the upper South of the United States. Both the name of the shelter and the names of the women in the study are pseudonyms to protect their identities.

[2] Ibid., 159.

[3] Ibid., 157.

[4] Ibid.

The suffering endured by women within abusive relationships is devastating, and thus theodicy questions are not uncommon for those who experience violence as part of their daily lives. Feelings of being abandoned by God in their darkest moments leave women in domestic violence situations feeling hopeless. While theodicies have focused on absolving God from responsibility for evil and demonstrating that sin exists as a result of human action, they do not fully acknowledge the questions of these women who are suffering as a result of injustice. Furthermore, with atonement playing a central role within the Christian tradition, women are often encouraged to embrace their suffering and victimization as their "cross to bear."

While Winkelmann acknowledges that traditional patriarchal ideologies can hinder the healing process for victims of domestic violence and states that "many battered women know that religion is a mechanism of social control,"[5] she maintains that religious faith, including theodicies, "can also serve to sustain the women through periods of profound suffering."[6] However, because theodicies focus on preserving God's attributes while exonerating God as responsible for the existence of evil, and laying blame on the individual sinner, they are very problematic, particularly for women living with daily violence. Consequently, women need resources that are not steeped in doctrine to offer support when suffering unjustly.

Based on a feminist standpoint,[7] which is informed by my activist roots (a decade of experience working in the trenches with survivors of rape and domestic violence), as well as my personal experience of losing my mother to an abusive relationship, I interpret the song "Grey Street" by the Dave Matthews Band as having great potential theological value and the capacity to act as a resource for women in abusive relationships. The song offers lyrics that lament a woman's suffering and express her theodical questions without the restrictions of Christian doctrine and

---

[5] Carol Winkelman, *The Language of Battered Women: A Rhetorical Analysis of Personal Theologies* (New York: State University of New York Press, 2004), 121.

[6] Winkelmann, "In the Bible, It Can Be So Harsh!," 149.

[7] Feminist standpoint theory acknowledges relationships between experience, knowledge, and identity. For additional information on feminist standpoint theory, see Sandra Harding, ed., *The Feminist Standpoint Theory Reader* (New York: Routledge, 2004); Sandra Harding, *Whose Science? Whose Knowledge? Thinking from Women's Lives* (Ithaca, NY: Cornell University Press, 1991); Sandra Harding, *Feminism and Methodology: Social Science Issues* (Indianapolis: Indiana University Press, 1987); Patricia Hill Collins, *Black Feminist Thought: Knowledge, Consciousness, and the Politics of Empowerment* (New York: Routledge, 2000).

can be interpreted as expressing the despair endured by women suffering within domestic violence situations. The lyric, "She says I pray, but my prayers they fall on deaf ears / Am I supposed to take it on myself to get out of this place?" symbolizes how this song articulates feelings of being alone and forsaken by God, left in isolation to survive a situation that seems impossible to escape.

In this chapter, I will argue that theodicies are unable to fully address questions that arise as a result of tragic suffering. In order to properly address the problem of suffering, I embrace Anthony Pinn's approach of "nitty-gritty hermeneutics," a method that pursues the questioning of evil without restricting its inquiry to the confines of doctrine, allowing for additional discourse and examination of the problem of suffering. Further, I examine music's ability to allow for explorations of anguish experienced as a result of injustice, as well as its ability to act as a coping mechanism and source of accompaniment for those sharing a similar experience expressed within a song.

A feminist standpoint will focus my analysis, my interpretation of the song "Grey Street," and its articulation of the emotional torment, affliction, and sorrow experienced by women who suffer in domestic violence situations. Because of the song's unrestricted exploration and articulation of suffering, it can act as a theological resource for women in abusive relationships. Because it does not conform to doctrine, "Grey Street" allows women to express their grief without limitations while validating feelings and offering a sense of accompaniment, providing momentary salvation.

Theodicies and "Nitty-Gritty Hermeneutics"

Theodicy, stemming from the Greek *theos* (God) and *dike* (justice), refers to theories that attempt to reconcile the coexistence of God and evil. The term was coined in 1710 by G.W.F. Leibniz, part of the title of his work that sought to explain how it was possible for evil to exist in a world created by God,[8] and from this point theodicy developed. These theoretical explanations seek to demonstrate that although evil exists, "God is just."[9] They aim to explain why a God who is loving and all-powerful

---

[8] See G.W.F. Leibniz, "The Theodicy: Abridgment of the Argument," ed. Philip P. Weiner, *Leibniz: Selections* (New York: Charles Scribner's Sons, 1951), 509–20.

[9] Kristine M. Rankka, *Women and the Value of Suffering: An Aw(e)ful Rowing toward God* (Collegeville, MN: Liturgical Press, 1998), 37. Also see Kenneth Surin, "Evil,

allows the existence of evil, and attempt to offer an explanation of how the theology of God overcomes this problem.

More specifically, traditional theodicies have focused on explaining the existence of evil alongside an omnipotent, omniscient, benevolent God and have differentiated between natural evil, such as disease, earthquakes, tsunamis, etc., and moral evil which is the result of human action and sin. Theodicies can be broken down into several types:[10]

- The dualistic model: Suffering exists due to an ongoing struggle between good and evil. Humanity is balanced between these dichotomies and thus endures suffering.

- The Augustinian or classic free will theodicy: Human sin has created suffering, and free will results in individuals' choosing to commit evil acts. Thus, God allows us to make choices and is not responsible for the suffering that results.

- The punishment/retribution model: Suffering is just retribution for humanity's sinfulness. Rankka explains, "God is understood as One who keeps track of individual and group actions and intercedes in history to exact punishment or retribution from sinful humanity."[11]

- The redemptive suffering/atonement theodicy: Human suffering is expiatory. Suffering is understood as one's "cross to bear," and humans are to suffer as Jesus did—willingly and obediently.

- The Irenaean or evolutionary model: Traced back to Irenaeus, this model argues that "evil [is] an integral part of an environment in which God shapes souls in a perfect likeness of the Divine."[12] Because we have knowledge of good and evil and the capacity to learn to conform to the image of God, evil occurs as a result of the abuse of free will.

Problem of," *Blackwell Encyclopedia of Modern Christian Thought*, ed. Alister E. McGrath (Oxford: Blackwell Publishers, 1993).

[10] For a comprehensive discussion on theodicy typologies, see Rankka, *Women and the Value of Suffering*; Richard Sparks, "Suffering," in *The New Dictionary of Catholic Spirituality*, ed. Michael Downey (Collegeville, MN: Liturgical Press, 1993), 950–3. Also see John Hick, *Evil and the God of Love* (San Francisco: Harper, 1977); S. Paul Schilling, *God and Human Anguish* (Nashville: Abingdon Press, 1977); Terrence Tilley, *The Evils of Theodicy* (Washington D.C.: Georgetown University Press, 1991).

[11] Rankka, 39.

[12] Ibid., 40.

- The remedial or instructive model: This typology is a variation of the Irenaean model merged with the retribution model and claims that suffering is "a test imposed by God for the refinement or strengthening of an individual or humanity as a whole."[13]

- The faith model: When one fails to understand the origin of suffering through other theodicies, like Job, she must "surrender in love to God's incomprehensibility."[14]

Each of these theodicies focus much attention on the individual sinner as the cause of evil, and do so with a clear purpose: they allow God to be exonerated from any responsibility for the existence or occurrence of evil and lay blame on the human being. Each of these models is focused on preserving the attributes of God and have failed to examine theodicy from the perspective of the individual suffering unjustly. Thus these theodicy arguments are flawed; they risk silencing those who suffer, while claiming their suffering is not only a duty, but also valuable.

In addition, as Sandra M. Schneiders argues, the examination of theodicies neglects to analyze the role of theological social institutions in creating and perpetuating suffering and evil, particularly for women. She explains that "not only were women excluded, marginalized, and degraded in the church, but they were also directly oppressed by church authorities, and the church legitimated and supported their oppression by men in family and society . . . [and is] a prime legitimator of patriarchal marriage and its attendant abuses."[15] Consequently, theological institutions, as well as theodicies, play a role in the problem of domestic violence, one of the greatest risks to women today.

In her examination of suffering, Dorothee Soelle explains that Christian theodicies "ignore distinctions between suffering we can and cannot end."[16] In addition, she states that designating sin as universal denies the distinction between those who are guilty and those who are innocent. Thus, according to Soelle, theodicies and interpretations of suffering call for masochism and affirm a "sadistic God" that punishes and "only becomes great when he makes us small."[17]

---

[13] Ibid., 41.

[14] Ibid., 43.

[15] Sandra M. Scheiders, *Beyond Patching: Faith and Feminism in the Catholic Church* (Mahwah, NJ: Paulist Press, 2004), 12.

[16] Dorothee Soelle, *Suffering* (Philadelphia: Fortress Press, 1984), 19.

[17] Ibid.

Terrence Tilley also acknowledges the extremely problematic nature of theodicies, stating that

> the usual practice of academic theodicy has marginalized, homogenized, supplanted, "purified," and ultimately silenced those expressing grief, cursing God, consoling the sorrowful, and trying practically to understand and counteract evil events, evil actions, and evil practices. I have come to see theodicy as a discourse practice which disguises real evils while those evils continue to afflict people. In short, engaging in the discourse practice of theodicy creates evils, not the least of which is the radical disjunction of "academic" philosophical theology from "pastoral" counsel.[18]

He concludes that "theodicies do falsify the picture and construct consoling dreams to distract our gaze from real evils."[19] Likewise, Anthony Pinn claims that "theodicy has functioned as a safeguard against assaults upon the substance of religious belief and structures. . . . It guards theological houses from the housecleaning horrific human experience periodically demands."[20] Because theodicies restrict the range of questions and perspectives that can be addressed when examining suffering, they must be rejected because they are insufficient as functional devices for explaining evil.

As Pinn argues, "religious thought concerned with alleviating the human existential condition must expose its questions and assumptions to the full spectrum of religious responses."[21] Rather than restricting analysis, a methodology that attends to a full scope of perspectives is necessary. Thus, in order to properly address the problem of suffering, I embrace Pinn's approach of "nitty-gritty hermeneutics."[22] This method does not limit inquiry and allows for expanded discourse and further examination of the problem of suffering and evil, which in turn offers a deeper understanding of the overall issue. The term "nitty-gritty" signifies the "rawest layer of truth"[23] and acknowledges the "rough edges" involved in suffering. It involves "hard labor" or strong and aggressive

---

[18] Terrence Tilley, *The Evils of Theodicy* (Washington, DC: Georgetown University Press, 1991), 3.

[19] Ibid., 249.

[20] Anthony Pinn, *Why Lord? Suffering and Evil in Black Theology* (New York: Continuum, 1995), 114.

[21] Ibid.

[22] For a comprehensive discussion of nitty-gritty hermeneutics see Pinn, "Blues, Rap, and Nitty-Gritty Hermeneutics," in *Why Lord?*, 113–37.

[23] Ibid., 180n8.

inquiry and does not "soften" the experience of those who suffer. Unlike theodicy, it allows for the freedom necessary to explore questions regarding evil.

According to Pinn, "The nitty-gritty 'thang,' so to speak, forces a confrontation with the 'funky stuff' of life and oddly enough, finds strength in the challenge posed."[24] The principles that shape this hermeneutic are found, among other places, in the blues. Unlike spirituals, which offer a glimpse at the collective reality of black life, the blues provide an individualized perspective and personal account of living within an antagonistic society and are concerned with "truth as it arises out of experience."[25] In addition, the blues address issues that are generally ignored or hidden by the church community. Pinn explains that "the positive expressions of this music suggest a hermeneutic which is worthy of investigation and implementation."[26]

While hermeneutics is an invaluable tool, it must be acknowledged that this method of interpretation is not without problems. As Pinn wonders, "How is meaning made objective when it must be filtered through subjective interpreters?"[27] Interpretations cannot be labeled universal or objective because of contextualities. Thus, various approaches have been developed in order to evaluate history, texts, and traditions with the purpose of rejecting universalist experience as supporting oppression and injustice. For instance, a feminist hermeneutic of suspicion exposes scripture as being written by men for men in order to support a patriarchal culture and thus identifies it as oppressive to women. This offers a theological platform that attempts to respond to women's experience; however it does not respond to the problem of evil as it specifically relates to women's issues. Instead it forces women to comply with Christian principles which undermine and refuse to fully acknowledge female experience. As Pinn states, "Nitty-gritty hermeneutics is not restricted by this theodical quagmire."[28] While Pinn utilizes this method in relation to black religious thought, I will employ it here to discuss domestic violence and the oppression women endure as a result of the patriarchal culture which can be and often is perpetuated by religion.[29]

---

[24] Ibid., 117.
[25] Ibid., 118.
[26] Ibid., 117.
[27] Ibid., 115.
[28] Ibid., 116.
[29] See Carol P. Christ and Judith Plaskow, eds., *Womanspirit Rising: A Feminist Reader in Religion* (New York: HarperSanFrancisco, 1992); Mary Daly, *The Church and the*

According to Pinn, nitty-gritty hermeneutics is free from theological predicaments and "is not wed to the same doctrinal or theological presuppositions [as Christian theology], thereby freeing inquiry to critique these presuppositions."[30] This methodology is non-restrictive, it does not conform to doctrinal rules and instead "ridicules interpretations and interpreters who seek to inhibit or restrict liberative movement and hard inquiries into the problems of life."[31] It confronts the tragedy in life while finding strength in that challenge. These principles, which give shape to nitty-gritty hermeneutics, can be found in the music of the Dave Matthews Band and specifically in the song "Grey Street."

Dave Matthews Band, Domestic Violence, and "Grey Street"

It is difficult to designate the music of the Dave Matthews Band as belonging to a specific genre. It has been referred to as a "mixture of rock 'n' roll, funk, jazz, and world rhythms," and its songs have been influenced by "such diverse musical fields as bluegrass, country, African rhythms, and South American vocal stylings."[32] Generally speaking, the music of this band seeks to acknowledge and combat existing social injustice and has been dubbed "music for the people."[33] Multiple social and political issues are addressed by the Dave Matthews Band including patriarchy and the oppression of women. The song "Grey Street" properly articulates the suffering of a woman in an abusive relationship. Through its questioning of God's attention to suffering, the song refuses to comply with Christian principles and does not restrict itself to theodicy; instead it engages in nitty-gritty hermeneutics. In addition, this song provides narrative through its lyrics and acts as a resource for women in abusive relationships. The energy of "Grey Street" expresses outrage while the lyrics bellow pain and despair. This song can be inter-

---

Second Sex (Boston: Beacon Press, 1985); Elizabeth Johnson, *She Who Is: The Mystery of God in Feminist Discourse* (New York: Crossroad Publishing, 2002); Rosemary Radford Ruether, *Sexism and God-Talk: Toward a Feminist Theology* (Boston: Beacon Press, 1993); Elisabeth Schüssler Fiorenza, *In Memory of Her: A Feminist Theological Reconstruction of Christian Origins* (New York: Crossroad Publishing, 1983).

[30] Pinn, *Why Lord?*, 116.

[31] Ibid., 117.

[32] Nevin Martell, *Dave Matthews Band: Music for the People* (New York: Simon Schuster, 1999), 1.

[33] See ibid.

preted as giving voice to the experience of suffering and injustice experienced within domestic violence.

When discussing lyrical interpretation, it is important to note that multiple interpretations are possible. While the Dave Matthews Band has not directly stated the intended meaning of the song "Grey Street," there has been speculation. Some claim that the song is about Julia Grey, Dave Matthews' ex-girlfriend; however it is more likely that the word "grey" is spelled as such because Dave Matthews is from South Africa and thus utilizes the British spelling.[34] It has also been claimed that "Grey Street" is about depression and that Dave Matthews' inspiration for the song was the poet Anne Sexton.[35] This being said, noting that Dave Matthews lost his sister to domestic violence,[36] it is appropriate to interpret this song as expressing the suffering and despair of a woman in an abusive relationship.

I employ feminist methodology in this interpretation, which according to Sandra Harding is characterized by three features: Women's experience is employed as new theoretical and empirical sources; the explicit benefit of women is at the heart of the research; and the researcher is not hidden from view, but rather is kept on the same critical plane as the overt subject matter.[37] Thus, I have disclosed my own experiences, social location, and agenda as they without doubt inform my interpretation of this song.

As a theologian and activist who has had extensive personal and professional experiences with domestic violence, I instantly recognize the symptomatic suffering of a battered woman within the song "Grey Street." The experience of abuse within an intimate relationship can result in depression, isolation, hopelessness, loss of self-confidence, anger, self-destruction, etc.[38] In addition, such violence ultimately gives rise to questions of theodicy. As Marie Fortune states,

[34] See Morgan Delancey, *Dave Matthews Band: Step into the Light* (Chicago: ECW Press, 2001).

[35] See Will Hermes, "Bartender's Blues: Dave Matthews Beats the Boots," *Spin* (August 2002): 107–8.

[36] See Christopher John Farley, "And the Band Played On," *Time Magazine* (March 26, 2001).

[37] Sandra Harding. "Introduction: Is there a Feminist Method?," in *Feminism and Methodology: Social Science Issues*, ed. Sandra Harding (Indianapolis: Indiana University Press, 1987), 6–9.

[38] See Holly Cefrey, *Domestic Violence* (New York: Rosen Publishing Group, 2009); Lyn Shipway, *Domestic Violence: A Handbook for Health Professionals* (New York: Routledge,

The particular experience of suffering that accompanies victimization by sexual and domestic violence raises particular issues in regards to theodicy. . . . Victims of domestic violence have a strong tendency to hold either God or themselves responsible for the abuse.[39]

The woman whose suffering is narrated throughout this song expresses such feelings while questioning God's role in her misery. Color is used as a metaphor for emotion throughout the song with the color "grey" being used to symbolize depression, loneliness, and despair. While the woman continually attempts to change her life using "colors bold and bright," those colors always mix to grey, returning her to her depressed state. She listens, but does not speak her thoughts. She gazes out at "Grey Street" and ponders her life, wondering how she came to be confined within her misery. All the while, the woman daydreams about escaping her life and wishes for something different, but is unable to change her circumstances on her own. She feels empty, lonely, and heartbroken and though she bleeds red, she feels as if there is "cold blue ice in her heart." She prays every night hoping God will listen, although she is certain God will not. Thus, "She says, I pray, but my prayers, they fall on deaf ears. Am I supposed to take it on myself to get out of this place?" Believing it is impossible to escape her misery on her own, she wants to "set fire to this life."

"Grey Street" can be understood as an emotional validation and response to the experience of women in domestic violence situations. Like the blues, its lyrics are concerned with truth as it arises out of experience and validate the extreme suffering endured within a violent relationship. As James Cone states in his analysis of the blues, "truth is experience and experience is truth."[40] According to David Tetzlaff, music "locates truth either in the lived experience of a community it aims to represent, or in the unique creative vision of the musician."[41] Examining this song

---

2004); Lenore Walker, *The Battered Women Syndrome* (New York: Springer Publishing, 2009).

[39] Marie Fortune, "The Transformation of Suffering: A Biblical and Theological Perspective," in *Violence against Women and Children: A Christian Theological Sourcebook*, ed. Carol Adams and Marie Fortune (New York: Continuum,1995), 85.

[40] James Cone, *The Spirituals and the Blues: An Interpretation* (New York: Seabury Press, 1972), 78.

[41] David Tetzlaff, "Music for Meaning: Reading the Discourse of Authenticity in Rock," *Journal of Communication Inquiry* 18, no. 1 (Winter 1994): 98.

from a feminist standpoint in relation to my personal and professional experiences with domestic violence, I have come to conclude that "Grey Street" is a powerful resource because it offers women in abusive relationships a language to express their grief and confusion about God's role in their suffering and the opportunity to become liberators for themselves. The surfacing of nitty-gritty hermeneutics in this song interprets theological themes based upon the complexities of living within an abusive relationship and encourages the listener to "remove the psychological comforting theological crutches and develop themselves as liberators."[42] As Dwight Hopkins explains, "The image of God planted in all creation, Christian and non-Christian, means a reflection of divine co-laborer and co-creator. In other words, God does not work alone. . . ."[43] The song does not limit women in their inquiry and does not insist they maintain specific qualities about God. "Grey Street" allows women to break free of doctrine and assert their genuine thoughts and feelings. It validates their suffering, provides comfort, and gives permission to speak their pain. Accordingly, this song can in fact act as a theological resource for women.

Music as a Source of Accompaniment and Salvation

According to Thomas Torino, "musical sounds are a powerful human resource, often at the heart of our most profound social occasions and experiences."[44] We utilize music to create and express emotion as well as to develop a sense of relationship, self-identity, and offer liberation from suffering. David Aldridge, whose work has given attention to transcending suffering, states that music offers spiritual healing and allows one to transcend a particular situation.[45] Likewise, Lucanne Magill explains that "music facilitates transcendence,"[46] meaning that the use of music can lead to one moving beyond her or his awareness to achieve

[42] Pinn, 121.

[43] Dwight Hopkins, *Shoes That Fit Our Feet: Sources for a Constructive Black Theology* (Maryknoll, NY: Orbis Books, 1993), 89–90.

[44] Thomas Torino, *Music as Social Life* (Chicago: University of Chicago Press, 2008), 1.

[45] David Aldridge, "Music Therapy and Spirituality: A Transcendental Understanding of Suffering," in *Music and Altered States: Consciousness, Transcendence, Therapy, and Addictions*, ed. David Aldridge and Jorg Fachner (Philadelphia: Jessica Kingsley Publishers, 2006).

[46] Lucanne Magill, "Music Therapy and Spirituality and the Challenges of End-Stage Illness," in Aldridge and Fachner, *Music and Altered States*.

a shift in consciousness and experience relief from suffering. In addition, Magill states "Music can help restore a sense of self-identity and a sense of relatedness. . . . [It] builds bridges, reduce[s] isolation, and re-establish[es] relationship."[47] That being so, women in abusive relationships can utilize music to alleviate feelings of being abandoned and alone to face a situation that seems impossible. Through achieving transcendence with music, victims of domestic violence can attain momentary salvation within their daily lives.

Lyrics that capture the experience of women's suffering alleviate feelings of isolation and thus sustain women who feel powerless. Songs are "texts of theological liberation because they respond to experiences of oppression and marginalization."[48] These lyrical texts function to raise questions about moral meaning for women in abusive relationships while acknowledging that moral structures are problematic. They "make sense of raw experience by (de)constructing systems of meaning and order,"[49] and thus are theological texts.

Meaningful music[50] provides stories that describe the lived experiences of women, a necessity for survival. As Carol Christ asserts,

> Women need a literature that names their path and allows them to use the emptiness in their lives as an occasion for insight rather than as one more indication of their worthlessness. Women need stories that will tell them that their ability to face the darkness in their lives is an indication of strength, not weakness.[51]

Like literature, music that offers substance provides narrative through lyrics and melody that offers women insight as well as a tool to connect with others and communicate their own feelings. According to Ann Savage, music affirms women's lives and acts as a great resource for them. She states that "As the soundtrack of our lives, we tie our memories, pleasures, and dreams to music as well as our sadness, struggles, and failures."[52] When particular lyrics ring true, the woman's connection

---

[47] Ibid., 178–79.

[48] David Fillingim, *Redneck Liberation: Country Music as Theology* (Macon, GA: Mercer University Press, 2003), 26.

[49] Ibid.

[50] Note that the meaningfulness of music here is determined by the listener.

[51] Carol Christ, *Diving Deep and Surfacing: Women Writers on Spiritual Quest*, 2nd ed. (Boston: Beacon Press, 1986), 17.

[52] Savage, 24.

with the music is heightened. Savage explains that when a woman recognizes her own lived experience within a song, it provides a sense of accompaniment. She is no longer alone in her suffering; rather she recognizes that others share her experience and she is liberated from feelings of loneliness and isolation. "It's about having a musical companion when dealing with sorrow."[53]

According to Savage, music is a coping mechanism for women, meaning that it is a tool used to respond to stressful or difficult situations in a way that allows care for the self. In a study Savage completed on the role of music in women's lives, she described how women utilized music as a means to cope. For instance, a study participant named Vivian stated that music offers her a way to "deal with the pressures of life."[54] Jo turns to different artists depending on the situation; she incorporates music into the process of "venting," or dealing with "emotional stuff," and finds "comfort" in particular songs. Terri stated, "I listen to songs to help me get through what I'm going through. . . . I want to stick in my CDs, I want to cry about them, I want to jam to them, I want to work out to them, and I want them to mean that to me, for me, all the time."[55] Each of these women identify with particular artists or songs and utilize music as a coping mechanism to survive the issues within their daily lives. Thus, music provides a way of making sense of lived conditions and offers comfort and support to those suffering.

Because music offers a sense of accompaniment and a means to cope with suffering for women, it also offers opportunity for momentary salvation within daily life. While salvation is often construed as occurring after physical death, in fact we also achieve salvation in our everyday routines. Momentary salvation does not eliminate our suffering once and for all; rather it is a step towards redemption, a moment of peace amid the anguish and despair felt in daily life. As Ivone Gebara explains, although salvation is at hand, we often search for it elsewhere with the misguided notion that it should be some remarkable event that will bring all suffering to an end. However,

> Salvation is not outside but mixed in with suffering; it is where one would not think to find it. Salvation is at hand, but we often look for it elsewhere, as if it could be some extraordinary event that might

---

[53] Ibid., 85.
[54] Savage, 80.
[55] Ibid.

> break the inexorable hold of certain sufferings. . . . Salvation is not
> a "once and for all" solution but a solution for a time, then another
> time, and then a thousand times. Salvation is like the breath of the
> Spirit—it blows where it will and as it can. . . . It is like a glass of
> water that quenches thirst for the moment, but thirst comes again,
> sometimes stronger than before. . . . The moment of the hoped-for
> salvation comes, sometimes seen, sometimes unforeseen. No sooner
> it comes than it is gone: it escapes, flying away to prepare another
> and another.[56]

Thus, salvation is not simply a promise, but rather it is all that sustains our lives, our bodies, and love. Music nourishes and can act as that glass of water and provide redemptive moments within a life of radical suffering. Vivian, Terri, and Jo describe this when discussing how music allows them to survive daily life.

"Grey Street" also has the ability to function in this way for women in abusive relationships. Because the song properly addresses theodicy questions for victims of domestic violence and acknowledges the overall feelings of isolation and despair experienced in this particular situation, this song allows for transcendence, a sense of accompaniment, a means to cope, and momentary salvation; thus women become their own liberators. It is through this experience that the divine is experienced; it points to God being at work within our lives in relation to others. Thus, God is not absent on "Grey Street," rather God accompanies us in our suffering and is experienced within momentary salvation.

Conclusion

Women within domestic violence situations experience a suffering that is meaningless and devastating. Their grief and despair is further impacted by theodicy questions. Because traditional theodicy responses are committed to maintaining specific attributes about God, they do not acknowledge the injustice women endure; rather theodicies encourage women to "bear their cross," suffer like Jesus, and embrace their victimization. Thus, traditional theodicy responses fail in addressing the radical suffering women endure within abusive relationships.

---

[56] Ivone Gebara, *Out of the Depths: Women's Experiences of Evil and Salvation* (Minneapolis: Fortress Press, 2002), 126, 123.

Pinn's method of nitty-gritty hermeneutics offers a means of exploring theodicy questions without restricting inquiries to the confines of Christian principles and doctrine. The song "Grey Street" engages in nitty-gritty hermeneutics through its unrestricted articulation of questions regarding suffering for women in abusive relationships. It validates women's experience, offers a sense of accompaniment, acts as a coping mechanism, and source of momentary salvation. Because "Grey Street" allows the listener to become a liberator of herself, this song is a theological resource for women suffering within domestic violent relationships. It acknowledges that traditional theodicies and their insistence on God's nature can be challenged. It is through listening to "Grey Street" that one comes to understand that in fact God is present in our suffering and at work within our world via other human persons.

Although some will question whether or not a song written by an all-male band can properly articulate the suffering, grief, and despair women experience within abusive relationships; it must be recognized that experience allows such a phenomenon to occur. Dave Matthews' loss of his sister to domestic violence has resulted in his ability to infuse this experience in his music. As Cone states, "truth is experience and experience is truth."[57] Matthews is able to create music that resonates with women who suffer domestic violence because his own life has been impacted by this injustice. Through my own experience of working with survivors of domestic violence and personal tragedy of losing my mother to an abusive relationship, I recognize the grief and despair felt by women trapped in battering situations in this song and thus claim it as a resource.

[57] Cone, 78.

PART THREE

Theology through Song

Chapter 6

Secular Music and Sacramental Theology

Christian Scharen

This chapter begins with the surprising fact that in Charles Taylor's monumental work *A Secular Age*, rock concerts are discussed as serious sites for understanding religion today.[1] Don't get me wrong. Having sung U2's song "40" with tens of thousands of others at the close of a rock concert, *I* thought rock concerts ought to be sites for serious thinking about religion today.[2] My surprise comes in finding perhaps the most important philosopher of our time saying it. Taylor's comments about the contemporary religious significance of rock concerts, brief though they are, are connected to a central strand of his argument in *A Secular Age* that details the fate of what he terms "the festive" or "festive Christianity" central to pre-modern Latin Christendom (and much antecedent religious experience cross-culturally).[3] The forms of religious ritual Taylor calls "the festive" were systematically repressed by waves of reform from the Middle Ages on, repression that accelerated in the seventeenth century. Yet repression of "the festive" was never totally successful, and his (brief) account of the religious role of rock concerts constitutes part of his articulation of a return of the festive in contemporary culture.

---

[1] Charles Taylor, *A Secular Age* (Cambridge, MA: Harvard University Press, 2007), 517.

[2] U2 closed their third album, *War* (Island, 1983), with a version of Psalm 40 with a chorus taken from Psalm 6. See Christian Scharen, *One Step Closer: Why U2 Matters to Those Seeking God* (Grand Rapids: Brazos, 2006), 30–33.

[3] Taylor, in *A Secular Age*, discusses "the festive," including Carnival and similar feasts of the liturgical calendar, as a recurrent theme in his argument. For the first comments on this theme, see 45–54.

In what follows, I propose an experimental method for reviving sacramental theology drawing on Taylor's work as theological provocation.[4] Beginning with three examples of "secular" music drawn from top Grammy award winners in 2011, I first suggest ways they perform a kind of "secular" sacramental theology. I put the term "secular" in quotes because while they are not performing explicitly Christian or sacred music by industry-standard categories, they nonetheless each have internal religious commitments shaping their art. Besides, my constructive theological position challenges such a notion of secularity as implicated in a dangerously reductionist version of Christian faith. Second, I unpack Taylor's argument about "the festive" with some care, tending to its pre-modern shape, the reasons for and consequences of its repression, and the shape of its return in contemporary culture. Finally, with Taylor's understanding of "the festive" in mind, I return to these "secular" artists with which I began to ask how they imply compelling revisions of sacramental theology and practice for churches in a secular age.

Performing "Secular" Sacramental Theology

In what follows I will briefly describe three pop music artists and their performances at the 2011 Grammy Awards. Of course the choice of pop music artists to engage could have been different. My engagements with Arcade Fire, Lady Gaga, and Esperanza Spalding work as exemplary cases, highlighting distinctive characteristics of, as Taylor terms them, "rock concerts, raves and the like" which embody elements of "the festive" and thereby provide key aspects of an enduring human response to and mode of seeking for God.[5] Following introductions to each, including their performances at the Grammy Awards, I suggest ways each can be read in relation to themes of sacramental theology including the Proclamation of the Word, Holy Baptism, and the Eucharist.

Arcade Fire

Arcade Fire, a seven-member indie rock band from Montreal, has been critically acclaimed since their beginnings a decade ago. Usually that is

---

[4] While Taylor is not a professional theologian, he is a Catholic and within *A Secular Age* he offers a constructive Christian theology as compelling as his historical and philosophical work that predominates in the book. For an example, see his account of a Christian version of ordinary human flourishing, 17–18.

[5] Ibid., 517.

the death-knell for a band, with awards too often going to artists with big sales numbers rather than critical praise. All three of their albums—2004's *Funeral*, 2007's *Neon Bible* and 2010's *The Suburbs*—were nominated for "Best Alternative Album."[6] *The Suburbs* was also nominated for the most prestigious of all the Grammy Awards, "Album of the Year," as well, a first for the band. While they lost "Best Alternative Album" to The Black Keys, they surprised everyone by winning "Album of the Year" over such megastars as Lady Gaga and Detroit rapper Eminem. Their win left award presenter Barbra Streisand looking confused, seeming to think the band's name was "The Suburbs" and the album called "Arcade Fire." The band, backstage preparing to play a final song live to wrap up the broadcast, shared looks of disbelief. They piled out from their cramped space behind stage, and Win Butler, the band's founder and lead singer, dropped to his knees to cross the last few feet onto stage as a spontaneous expression of humility and gratitude. Upon reaching the microphone, the shocked band expressed jubilant thanks, and then declared, "We're going to play another song 'cause we like music!"

After a few moments of darkness, a few more thanks, and the squealing sound of guitars being plugged in, the band launched into the second song from *The Suburbs* titled "Ready to Start." The song begins with Win Butler's pulsating fuzzy guitar, almost like a busy signal one used to get on the phone, picked up and carried along in a frenetic pace by the pounding tempo of Régine Chassagne and Jeremy Gara each on their own drum kits. Suddenly, Tim Kingsbury's insistent, propulsive bass leads the rest of the band (Will Butler, Win's brother, on piano and Sarah Neufeld on violin) and in fact the whole audience into a joyfully earnest proclamation of the possibility of beginning again despite the compromises of life in "The Suburbs." The faces of the band were clearly caught up in the joy of the moment. The performance offered an intensity of surprising proportions for a highly scripted broadcast, as if the fully realized possibility of rock and roll concerts to take people outside of themselves broke open even this jaded audience. They were, in this moment, exactly as the English rock critic Paul Morley has labeled them: "a scholarly post-punk gospel choir merrily identifying the menace of the world."[7]

[6] Arcade Fire, *Funeral* (Merge Records, 2004); Arcade Fire, *Neon Bible* (Merge Records, 2007); Arcade Fire, *The Suburbs* (Merge Records, 2010).

[7] Paul Morley, "Keep the Faith," *The Guardian* (Sunday, 18 March 2007) available at: http://www.guardian.co.uk/music/2007/mar/18/popandrock.features11.

Lady Gaga

Earlier in the night, Lady Gaga's dramatic red-carpet entrance inside a large egg transitioned to a birth on stage that grew into a high-energy performance of Gaga's hit single, "Born This Way." Perhaps the planet's biggest and most flamboyant pop singer and performance artist, her second album, 2009's *The Fame Monster*, received six Grammy nominations in 2011, including the coveted "Album of the Year," and won awards for "Best Female Pop Vocal Performance" for the single "Bad Romance" and "Best Pop Vocal Album."[8] While early records stayed within typical bounds for pop dance music, her latest album *Born This Way* embodies a countercultural imagination.[9] Her commitments to inclusion and diversity emerged as she began to publicly speak on behalf of lesbian, gay, bisexual, and transgender rights. Commenting on this shift in her life and her music, she said: "For three years I have been baking cakes—and now I'm going to bake a cake that has a bitter jelly."[10] That bitter jelly is embodied in *Born This Way* and its title track. The lyrics of "Born This Way" work the typical categories of rejection in our society: race, class, gender, ability, and sexual orientation, in addition to the generalized bullying and teasing typically suffered by those deemed "misfits." Taking off from her *The Fame Monster* album and subsequent worldwide Monster Ball Tour, her fans began calling themselves "little monsters" and Lady Gaga "Mother Monster": the one who offers inclusion to those who feel excluded, community to those who feel isolated, a place to fit for those told they are misfits.

In her Grammy performance, Lady Gaga was rolled out from stage left in darkness, chanting the opening lines of "Born This Way" from within her translucent egg: "It doesn't matter if you love him, or capital H-I-M: just put your paws up because you were born this way, baby." She climbed out of the egg, surrounded by a wonderfully diverse group of dancers all keeping artful time with the infectious dance beat of the song. Typical of her performances, the musicians are hidden in darkness at the rear of the stage dominated by the drama of Gaga and her dancers. She begins by evoking the love of "capital H-I-M," a sort of ham-fisted reference to God, before channeling her mother's teaching that God made

---

[8] Lady Gaga, *The Fame Monster* (Interscope, 2009).

[9] Lady Gaga, *Born This Way* (Interscope, 2011).

[10] "Lady Gaga Tells All," Rolling Stone Issue 1308-1309 (June 21, 2010) http://www.rollingstone.com/music/news/lady-gaga-tells-all-rolling-stones-new-issue-20100621 [Accessed January 12, 2012].

her perfect. As a result, Gaga declares, you should hold your head up and believe that in all your particularity you are God's good creation ("cause God makes no mistakes"). "To paraphrase Will Campbell," theologian Rodney Clapp writes, "the Gospel message is that we're all misfits but God loves us anyway." Calling her a "Kierkegaard in fishnet stockings," Clapp points out how Gaga reminds us of Jesus' own "lack of fit" and the accusations that he was not at all a proper Messiah, beginning from his ignoble birth among the animals in a stall to his death hung between two criminals on a cross.[11]

Esperanza Spalding

Esperanza Spalding, a twenty-six-year-old virtuoso bassist, singer, and composer, co-hosted the "Pre-Grammy Telecast" when the bulk of the awards are given. She co-hosted with Bobby McFerrin, himself a virtuoso vocalist and conductor as well as ten-time Grammy winner. Walking out to begin the telecast, McFerrin checked his mic, Spalding picked up her bass, and they launched into an inventive and deliciously fun version of the Eddie Harris tune, "Freedom Jazz Dance," made famous by Miles Davis on his 1967 album *Miles Smiles*.[12] Later that evening, much to her (and most people's) surprise, Spalding received the award for "Best New Artist," winning over teen pop icon Justin Bieber and hip-hop star Drake. As she took the stage in disbelief, she began by saying, "Thank you to the academy for even nominating me in this category." She thanked all her friends, family, and teachers, a community she described as "such a blessing" in her life and music. Spalding has particular aims to communicate through her music, some that are self-evident as she and McFerrin begin with a firm yet measured groove, but exploring a dynamic range and emotional breadth marked by intensity from a whisper to playful scat to a head-back, full-throated, soulful cry. Their interrelated improvisation of jazz communion joined themselves to the band behind them and the audience in front of them.

Growing up, Spalding explored jazz but also played bass and sang in a popular Portland indie rock band, Noise for Pretend. Her musical range and interest is enormous—one report lists her iPod collection at eleven thousand songs—from Johann Sebastian Bach to Stevie Wonder (enough

---

[11] Rodney Clapp, "From Shame to Fame," *Christian Century* (July 13, 2011) http://www.christiancentury.org/article/2011-07/shame-fame [Accessed June 20, 2012].

[12] Miles Davis, *Miles Smiles* (Columbia, 1967).

music to play continuously for nearly two months).[13] Her range of influences matches her iPod collection, causing some critics to describe her work as too broad in style, unfocused, in need of editing. Others describe her eclecticism as particularly fitting—a representative of a post-hip-hop generation. Her very identity embodies a kind of multiracial (she has an African American father and a Welsh-Mexican-Native American mother) and multilingual (she sings in Portuguese, Spanish, and English) complexity fitting for the internet-driven twenty-first-century global music scene of which she is now a leader.[14] While her recent album, *Chamber Music Society*, employs classical depth and enhanced string arrangements (done by Spalding herself), her next album is titled *Radio Music Society*, a decidedly populist move.[15] A look at her playing schedule shows the same range, touring with jazz luminary Joe Lovano's Us Five group and opening for a series of concerts by Prince in New York and Los Angeles. The spirited nature of her music is rooted, she says, in a similarly dynamic understanding of God "whose beauty, presences and effect in and on my life invokes infinite inspiration, admiration and wonder."[16]

To conclude this section, I must say clearly the ways each performer and performance gestures toward aspects of sacramental theology. While I do this in brief fashion here, I will develop this a bit further in the third part in relation to congregational worship practices. I hope aspects of this "leaning into" theology have been evident already. Arcade Fire—and its charismatic front man, Win Butler—embodies the voice of preacher-prophets, like Jesus and his followers, who were accused of turning the world and its values upside down. Such prophetic voice is evident on all their albums, *The Suburbs* included. While they lament the trap of the vampire relationship between workers and their corporate bosses in suburbia, they see the possibility of saying no to this reality and starting again with something true. Lady Gaga draws upon the baptismal sen-

---

[13] John Colapinto, "Profiles: New Note: Esperanza Spalding's Music," in *The New Yorker* (March 15, 2010): 37.

[14] Colapinto, "Profiles: New Note: Esperanza Spalding's Music," 34. Colapinto visited her in her Austin, Texas home and filmed her talking about her creative process working on a new song. It is incredible to hear her say and show a humility that knows "sometimes a musical idea comes to me that I don't have the maturity to fully realize yet." http://www.newyorker.com/online/blogs/goingson/2010/03/video-esperanza-spalding.html [Accessed January 7, 2012].

[15] Esperanza Spalding, *Chamber Music Society* (Heads Up, 2010); *Radio Music Society* (Heads Up, 2012).

[16] Esperanza Spalding, *Junjo* (Ayva Music, 2006), liner notes.

sibility of dying and rising, saying no to the inequality that makes some powerful and others marginal, and saying yes to a God-given equality and created goodness. Her embrace of design, costume, and dance performance lend an explicit sense of creative freedom to her call to be true to God's creative intentions for each person. Esperanza Spalding's intimate and passionate merger of instrument and song evokes a joining not unlike communion, becoming one body with musical forebears (Eddie Harris and Miles Davis), musical community in the present (Bobby McFerrin, the band, the audience) and the depth of her connection to God whose creative gifts overflow as healing and joy in the midst of it all. The word and sacrament of pop music gospel, sung and played for the sake of the gathered assembly of believers, a gathered assembly at the Grammys who despite their music industry status are nevertheless continually taken out of the moment and transported to that other place, a place where time shifts to no time and one can join in a communal experience of music with body and soul. This is not, of course, to say that these artists offer traditional Christian theological perspectives in general, let alone on preaching and sacraments. Yet the combination of the fact that they all describe their work in religious terms and that their performance offers variations of "transcendent" experience sets up my discussion of Charles Taylor's notion of "the festive" and its religious role in culture, mostly now lost, but perhaps returning through such live pop music performance.

On "The Festive": Repression and Return

Of course it is not at all clear that Arcade Fire, Lady Gaga, and Esperanza Spalding are commonly heard as I presented them: as participants in the work of God. Not only that: pop music is, as theologian and musician Jeremy Begbie has noted, mostly considered "god-forsaken."[17] Among other things, I want to ask in this next section about how we ended up with a dominant culture in North America that divides sacred from secular, reduces faith to morality, and reduces worship and religious ritual to what is proper, decent, and manageable. If we are to understand at all how the past frames the particular forms of life we inhabit in our

---

[17] A phrase taken from the endorsement by Begbie on the back cover of my book *Broken Hallelujahs: How Pop Music Matters to Those Seeking God* (Grand Rapids: Brazos Press, 2011).

present age, we'll need to find some way of asking about this history, and wondering about music's role in it.

As a key notion to guide us, it is important to have a definition of "the festive." Charles Taylor uses this notion of "the festive" to refer to "large numbers of people coming together outside of quotidian routine, whether the 'outside' is geographic, as in the case of pilgrimage, or resides in the ritual of the feast, which breaks with the everyday order of things."[18] He means such events as Carnival, still surviving as a major festival in Brazil and New Orleans, for example, or what he calls the "feasts of misrule" including the medieval Feast of Fools typically held near year's end.

Historian Peter Burke writes that the Feast of Fools was typically held on December 28, organized by junior clergy. The feast would begin with the election of a bishop of the fools, and include:

> dancing in church and in the streets, the usual procession, and a mock mass in which the clergy wore masks or women's clothes or put their vestments on back to front, held the missal upside down, played cards, ate sausages, sang bawdy songs, and cursed the congregation instead of blessing them.[19]

The Feast of Fools embodies, Burke writes, the typical character of these feasts: reversals of roles, especially, but also suspension of typical social norms allowing an experience of "the world turned upside down."[20] Many of these "feasts of misrule" fell during Christmastide, the traditional season of the twelve days of Christmas, "since the birth of the son of God in a manger was a spectacular example of the world turned upside down."[21] Festivals were often very localized to begin with, and as Taylor notes, tended to mix some "sacred ritual with a lot of very earthy eating, drinking and dancing, with often unmentionable consequences for the sexual morality of young and old alike."[22]

"The festive," as Taylor describes it, has multilayered meaning. It connected people to one another and to something "more," be that explicitly sacred or not. Integral to these festivals was a kind of overflowing, an

---

[18] Charles Taylor, *A Secular Age* (Cambridge: Harvard University Press, 2007), 469.

[19] Peter Burke, *Popular Culture in Early Modern Europe* (New York: New York University Press, 1978), 192.

[20] Burke, *Popular Culture,* 192.

[21] Ibid., 193.

[22] Taylor, *A Secular Age,* 465.

abundance of what anthropologist Victor Turner called *"communitas"* in which one can "forget oneself" and the distinctions of the established order give way to another sort of common unity or belonging that is deeply moving.[23] They were, in a sense, a time out of time, when the ordinary routines of daily life fell aside and all joined in celebrations, merriment, and play. For example, a Scandinavian Christmas cookbook records that the length of the Christmas festival was concurrent with the Christmas beer supply.[24]

These many festivals that developed as part of "festive Christianity" in the West are largely known because of the waves of reform that sought to suppress or at least downplay the "elements of collective ritual and magic, in favor of personal commitment, devotion, and moral discipline."[25] Erasmus, the Dutch Renaissance scholar, wrote in horror about his first-hand experience of the Carnival he witnessed in Siena in 1509. It was a decidedly unchristian feast, he argued, because it contained: *"veteris paganismi vestigia"* (traces of ancient paganism) and *"populus . . . nimium indulget licentiae"* (the people over-indulge in license).[26] One can trace these two kinds of religious objections, the one theological (against idolatry) and the other moral (against sin). A common strategy employed in efforts to control or even eliminate the Carnival, Feast of Fools, and other similar festivals was to trace their roots to the ancient Greco-Roman *Bacchanalia*, and especially the New Year's festival, *Saturnalia*.[27] These celebrations tied together the theological and moral concerns, and united Protestant and Catholic reforms.

The whole drive of reform "from the High Middle Ages through the Reformation and Counter-Reformation right up through evangelical renewal and the post-Restoration Church," was to make Christians with a strong and personal devotional commitment to God and the faith.[28] I think of the iconic Eric Enstrom photograph that hung in our dining room during my childhood. Taken in 1918, the photo shows Charles Wilden in Bovey, Minnesota, head bowed and hands folded, a loaf of

---

[23] Victor Turner, *The Ritual Process: Structure and Anti-Structure* (Chicago: Aldine, 1969), 94.

[24] Kathleen Stokker, *Keeping Christmas: Yuletide Traditions in Norway and the New Land* (Saint Paul: Minnesota Historical Society Press, 2001), 34–38.

[25] Charles Taylor, *Dilemmas and Connections* (Cambridge, MA: Harvard University Press, 2011), 257.

[26] Burke, *Popular Culture*, 209.

[27] Ibid.

[28] Taylor, *A Secular Age*, 465–66.

bread, bowl of soup, and a large Bible on the table before him. Like many devotional images of its time, it portrays the morals of modernity that Taylor argues were the successors to "festive Christianity": individual devotion, modesty, and decency. This same reforming ethic drove the nervous reaction to Handel's first London performances of his new oratorio *The Messiah*, staged in a theater and using its performers. As one writer at the time put it, "I ask if the Playhouse is a fit Temple to perform it in, or a Company of Players fit Ministers of God's Word." [29] Handel himself, worried about such criticism, advertised the performances without using the word "Messiah" simply calling it "A New Sacred Oratorio." [30]

The trouble that faced the London debut of *The Messiah* was part of the rise of what Taylor calls an Age of Mobilization. [31] During this era, nation-states took center stage and capitalism became the dominant economic system, and both depended on disciplined individual citizens doing their duty. [32] What the early response to *The Messiah* represents, then, is continuing pressure against "the festive" and for decency and uprightness. Yet the long history of jubilant performances of *The Messiah* highlights how hard it is to suppress "the festive" as communal expression of musical joy—a factor that points forward to the role Taylor assigns to rock concerts. While it is true that "the festive," as Taylor outlined it, is a deep and abiding feature in human social life, it has had to exist in marginal settings and has suffered many efforts at control (no bawdy performers or theater context for *The Messiah* these days!).

Today, one might say, the return of the festive is a remarkable part of the breakdown of modernity and its moral order of "decency." Of course the breakdown of traditional sexual mores is most prominent but the overall pattern of rejection of the modern moral order from Romanticism onward seeks to escape from the reduction of experience underwritten by the modern moral order. Its rejection of the earthy, experiential, and communal in favor of the heavenly, cognitive, and individual left moderns alone in a disenchanted world of sober discipline. To make sense of the effects of the trajectory of reform, Taylor coins the term "excarna-

---

[29] Calvin R. Stapert, *Handel's Messiah: Comfort for God's People* (Grand Rapids: Eerdmans, 2010), 45.

[30] Ibid.

[31] Taylor, *A Secular Age*, 471, demarcates the Age of Mobilization as 1800–1950.

[32] Aspects of this longer story in the Latin West are found in Norbert Elias, *The Civilizing Process*, trans. Edmund Jephcott (Cambridge: Blackwell, 1994).

tion" by which he means "the transfer of our religious life out of bodily forms of ritual, worship, practice, so that it comes more and more to reside 'in the head.'"[33] With respect to three modes of human communication (embodied *habitus*, symbolic expression and language), "the festive" was mainly rooted in the first two, while the "excarnating" reforms led to a restriction of the life of faith to the third: language and especially propositional truths.[34] Taylor goes so far as to say such constriction of modern society ordered by what he calls "code fetishism" not only makes us blind to "the vertical dimension" but actually "dumbs us down, morally and spiritually."[35]

"The festive" breaks open such sober discipline, opening into a renewal of experiences that fuse common action and experiential feeling, a powerful sense of connection and even transcendence. In our contemporary age (post-1950s), in what Taylor calls the "Age of Authenticity," the expressive individualism rooted in the elite thinkers of the Romantic era now has become broadly distributed in society. The manifold impacts include an imperative of self-cultivation: be (or find) yourself! Individuals search for depth experiences, renewal, experiences of fusion, of common action and purpose with others. This might happen at sports games, for instance, when the crowd rises as one to cheer a last-minute goal.[36] Spiritual seekers, Taylor writes, are likely to find such connection and transcendence via pilgrimage and communal song at rock concerts and festivals. Either way, something key happens that taps the dimension of religious experience meant by the concept of "the festive": "moments of common action/feeling, which both wrench us out of the everyday, and seem to put us in touch with something exceptional, beyond ourselves."[37] While not explicitly religious, such experiences at concerts "sit uneasily in the secular, disenchanted world." Many people who experience these momentary senses of "wow" are not satisfied; they want to take that experience further, and thereby "seek practices which are their main access to traditional forms of faith."[38] Taylor acknowledges

[33] Taylor, *A Secular Age*, 613.

[34] Ibid., 615.

[35] Ibid., 707.

[36] Ibid., 482; See also Hubert Dreyfus and Sean Dorrance Kelly, *All Things Shining: Reading the Western Classics to Find Meaning in a Secular Age* (New York: The Free Press, 2011), 190.

[37] Taylor, *A Secular Age*, 482–83.

[38] Ibid., 518.

that while these experiences—at rock festivals or elsewhere—are the "closest analogues" to the festivals of prior times, they are not (usually) set within a public or social frame of structure and anti-structure (to recall Turner's phrase).[39] Such contemporary experiences of "the festive" may involve aspects of anti-social behavior, of many sorts, but this is the point. They tend to be rather uncoordinated, wild, as much for fear as for hope that such energy could revive a fuller experience of faith and practice in modern life. Nonetheless, Taylor concludes, the rise of such experiences over the last fifty years heralds the need for the deep power of "the festive as a crucial feature of modern life."[40]

What I have tried to open up here is a way of showing how the repression of "the festive" marks a constriction of how we understand God, how and where we imagine God to be at work, and our place in that. This constriction of the life of faith is a Puritan impulse, dividing clean from dirty, Godly from the God-forsaken. While this is indeed an ancient impulse in culture, it has had a particularly powerful hold on western modernity and its moral imagination.[41] Under this influence we might forget God's abundant and surprising ways. We might then be formed with constricted imagination, worrying that the wrong people in the wrong place could never be "fit Ministers of God's Word." We might then struggle to see pop singers at the Grammy Awards as an inspiring example of God's people singing. Yet exactly because of the power of "the festive" and the spiritual longing that emerges there, the sound track for the "Age of Authenticity" seems to be bursting with religious questions and experiences, often sung by the most surprising people in the most unlikely places. Given this, those who inhabit contemporary communities of faith, who are the conservators of the practices of traditional faith, ought to take seriously that they may be the means through which the concertgoer could find means to sustain and deepen the "wow" they experience in the live music performance. Because the church is the body of Christ, formed into the very character of God who listens to the cries of human life from sorrow to joy that emerge in popular music, and whose very gift of communion it is that festival goers experience there, Christians of all people ought to see the connections between "secular music" and "sacramental theology and practice" as

---

[39] Ibid., 715.

[40] Ibid.

[41] Mary Douglas, *Purity and Danger: An Analysis of the Concepts of Pollution and Taboo* (London: Rutledge and Kegan Paul, 1978).

crucial. It is exactly such festival communion that we already know in our bones, can articulate and ought to enact ourselves with great integrity and imagination. Were we to do so, those same hoards who are shouting "Now I'm ready to start" with Arcade Fire may just be in the assembly at the great festival of the vigil of Easter shouting "This is the night." Give them the full stretch of living, cries real and deep, sorrowful and ecstatic, and something of the festival of old will capture their full selves in the life possible for all.

Beyond Excarnation:
The Festive in Word and Sacrament

For now, I want to conclude with some practical comments about what the intersection of "secular music" and "the festive" says about the proclamation of the word and celebration of the sacraments as key elements of Christian worship. The proclamation of the Gospel is, of course, first of all a living word, Jesus Christ, who comes despite our well-defined expectations about how a proper God should act. That this Word might find ways to "speak" in our day through music should not surprise us. Ministers of music know this in their bones: their gift and task is to proclaim the word in song and music. The whole musical tradition of the Christian church globally shows this power of music to proclaim the Gospel. It should not surprise us then to find in "secular" music a word of the Lord speaking in prophetic or any other scriptural mode. When we do hear such a pop music word, we find ourselves opened to what theologian David Ford calls "the logic of superabundance."[42] It is an "overwhelming" that either threatens us or opens us to transformation and, Ford would say, salvation. The experience of overwhelming, of transformation and salvation, is a key feature of "the festive."

Likewise, baptism is into Christ's own death and resurrection, and although this saving plunge happens only once, in it the Christian has, as Martin Luther taught, "enough to study and practice all his or her life."[43] Daily practice amounts to saying "no" to death, the devil and all his empty promises, and "yes" to the God of all creation who in mercy loved us and freed us for abundant life. Yet baptism too often is merely

[42] David F. Ford, *Self and Salvation* (Cambridge: Cambridge University Press, 1999), 98.
[43] Martin Luther, "The Large Catechism," *The Book of Concord*, ed., Robert Kolb and Timothy Wengert (Minneapolis: Fortress Press, 2000), 461.

a sentimental light wetting of an infant's head, a public means to acknowledge a child's birth, but no dramatic dying dare be invoked or the sentimental magical moment would be broken. Too often the font is put away when not in use (as it was last summer when we went to celebrate my son's thirteenth baptismal anniversary and we literally had to pull it out, uncover it, and fill it with water).

Given the surprising abundance of spirituality in pop culture, ought Christians claim a baptismal practice like Lady Gaga, shaped by a baptismal "no" to the death-dealing world's order of things and a "yes" to new identity as beloved, as opened to the fullness of all God intends? Christians might 'chime in' with Gaga's effort to drown the identities that divide them and us and open us to life in a body of many members, all blessed and gifted. David Ford's notion of "overwhelming" helps us again here. Ford says, "Baptism is the clearest Christian testimony to the fundamental and inescapable reality of being overwhelmed. Those of us who are baptized have taken on an identity shaped by the overwhelming of creation, death, resurrection, and the Holy Spirit." [44] Too often our sin is holding on to death-dealing aspects of lives. This overwhelming of baptismal saving from sin is desperately needed in our time, and the flamboyant display by Lady Gaga only serves to make that point more dramatically.

Lastly, some practical comments about what this experience of festive joy says about the meal we share called Eucharist. This eschatological meal both remembers all God has done and most especially in the life, death and resurrection of Jesus, but it also makes present now a foretaste of that great festival banquet promised on that day when all shall be well, all whole, the lamb sleeping with the lion. Such an eschatological presence filling our cup to overflowing suggests ways we might enact a Eucharistic practice that is more like wisdom's feast, reviving the deep logic of "the festive" in which our bodies are brought together into one Eucharistic body and formed in a life of healing that is not our own but gift, offered in the interplay of the body taken, blessed, broken, and given. The effervescent jazz-pop improvisation between Esperanza Spalding and Bobby McFerrin captures this joining, this communion, exhibiting an interplay as one musical experience that, like the liturgy of communion, might allow us to be caught up into the action of being given for the sake of the world. Great music played together in joy, just as the

---

[44] David F. Ford, *The Shape of Living* (Grand Rapids: Baker Books, 1997), 49.

bread and wine of Eucharist, proclaim the feast as a living word, an echo and embodiment of the promised eschatological feast. That festival in heaven, shared as a foretaste even now, has the spirit-filled power to draw us body and soul into festival celebration of life in its fullness.

Chapter 7

Erase This from the Blackboard: Pearl Jam, John Howard Yoder, and the Overcoming of Trauma

Myles Werntz

In this chapter, I will be examining Pearl Jam's seminal album *Ten*, to ask what Christian theology is to do with suffering and trauma. In doing this, I am not saying that Pearl Jam is an "anonymously Christian" band, or that their continually changing catalog must be read as an extended exercise in theological discourse; Pearl Jam's music has, for the most part, avoided any lyrical discussion of religion.[1] Rather, I will be arguing that *Ten* provokes the narrative question of what destiny awaits victims of trauma: accepting an endless recurrence of violence, or breaking out of the cycle in a new hope. In light of the problematic evoked by *Ten*, I will explore how Christian theology might endeavor to answer this question.

The argument will unfold in three parts. In the first part, I will examine the album, *Ten*. The album has been noted for its negative themes, including childhood trauma, homelessness, and abuse. I will challenge the presumption that the album is simply a dystopian collection of songs, showing instead that it is a work designed to question whether past violence inevitably leads to future violence. In the second part, I will explore what is at stake in articulating *how* this violence is rejected, by posing a choice between a recurrence of violence and an "apocalyptic"

---

[1] A few notable exceptions to this rule include "God's Dice" from Pearl Jam's *Binaural* (Sony, 2000), "Man of the Hour" from *Rearviewmirror: Greatest Hits 1991–2003* (Epic/Sony, 2004), and "Just Breathe" from *Backspacer* (Mwr, 2009).

approach that opens the space for a rejection of violence. Apart from this "apocalyptic" approach—by which I mean the unveiling of a new possibility which transcends present possibility—I contend, we are left with a Nietzschean "recurrence of the same," a revisiting of trauma rather than an emergence of genuinely new social possibilities. In the third part, I will explore the work of John Howard Yoder to explore how the hopes of *Ten* might be theologically narrated, and how Yoder—alongside Pearl Jam—envisions violence and trauma being overcome.

In an age of digital downloads, it is inconceivable that there could have been an era in which music was listened to in an "album" format. The singular manner in which tracks are encountered through file-sharing networks has, according to one study, significantly decreased the life cycle of whole works, reducing the probability that a hearer will ever hear the totality of work.[2] My reading of Pearl Jam's *Ten* is thus, in part, an apology for an older way of listening which not only necessitates attention to a musical work as originally crafted by the artist, but with an ear to the social circumstances surrounding the work's composition.[3] My contention will be that the composition of *Ten* as a whole yields a significantly different meaning than can be gleaned by listening to the tracks in isolation.[4] While anthems such as "Alive" and "Black" may immediately resonate with listeners apart from other tracks, when the album is encountered as a totality, the work as a whole breathes forth a fulsome narrative that may provide a new context to hear the individual components.[5]

---

[2] Sudip Bhattacharjee, Ram D. Gopal, Kaveepan Lertwachara, and James R. Marsden, "Stochastic Dynamics of Music Album Lifecycle: An Analysis of the New Market Landscape," *International Journal of Human Studies* 65 (2007): 85–94.

[3] What I am arguing for here is not a return to a kind of "authorial intent." Insofar as interrogating a work—musical, literary, or scriptural—for its "original intent" attempts to be within the mind of the author, this is impossible. Music as a symbolic product necessarily creates multiple meanings for both songs and text. See Peter Manuel, "Music as Symbol, Music as Simulacrum: Postmodern, Pre-Modern, and Modern Aesthetics in Subcultural Popular Musics," *Popular Music* 14 (May 1995): 227–39.

[4] For the impact of peer-to-peer file sharing on album format sales, see Stan J. Liebowitz, "Testing File Sharing's Impact on Music Album Sales in Cities," *Management Science* 54 (2008): 852–60. The study draws a correlation between the ubiquity of digital formats through which new music can be accessed and the sale of whole albums.

[5] As Simon Frith, *Performing Rites* (Cambridge, MA: Harvard University Press, 1996), has argued, lyrics create a kind of "speech-symbol" which hearers inhabit,

The Structure of *Ten*:
Inevitable Violence or "Release"?

Ten was, in many ways, the birth of Pearl Jam itself.[6] In the wake of the demise of the seminal Seattle band Mother Love Bone in 1990, guitarist Stone Gossard and bassist Jeff Ament began work on a new set of demos, culminating in five instrumental tracks, four of which would be on *Ten*.[7] Bandmate Jack Irons sent the tape to the relatively unknown San Diego vocalist Eddie Vedder, who sent the tape back with lyrics of what Vedder described as a "mini-opera."[8] Vedder's triad of songs, which he named "Mamasan," would become the backbone of *Ten*, though at the time, it was not clear to Vedder's bandmates what the songs were truly about.[9] Over the next few months, Gossard, Ament, and Vedder, together with guitarist Mike McCready and drummer Dave Krusen formed Mookie Blaylock, the predecessor of Pearl Jam.[10] The songs which created this lineup—the tracks of *Ten* —were thus the creation of the band itself.[11]

The creation of the band was the appearance of a new musical force out of other fragments; Vedder joined the band upon departing his San Diego group Bad Radio, and the remainder of Pearl Jam's lineup ap-

---

which prevents lyrics from being the totality of music's "meaning" (159–73). While I do not deny that a composition cannot be understood simply as what is communicated by its libretto, the linguistic aspects of music provide a guide toward how the different performances might fit together. Such will be my approach in reading the texts of the songs of *Ten* for their overarching narrative, acknowledging that in isolation from one another, the songs of *Ten* may yield any number of meanings.

   [6] The authoritative work on Pearl Jam's history remains Kim Neely's *Five against One: The Pearl Jam Story* (New York: Penguin Books, 1998). This biography has been updated in part in Martin Clarke's *None Too Fragile: Pearl Jam and Eddie Vedder* (Medford, NJ: Plexus Publishing, 2010). Other invaluable resources for understanding the grunge era of American music include Greg Prato's *Grunge Is Dead: The Oral History of Seattle Rock Music* (Ontario: ECW Press, 2009), and Clark Humphrey, *Loser: The Real Seattle Music Story* (New York: Harry N. Abrams, 1999).

   [7] Neely, *Five against One*, 50.

   [8] Neely, *Five against One*, 59–61. There are conflicting accounts of how Vedder came into contact with Gossard and Ament. Cf. Neely, "Right Here, Right Now," *Rolling Stone* (October 31, 1991).

   [9] See Cameron Crowe, "Five against the World," *Rolling Stone* (October 28, 1993).

   [10] Mookie Blaylock was a popular point guard in the NBA, playing between 1989 and 2002.

   [11] In 1991, the band dropped the Mookie Blaylock moniker for Pearl Jam, and recorded the album *Ten*, in honor of Blaylock's jersey number.

peared out of the demise of Mother Love Bone.[12] But in another sense, this was not simply something preexisting, in that the band came into existence alongside the album itself, such that it makes no sense to talk about Pearl Jam apart from the creation of these tracks. *Ten*, as the birth of Pearl Jam itself, is a kind of emergence of "newness," in that prior to the creation of *Ten*, there was no Pearl Jam; in and through the drawing together of Gossard's tracks and Vedder's words, a band was born. But what kind of "newness" exists here, and how does this aid in interpreting the movement of *Ten*? Describing the band in terms of its "newness" is a fragile statement; as *Ten* points out, the world is not a place characterized by kindness, with the constant threat of being swept away by the violence of the world. The tracks of *Ten*, thus, can be read as an extended argument of *how* then this "newness"—of life, of music, and of existence, and of Pearl Jam—can be possible.

Vedder has noted in interviews that three of the original tracks of *Ten* ("Once," "Alive," and the recently released "Footsteps") create a narrative of a child who undergoes abuse, only to repeat it as an adult.[13] Other tracks of the album, while not a part of this "rock opera," continue this theme of childhood trauma, describing children overlooked by their parents and schoolmates ("Jeremy"), left on the street ("Even Flow"), and put into institutions by their parents ("Why Go"). In sum, the lyrics of the work describe the journey of childhood trauma resulting in a repetition of the sins of the parent by the son. But in contrast to other albums of its day that deal with these themes, *Ten* goes beyond simply describing the trauma and asks the question of whether the continuation of this trauma and violence in the future is a *necessity*, or whether there is a way to truly break the cycle. The album's teasing out of the "mini-opera" of childhood abuse, which consummates in further abuse, is bookended by the instrumental "Master/Slave," a wordless riff that appears prior to the first track and after the last track. The riff links together two of the most oddly juxtaposed songs on the album: "Once,"

---

[12] Neely, *Five against One*, 51–56.

[13] As Vedder has explained it, "Alive" is the first movement, describing the abuse of a child by his mother; likewise, "Once" is the story of that child—now grown—acting out this abuse on another, and "Footsteps" is that boy (now a man) walking down death row for his crimes. See Neely, *Five against One*, 60, where Vedder describes the trilogy, saying that "half of it was real, and half of it was extensions of reality." For the contradictory biographical facts behind this trilogy, see ibid., 201–48, particularly 239ff., where Vedder's claims about his childhood are called into question.

a song about a murderer, and "Release Me," Vedder's moving plea to be able to be his own person. The flowing of the "Master/Slave" track from the end of the album back into the beginning creates a loop, with the plea for freedom forever careening back into the violence that is a result of trauma.

While the continuous nature of the album (looping from back to front) could be read as a failure of the "release me" refrain, in that the child will *always* become the killer, this reading of *Ten* fails for two reasons. First, Vedder's own biography, which gives rise to "Once," "Alive," and "Footsteps," leads him to become not the figure of "Once" but rather a musician seeking to exorcise his demons through the lyrics of *Ten*. Second, the presence of the "Master/Slave" track at *both* the beginning and end of the album points toward reading "Once" in light of "Release," not vice versa, meaning that we should view "Once" as a possibility but not an inevitability, a question mark on the cyclical nature of violence rather than an exclamation point.[14]

Whither the Way Out? Eternal Return or Apocalypse?

The final notes of "Release" leave us, then, with two primary options for understanding *Ten*'s vision of violence: recurrence of the same, or apocalypse. It can certainly be argued that the presence of trauma does not necessitate these two options—either a cycle of violence or a breaking of the cycle of trauma altogether. And indeed, as I will argue in the conclusion, neither option is perfect, in that trauma—even if overcome—still lingers and must be borne for years, if not decades. But as I will suggest, "recurrence" and "apocalypse" name the two approaches which *Ten* suggests are the most plausible solutions to how one addresses trauma, sharing enough to be recognizable to one another, but also different enough that one must ultimately choose between them. In any event, one cannot simply flee the problem of *whether* violence and trauma is

---

[14] In subsequent albums, particularly the follow-up *Vs.*, Vedder continues to tease out the desire for relief from trauma initiated in "Release Me," particularly "Leash," "Blood," and "Rearviewmirror." In more recent works, songs of protest have given way to songs of new possibility, attempting to articulate a new vision, often cast by critics as a more "optimistic" Pearl Jam. I would read this, however, not as optimism, but as the ongoing attempt to flesh out *Ten*'s "Release."

dealt with; we can "try to erase [trauma] from the blackboard" as much as we like, but the problem—quite simply—remains.[15]

The two primary roads which *Ten* leaves us—recurrence of violence or bursting forth into a new possibility—are best seen, I suggest, in a contrast between Friedrich Nietzsche and John Howard Yoder.[16] In Nietzsche's work, any thought of "escape" from the violence of existence was akin to a Platonic mistake of wanting to transcend the world rather than live within it; Christianity as much as Platonism had been formed around this core and, thus, must be rejected if one is to truly live within the world as it is.[17] For Nietzsche, the way through the harshness of the Dionysian world was not to flee from it, as with the Platonists, but to continue to exercise one's will.[18] The exercise of will, as an affirmation of one's own life, leads Nietzsche to hope for "eternal recurrence," or the return of one's life in all of its particularity. If one's life is an expression of one's will which has created life in one's own image, then the return of life—the context within which one receives one's true self and

---

[15] "Jeremy," *Ten*. "Try to erase this from the blackboard" appears at the end of "Jeremy" as the reminder that the story of Jeremy—the neglected child who kills himself in front of his class—cannot be simply escaped but must be lived with.

[16] My reading of Nietzsche here owes much to the reading of Gianni Vattimo, *The End of Modernity: Nihilism and Hermeneutics in Postmodern Culture* (Baltimore: Johns Hopkins University, 1988), who describes Nietzsche's legacy as a coincidence of value and exchange, such that there can be no value which is no longer unable to be circulated and reformulated, the end result of which is materiality as an endless reformulation of that which is already present, but nothing "new" as such (19–29).

[17] This movement is seen most forcefully in Nietzsche's two early works, *Birth of Tragedy out of the Spirit of Music*, trans. Clifton P. Fadiman (New York: Dover, 1995), and *Philosophy in the Age of the Greeks*, trans. Marianne Cowan (Washington, DC: Regnery Publishing, 1962). In *Philosophy*, Nietzsche makes the case that the absolutizing of the Platonic vision of reality, while reading the current world as shadow, served to bring moral order to primal impulses (113ff.). For a powerful and provocative challenge to this reading of Nietzsche's religion, see Bruce Ellis Benson, *Pious Nietzsche* (Bloomington: Indiana University Press, 2009).

[18] See *The Gay Science*, trans. W. Kaufmann (New York: Random House, 1974), aphorism 13: "A living thing seeks above all to discharge its strength—life itself is will to power; self-preservation is only one of the indirect and most frequent results." Later works, specifically *Ecce Homo: How One Becomes What One Is* (New York: Penguin Classics, 1992) will point to more physiological understandings of the most basic impulses of humanity, but it is not necessary that will and physiology are competing ideals. Rather, the body is that vehicle by which the will finds expression.

exercises one's will—is the greatest hope, not a release *from* life.[19] The recurrence of life in all its particularity—including the traumas to be overcome—was the ultimate affirmation of existence and the ultimate rejection of any sense of flight from the world.

Aside from making evil and trauma moral necessities (the occasion by which one's will is forged), Nietzsche's formulation also bears with it the necessity of certain traumatic outcomes. In the context of *Ten*, thus, Nietzsche's proposal for the will as the solution to overcoming trauma is coupled with an *inevitability* of becoming the monster who repeats the sins of the father (and mother). While the narrator of *Ten* learns from the experiences of childhood and (in the case of Vedder) is offered a chance to overcome these experiences, eternal recurrence binds together the opportunity to learn from these events and their inevitable return, such that one can only resist from within the confines of the original trauma; the narrator can only do differently from within the confines already established by the original violence. Yoder's work, as I will describe it shortly, short-circuits this either/or question of embracing either violence's inevitability or flight from the world, by focusing on new social possibilities breaking into the world from outside, but along lines that are recognizable to that world. This is where, for the protagonist of *Ten*, Nietzsche's approach becomes most problematic. Nietzsche is right to affirm the pursuit of new social possibility in and through creaturely acts, but this kind of aspiration for newness can only be a reorganization of existing material, through affirming the necessity of the original violence; such an approach offers little hope for the one whose own self and situation have contributed *in toto* to them walking "with . . . hands bound."[20]

From a Christian perspective, Nietzsche is to be commended for affirming the materiality of religion; indeed, the central tenet of Christianity—the incarnation of God in Jesus of Nazareth—rests upon an affirmation of materiality and the world as that which God has loved.

---

[19] *Gay Science*, aphorism 341: "What if some day or night a demon were to steal after you into your loneliest loneliness and say to you: 'This life as you now live it and have lived it, you will have to live once more and innumerable times more'? . . . Would you not throw yourself down and gnash your teeth and curse the demon who spoke thus? Or have you once experienced a tremendous moment when you would have answered him: 'You are a god and never have I heard anything more divine.'" As Nietzsche notes, this concept forms the backbone of *Thus Spake Zarathustra*, trans. Walter Kauffman (New York: Random House, 1954), aphorism 1.

[20] "Garden," *Ten*, Pearl Jam.

But in describing new social possibility by more deeply plumbing the limitations of our situation, we are left with the trauma of the present, reinscribed mimetically in perpetuity.[21] As Karl Barth's writing on the incarnation suggests, however, the materiality of the world is never a matter of immanence; describing the second person of the Trinity as the "elected human" means in part for Barth that there is no insoluble break between God and the world, but rather that the conditions of immanence are *always* included within and open to transformation and permutation by the transcendent.[22] As Paul Daffyd Jones has described this:

> Such is the extremity of God's love. God does not rest content with the perfections of deity; God intends the radical alterity of a particular creature with whom God can live in fellowship. . . . For the sake of validating, ensuring and upholding God's relationship with humankind, God makes this representative human, this "first work" of God, a permanent dimension of God's being *qua* Son, thereby securing for all humans the favor of divine companionship.[23]

But far from this being an over-determining of the material world, Jones suggests that

> the human individual, identifiable as the man Jesus, is not overrun by God, even as he is determined by God, even as he is drawn into the divine life. . . . This "enclosure" does not compromise the integrity of Christ's humanity any more than it compromises the integrity of those who live "in Christ."[24]

The upshot of the incarnation, then, is that "God does not overbearingly dictate the life history of God's creatures . . . [but] allows it to develop

---

[21] This point has been made particularly forcefully by Rene Girard, *Violence and the Sacred* (Baltimore: Johns Hopkins, 1977).

[22] Karl Barth, *Church Dogmatics*, vol. 2, bk. 2, 121ff. Barth describes the incarnation as "God [making] the being of this other God's *own* being, that he allows the son of man Jesus to be called and actually to be his own *Son*." In describing this movement as the immanent (world) being open to the transcendent (God), I am doing violence to Barth's formulation in that Barth never sees description of God as "transcendent," but only specifically as the God of Israel in the Bible.

[23] Paul Daffyd Jones, *The Humanity of Christ: Christology in Karl Barth's Dogmatics* (London: T&T Clark, 2008), 88–89.

[24] Ibid., 91.

in freedom."[25] Such divine self-gifting creates the possibility for a life other than the prison of pure immanence.[26]

Such a relation between the transcendent and the immanent, as described by the incarnation, facilitates the possibility of genuine newness of social life which is neither reducible to our construction from existing pieces nor an esoteric existence devoid of social shape. If the incarnation describes a divine "enclosure" of the material world that does not over-determine human freedom, then two effects follow. First, the material world remains open to the movement of the transcendent, in ways that radically reconfigure social possibilities. Following Barth, God's taking up of the world effects a reconciliation of humanity, with God and with one another, making possible a rejection of violence by immanent cycles of violence being punctured by transcendent hopes.[27] Second, the transcendent appears along lines which are perceptible and visible, not the invisible and esoteric. In the incarnation, God appears to us *in and through* the human person of Jesus, implicating all created life in the process as both open to God and made free to live as God's creatures.

This irruption of God into immanence in the person of Jesus, which opens the world to transcendence and frees the world toward new social possibility, is what I want to name "apocalyptic." This kind of "apocalyptic" has little to do with what Kelton Cobb has labeled "scripts of escape," narratives which seek to flee the created world for some immaterial alternative, but rather, as David Dark has named them, the "announcing [of] a new world of unrealized possibility . . . [serving] to invest the details of the everyday with cosmic significance while awakening its audience to the presence of marginalizing forces otherwise unnamed and unchallenged."[28]

It is here that I want to give Barth's insights a more communal focus by moving to one of Barth's students, John Howard Yoder. Whereas in

---

[25] Ibid., 97.

[26] Ibid., 184–85. What is important here is the insight that God communicating with the world in the incarnation does not involve an over-determination of the world. By Jones' interpretation, Barth allows for the presence of the transcendent within the immanent but *not* as a competitive force to the immanent; it is, rather, as Kathryn Tanner describes it, a noncompetitive relation between God and the world. See Kathryn Tanner, *God and Creation in Christian Theology* (Minneapolis: Fortress Press, 2004).

[27] Jones, *Humanity of Christ*, 182–86.

[28] For Kelton Cobb on "scripts of escape," see *The Blackwell Guide to Theology and Popular Culture* (Malden, MA: Blackwell Publishing Co., 2005), 18–20. See David Dark, *Everyday Apocalypse* (Grand Rapids: Brazos Press, 2002), 11.

Barth, this "apocalypse" takes the form of the person Jesus, for Yoder, this apocalyptic presence of God expresses itself derivatively in the creation of a new community which *is* the witness to the rejection of the necessity of violence within the world. I will now turn to Yoder to explore what an "apocalyptic" rejection of violence might look like and then, specifically, how such a proposal illuminates toward what the structure of *Ten* gestures.

The Apocalyptic Breaking of the Logic of Trauma

In this section, I will briefly explore Yoder's work as a theological proponent whose work puts forth an overcoming of violence and trauma, not by advocating further retributive violence, but through a rejection of *both* the logic and apparatus that enable trauma. Yoder wrote prolifically on a number of doctrinal and ethical topics but is best known for his relentless writing on nonviolence.[29] For Yoder, embracing nonviolence and rejecting cycles of violence was not a self-evident choice.[30] What enabled him to embrace nonviolence and reject violence as inevitable for human relations was his eschatology; for Yoder, the nonviolent Jesus of Nazareth who suffered and refused to fight is the Lord over all history; as such, history itself is not moved by violence but by a God who has come among us in nonviolence.[31]

Yoder's argument for nonviolence thus turns on the moral example of Jesus being identical with the Christ spoken of in Revelation, the "Lamb who was slain" who rules over history. The character of this God,

[29] For introductions to Yoder's life and thought, see Mark Theissen Nation, *John Howard Yoder: Mennonite Patience, Evangelical Witness, Catholic Convictions* (Grand Rapids, MI: Eerdmans, 2005), and Earl Zimmerman, *Practicing the Politics of Jesus: The Origin and Significance of John Howard Yoder's Social Ethics* (Telford, PA: Cascadia Publishing House, 2007). For a more critical introduction, see Paul Martens, *The Heterodox Yoder* (Eugene, OR: Cascade Books, 2011).

[30] Yoder appeals on occasion to "common sense" when arguing for nonviolence outside Christian circles. See "The Way of the Peacemaker," *Peacemakers in a Broken World*, ed. John A. Lapp (Scottdale, PA: Herald Press, 1969), 111–25, and "The Church and Change: Violence Versus Nonviolent Direct Action," in *War of the Lamb*. For the fullest argument for nonviolence as a possibility within multiple idioms and cultures, see his posthumously published, *Nonviolence: The Warsaw Lectures*, ed. Paul Martens, Matthew Porter, and Myles Werntz (Waco, TX: Baylor University Press, 2010).

[31] John Howard Yoder, *The Politics of Jesus* (Grand Rapids, MI: Eerdmans, 1972), 238–39.

revealed through the person of Jesus, is that of non-coercion and of re-
nunciation of any mode of violence that subjects others to its whims.[32]
This nonviolence is not the possession of Jesus of Nazareth alone, however, but is made manifest in a new community which Jesus founds: the
church.[33]

What has been typically meant by the claim that Yoder's ethics are
"apocalyptic" is that for Yoder, the possibility for real social alternatives
emerges out of the singularity of Jesus' person in the form of a "new
peoplehood," an alternative community which challenges "the powers"
of violence and coercion by its very existence, creating a witness to transcendent possibility within immanence.[34] While David Toole, the pioneer
of this approach, is correct to point out Yoder's "apocalyptic style," Toole
downplays Yoder's work on an important point. Toole is correct to argue
that, for Yoder, the "new humanity" or the "new community" which
lives in an alternative way is the continuation of Jesus' life (and as such,
is able to reject violence and model new social alternatives), but Toole
underplays the role nonviolence plays for how this social body appears.[35]

---

[32] Ibid., 244–45. In a slightly earlier work, *The Original Revolution* (Scottdale, PA:
Herald Press, 1971), Yoder goes as far as to say that "We do not, ultimately, love our
neighbor because Jesus told us to. We love our neighbor because God is like that. It
is not because Jesus told us to that we love even beyond the limits of reason, even to
the point of refusing to kill and being willing to suffer—but because God is like that
too" (52).

[33] In contrast to Reinhold Niebuhr's "impossible possibility" of love in the world,
Yoder held that Jesus in fact makes possible a new social community committed to
nonviolence, not as an ideal but as a reality. For Niebuhr, cf. *An Interpretation of Christian Ethics* (New York: Meridian Books, 1956), 44–62.

[34] This approach was pioneered by David Toole, *Waiting for Godot in Sarajevo*: *Theo-
logical Reflections on Nihilism, Tragedy, and Apocalypse* (Boulder, CO: Westview Press,
1998), 210. Toole's initial work has been modified and amplified in different ways by
Doug Harink, Daniel Barber, and Nathan Kerr. See Douglas Harink, *Paul among the
Postliberals*: *Pauline Theology Beyond Christendom and Modernity* (Grand Rapids, MI:
Brazos Press, 2003); Daniel Colucciello Barber, "Immanence and Creation," *Political
Theology* 10 (2009): 131–41; "The Particularity of Jesus and the Time of the Kingdom:
Philosophy and Theology in Yoder," *Modern Theology* 23 (2007): 63–90. See also Nathan
R. Kerr, *Christ, History, and Apocalpytic: The Politics of Christian Mission* (Eugene, OR:
Cascade Books, 2009), and "Transcendence and Apocalpytic: A Reply to Barber,"
Political Theology 10 (2009): 143–52.

[35] As far back as Yoder's *Discipleship as Political Responsibility* (Scottdale, PA: Herald
Press, 1964), the church's continuation of Jesus' work is linked intrinsically to the
rejection of violence (22–32). Apart from this commitment, the community fails in its
commitment to Jesus. See *The Christian Witness to the State* (Scottdale, PA: Herald
Press, 1964), 8–16, where the church's distinction from the state is described in terms

For Yoder, Jesus emerges as the nonviolent one; the "new humanity," following its founder, emerges along the lines of nonviolence first and foremost, and not any institutional "marks."[36] Likewise, the God who overcomes violence in the eschatological culmination of the world is for Yoder identical with the Jesus who establishes a new social body capable of rejecting further violence.[37] In other words, the rejection of violence is central to this community existing as a new social possibility—the inbreaking of transcendence into immanence, disrupting the normal cycles of violence.

Returning to the dilemma of *Ten*, the question is framed by Yoder in this way: will the trauma visited upon the central character in the songs of *Ten* be a recurring nightmare (visited upon others), or will the original violence be undone with a new way of existence breaking forth? Whereas for Nietzsche, the way out of trauma is to embrace it and grow from it—an approach which necessitates violence being repeated in the future—Yoder's emphasis on a "new humanity" which is made possible by Jesus' rejection of violence opens up another possibility: the utter rejection of trauma through the establishment of a new community which can tell a new narrative about the nature of social existence.

For Yoder, it is not enough to simply "unmask" violence. Violence can return in any number of ways, and simply making it *visible* does not banish it. Rather, a new community which exists *as a rejection* of violence is called for, a new social alternative which is able to tell a new story about how violence is undone, and what kind of life can be lived instead. Yoder emphasizes that the rejection of violence is not simply an unmasking of an immanent problem but the unveiling of a transcendent solution *within* immanence. Because the one who exemplifies nonviolence in history (Jesus) reveals the character of the God who rules *over* history, the community that is established is able to exist as a new social alternative, free to reject the logic of violence and trauma's "necessary" repetition.

---

of acts of violence. Stanley Hauerwas has noted this as perhaps the most enduring feature of Yoder's ecclesiology, in *The Peaceable Kingdom* (Notre Dame: University of Notre Dame Press, 1984), xxiv–xxv.

[36] See *Original Revolution*, 116–17. Yoder is consistently critical of attempts to name "church" by marks that have nothing to do with obedience to Christ's witness. See Yoder, *The Ecumenical Movement and the Faithful Church* (Scottdale, PA: Mennonite Publishing House, 1958), and "The Nature of the Unity We Seek: A Historic Free Church View" and "The Free Church Ecumenical Style," both in *The Royal Priesthood*, ed. Michael G. Cartwright (Grand Rapids, MI: Eerdmans, 1994).

[37] See Yoder, *The Politics of Jesus* (Grand Rapids, MI: Eerdmans, 1994), 228–41.

One of the concerns with this approach—immanent violence rejected by a transcendent narration of nonviolence—is best expressed by Gavin Hyman, writing that such approaches reproduce the violence of one kind only by eliminating all other competing interpretations of the world.[38] This criticism is relevant to Yoder insofar as Yoder posits that it is the *Christian* God who provides meaning not only to nonviolence but to a world in which nonviolence bears witness to new social possibility. But for Yoder, the presence of a specifically Christian ethic—a nonviolence rooted in the witness to Jesus—does not entail the negation of other forms of nonviolence; throughout Yoder's writings, dialogical engagement with others concerned about violence happens as a way of exploring how others have come to this conclusion of nonviolence.[39] With Yoder's vision of "apocalyptic" nonviolence in hand, we are in position to see most fully how *Ten*, for Christian theology, constitutes a kind of "parable of the kingdom of heaven"—not identical to Christian witness, but an analogy made possible by the grace of God.[40]

This is the point at which reading *Ten* as an apocalyptic work matters the most. As I have argued, *Ten* is best understood as a work which leaves the question of violence's necessity an *open* question. Rather than spelling out what the overcoming looks like, *Ten* leaves us with a wordless track

---

[38] Gavin Hyman, *The Predicament of Postmodern Theology: Radical Orthodoxy or Nihilist Textualism?* (Louisville, KY: Westminster John Knox Press, 2001), 65–75.

[39] Romand Coles' article, "The Wild Patience of John Howard Yoder: 'Outsiders' and the 'Otherness of the Church,'" *Modern Theology* 18 (2002): 305–31, best expresses the possibilities found in Yoder's dialogical method with those outside of the church. Yoder's engagements with a variety of alternate positions on war, particularly just-war forms of reasoning, can be seen in a variety of places. See *Karl Barth and the Problem of War* (Nashville: Abingdon Press, 1970); "Vietnam: A Just War?" *His* (April 1968): 1–3; "The Way of the Peacemaker," in *Peacemakers in a Broken World*, ed. John A. Lapp (Scottdale, PA: Herald Press, 1969), 111–25, and most preeminently *Nevertheless: Varieties of Religious Pacifism* (Scottdale, PA: Herald Press, 1971). For Yoder, this dialogue was not a *consequence* of the church's identity but intrinsic to *being* church. See *Anabaptism and Reformation in Switzerland: An Historical and Theological Analysis of the Dialogues between Anabaptists and Reformers*, ed. C. Arnold Snyder, trans. David Carl Stassen and C. Arnold Snyder (Kitchener, ON: Pandora Press, 2004), 219–27.

[40] The term "parables of the kingdom of heaven" is one that Karl Barth used to describe those forms of goodness which are not explicitly Christian but which bear certain contours to the Christian Gospel. See Barth's analysis of Mozart's music in this fashion in *Wolfgang Amadeus Mozart*, trans. Clarence K. Pott (Grand Rapids, MI: Eerdmans, 1986), 57.

that binds the ending to the beginning, gesturing toward either a form of inevitable repetition or a new narrative altogether. It is important to remember that *Ten* is not a *solo* work, i.e., the production of a singular artist against the masses. Rather, *Ten* is both the production of a new community—the opening shot from a band now celebrating their twentieth anniversary—and the *occasion* for the community's origin. In other words, to hear *Ten* is to hear the witness of a new social community, in that the album is the performance of a new community *and* that which produces the community.

For Yoder, the new community which rejects violence is ordered around the one who inaugurates the community: Jesus—the nonviolent one who bears out the character of God. For Pearl Jam, however, the rejection of further violence does not immediately yield a new orientation. In their follow-up album, *Vs.*, themes of trauma continue to permeate the lyrics in nearly every song. Declaring in "Go" that he is just "passing it on," Vedder continues to exorcise the demons first addressed in *Ten*. Struggling to leave behind the sins of the parent(s), "Rearviewmirror" and "Leash" continue to try to leave behind the horrors of the past.[41] These desires, for example, are described in "Jeremy"-esque terms in "Daughter," with the central character who "can't deny nothing's wrong" struggling to leave behind her family.[42]

But whereas in *Ten*, the future beyond this pain is left an open question (having negated trauma without a defined alternative), a new sense of determination is present in *Vs.*'s desire to "make my way through one more day in hell."[43] While "Indifference" might lead us to suspect that the narrator's ability to "rise above" ("Daughter") is the result of a Nietzschean will-to-power, what the lyrics point us to continually is what we have seen as nascent in *Ten*: the "five against one," the band against the world.[44] As the band has discussed, the subsequent fame of *Ten* resulted in their feeling hemmed in by fame and attention, only drawing them more closely to one another as the only way forward into

[41] "Leash": "Troubled souls unite. We got ourselves tonight. . . . Drop the leash"; "Rearviewmirror": "I took a drive today / Time to emancipate / I guess it was the beatings, made me wise / But I'm not about to give thanks or apologize."

[42] "Daughter": "Alone, listless / Breakfast table in an otherwise empty room / Young girl, violence. Center of her own attention. . . . She holds the hand that holds her down / She will rise above."

[43] "Indifference," *Vs.*

[44] This phrase of "five against one" is repeated throughout "Animal," referring to their creating a new band against the world.

the world. In the creation of music, Pearl Jam was created, the new community able to embody a truly different way forward.

Whereas for Yoder the new community-as-social-alternative is a *secured* community, made possible against all odds by the nonviolent presence of God, for Pearl Jam, this new community must continue to be reasserted if it is to survive.[45] But what both Pearl Jam and Yoder emphasize is that this new community—a new social alternative to trauma—can only emerge *within the world*. For Yoder, the apocalyptic breaking of violence's recurrence as the presence of a new social body is possible because of the transcendent's being known in history; for Pearl Jam, the apocalypse is one which is gestured toward, longing for what it cannot yet grasp but hopes for nonetheless: a community which *is* the way out of the past.

Conclusion: Melodies in Search of Resolution

In sum, I suggest that *Ten* represents a real struggle with the question of violence's inevitability, suggesting that (for Pearl Jam) the solution to trauma and violence lies not in repeating it, but in breaking free of its bonds and presuppositions. For Yoder, this possibility emerges only because of eschatology—that new possibilities emerge within the world as witnesses to the way things truly are. Whereas Yoder can claim this on the basis of the witness of Jesus, for Pearl Jam, this is a conclusion which must be arrived at not by means of divine fiat or revelation, but through the continual working out of the "release"—or as I have termed it, the apocalyptic solution—through future albums. For Pearl Jam, longing for "newness" is more apophatic than positive, a hope for newness named as "release" rather than specific content; for Yoder, the hope for the future is connected with the person of Jesus.

Similarly, Pearl Jam's own story—the creation of a new community that articulates an alternative social vision—is akin to Yoder's church, with one distinct caveat. For Yoder, this community is intimately related to the person of Jesus, whereas for Pearl Jam, this newness is looking for that which is unnamed, wordless, undiscovered. But rather than see these two approaches as antithetical, I would describe this with Barth

---

[45] This is not to say that the church is for Yoder a *closed* community. A number of good works have emphasized the manner in which the church for Yoder is a dialogical body. See J. Alexander Sider, *To See History Doxalogically: History and Holiness in John Howard Yoder's Ecclesiology* (Grand Rapids, MI: Eerdmans, 2011).

as a kind of "secular parable" which gestures toward the methodology and structure of a Christian rejection of the inevitability of violence but which does so apart from an explicit theological confession.

That which *Ten* gestures toward is parabolic of what Yoder describes, but lacks, for Barth and Yoder, a grounding of the transcendent into the immanent.[46] As a Protestant theologian listening to Pearl Jam, this is where I must part ways with Vedder and company: grateful for the companionship and surprised by the overlap between a Christian confession and the structure of *Ten*, but recognizing that there remain material differences between how I understand violence to be overcome and the resources which *Ten* in and of itself provides.

This is not to say that Yoder's proposal is not without its own fragility. What Yoder's account lacks, as Cynthia Hess argues, is an account of how to speak not only about the trauma's *overcoming* but of the trauma *itself*; whereas Yoder's account of the new community emphasizes speaking of how the rejection of violence is rooted in God's overcoming of violence, Yoder is often silent on what the church is to do with its own experiences of violence, of how to speak of real, past violence while it confesses the primacy of nonviolence. Helpfully bringing Yoder's work on nonviolence into conversation with trauma studies, she has explored the manner in which Yoder's nonviolence embodied in social form means, in part, the ability to tell new stories which do not conform to the old "script."[47] Emphasizing the manner in which "church" for Yoder is a voluntary, egalitarian, and witnessing community, Hess notes that, for those seeking a way out of violence, the church as a place of "witness" is essential.[48] The church, as it rejects violence and offers a new social reality, participates in a new way of life brought forth by God into the world, bearing witness to a new social possibility that testifies to the way things truly are.[49]

But as Hess notes, in church, those experiences which are dissonant from the hope of violence being overcome find themselves sublimated,

[46] See Søren Kierkegaard, "The Genius and the Apostle," in *The Book on Adler: Kierkegaard's Writings*, vol. 24, trans. Howard and Edna V. Hong (Princeton: Princeton University Press, 1998).

[47] Cynthia Hess, *Sites of Violence, Sites of Grace: Christian Nonviolence and the Traumatized Self* (Lanham, MD: Lexington Books, 2009). On the scripting of repetitive forms of violence into social relations, see James C. Scott, *Domination and the Arts of Resistance: Hidden Transcripts* (New Haven, CT: Yale University Press, 1992).

[48] Hess, *Sites of Violence*, 102–5.

[49] Ibid., 103.

whereas in Scripture, these experiences of unresolved trauma and disappointment are given voice from the first book of Scripture to the last.[50] If, for Yoder, the practices of the church arise out of its narratives, then giving voice to the unresolved and lingering effects of trauma is a practice that has scriptural warrant.[51] In articulating individual trauma narratives (the most paradigmatic being that of Jesus) as not being *antithetical* to the life of the community, churches become the location in which stories of trauma are contextualized, given voice, and reworked into stories of hope. As survivors of trauma join their stories to the stories of others, in a new community, trauma victims are enabled to identify themselves not as "victims" but as agents capable of new narratives, making life out of death.[52]

It is here perhaps that Pearl Jam's journey exposes a particular weakness in Yoder's account, which Cynthia Hess highlights: the need to tell stories about trauma, for this is, in part, *how* the trauma is overcome. In song after song, Pearl Jam continued to address this theme, working out this question in a way that allowed others to work it out alongside them. One could argue that Pearl Jam's journey to resolve the question of *Ten* is unnecessarily circuitous by comparison to what Yoder provides; continuing into *Vs.* and beyond, Pearl Jam continued to explore *how* to "erase this from the blackboard," without resolution.

My own initial encounter with Pearl Jam was as a fifteen-year-old whose life bore no resemblance to the characters of "Alive," "Jeremy," "Once," or "Release." And yet, hearing them articulate the sense of longing for something different, for something "new," gave voice to the longings that my adolescent self did not, at that point in my musical life, have the words for. It was through the work of those such as Pearl Jam that I was able to return to the psalms, to Job, to the laments of the gospels, and see for the first time what had been there all along: that bearing witness to the "new life" that Christian theology describes was not simply a matter of asserting a confession. Rather, speaking of this "newness" is intimately bound up with telling stories about how the old violence has been done away with, for it is *through* these stories that the violence is overcome—the irruption of the apocalyptic "new" within history is

---

[50] Ibid., 104–5. Hess argues that, oftentimes, the church's own constitutive practices suppress trauma victims' experiences, emphasizing, for example, the trauma done to Jesus while neglecting how other victims of trauma will react to these narratives.

[51] Ibid., 111.

[52] Ibid., 113–16.

not, in other words, *knowledge* so much as it is a new *way of life*. And in this sense, Christian theologians can listen to *Ten* and say with Jesus that it is "not far from the kingdom," in that *Ten*—in its stories and in its structure—gestures in hope toward what Yoder sees Jesus displaying in fullness.

Chapter 8

Baptized in Dirty Water: Locating the Gospel of Tupac Amaru Shakur in the Post-Soul Context

Daniel White Hodge

Here on Earth, tell me what's a black life worth
A bottle of juice is no excuse, the truth hurts
And even when you take the shit
Move counties get a lawyer you can shake the shit
Ask Rodney, LaTasha, and many more
It's been goin on for years, there's plenty more
When they ask me, when will the violence cease?
When your troops stop shootin niggaz down in the street
Niggaz had enough time to make a difference
Bear witness, own our own business
Word to God cause it's hard tryin to make ends meet[1]

Tupac Amaru Shakur. Just the name causes many hip hoppers to stand still and pause for a moment. When asked what he did on hearing the news of Tupac's death, Marlon Wayans stated that he cried like his momma cried when Marvin Gaye was murdered. Young girls and boys who were not even alive during Tupac's life remember him and adore him as if they had grown up in his era. Further, even mildly liberal parents today (who were teens in the 1990s) pause and think about the effect Tupac had on their own lives.[2] Tupac was iconic. Recalling Tupac's ac-

---

[1] Tupac, "I Wonder If Heaven Got a Ghetto?," *R U Still Down* (1997).

[2] As seen in my 2004–2008 interviews on Tupac's theological mystique in Daniel White Hodge, *Heaven Has a Ghetto: The Missiological Gospel & Theology of Tupac Amaru Shakur* (Saarbrucken, Germany: VDM Verlag Dr. Muller Academic, 2009).

complishments at such a young age, Quincy Jones recalls Tupac's death by stating that if Martin Luther King Jr. had died when he was twenty-five, he would have been a struggling black Baptist minister; if Malcolm X had died at twenty-five, he would have been a street hustler; and if he himself had died at twenty-five, he would have been a struggling trumpet player; but Tupac died at twenty-five, leaving a legacy of life, love, rage, pain—and theology. "Tupac was touched by God[;] not very many people are touched by the hand of God."[3]

What makes for such an iconic figure? What makes him what some scholars call an urban theologian?[4] What makes Tupac's music, life, and poetry continue to ring true fifteen years after his death? Is there something deeper and more meaningful in Tupac's lyrics, which percolate with a type of ghetto spiritual essence and urban contextualized spiritual authority entrenched in the murky waters of the profane and the sacred?[5] Yes, there is.

Tupac was more than just a fad or an "estranged artist." Quincy Jones had it right: Tupac was touched by God; God had a special message and mission for Tupac. It was a mission and message that few are able to embrace. The cost is high—your life. Tupac saw life and culture beyond the routine and ordinary; he approached life full of passion, rage, anger, love, thoughtfulness, and even carelessness; he was the product of a post-soul society which had been groomed on the ambiguous consumer

---

[3] Interview taken from the DVD documentary *Thug Angel: The Life of An Outlaw* (2002).

[4] See Michael Eric Dyson, *Between God and Gangsta Rap: Bearing Witness to Black Culture* (New York: Oxford University Press, 1996); Daniel White Hodge, *The Soul of Hip Hop: Rims, Timbs and a Cultural Theology* (Downers Grove, IL: InterVarsity Press, 2010); Ralph Basui Watkins, *Hip-Hop Redemption: Finding God in the Rhythm and the Rhyme*, Engaging Culture Series (Grand Rapids, MI: Baker Academic, 2011).

[5] I argue that for too long religious discourse and rhetoric has placed a polarized stance on "good" and "evil": the sacred and the profane. However, what emerges in the post-soul context is a type of third area: between good and evil, sacred and profane, making this murky ground. In this world, Tupac found God. For further review, see Esther Iverem, "The Politics of 'Fuck It' and the Passion to be A Free Black," in *Tough Love: The Life and Death of Tupac Shakur*, ed. Michael Datcher and Kwame Alexander (Alexandria, VA: Black Words Books, 1997); Jack Miles, *Christ: A Crisis in the Life of God* (New York: Alfred A. Knopf, 2001); Anthony Pinn, *The Black Church in the Post–Civil Rights Era* (Maryknoll, NY: Orbis Books, 2002); Teresa L. Reed, *The Holy Profane: Religion in Black Popular Music* (Lexington: The University Press of Kentucky, 2003).

culture of the 1980s.[6] In this consumer culture, Tupac became a type of popular critical pundit for the hip-hop community—which was established early on in hip-hop culture in its critique of US social structures—particularly religion and economics. He was a by-product of the post-revolutionary black spirit alive in the early 1970s.[7] He was the voice of the ghetto/'hood marginalized, oppressed, and downtrodden,[8] connecting God to a people who would never imagine gracing the pristine hallways of a church. He related God, culture, hip hop, life, pain, and even "sin" to Jesus, and forced the listener to deal with those issues while providing an accessible pathway and access to a God that was not marred with a blonde-haired, blue-eyed embodiment of perfection. Tupac's God was the God of the 'hood. As Cheryl Kirk-Duggan so eloquently states of Tupac, "amid his deep hurt and alienation, he often expressed profound religious sensibilities—a kind of street spiritualty that invokes traditional faith categories [and] ranging from irony and sarcasm to humility and sincerity, aware of the life and death issues that people face daily on the street."[9]

This chapter is concerned with demonstrating the post-soul theology of Tupac Amaru Shakur,[10] while providing an alternative space for those who do not fit the white evangelical model of "finding God" to *seek* God.

---

[6] Tawnya Adkins Covert, "Consumption and Citizenship During the Second World War," *Journal of Consumer Culture* 3, no. 3 (November 1, 2003).

[7] Also see Anthony Pinn, *The Black Church in the Post-Civil Rights Era* in which he discusses the effects of the civil rights movement, post-soul creations, and post-revolutionary elements for the black church and black theology.

[8] While this was Tupac's main audience, there have been numerous suburban, wealthy, white persons who connected with Tupac's message simply because they themselves were marginalized, oppressed, and/or downtrodden by parents and/or other structural forces similar to that of the urban poor.

[9] Cheryl A. Kirk-Duggan, "The Theo-poetic Theological Ethics of Lauryn Hill and Tupac Shakur," in *Creating Ourselves: African Americans and Hispanic Americans on Popular Culture and Religious Expression*, ed. Anthony B. Pinn and Benjamín Valentín (Durham, NC: Duke University Press, 2009), 214.

[10] This is not to say that Tupac did not have his issues. Tupac was aware of these failures as it related to his own anger, hurts, and pain. Moreover, Tupac struggled with both sides of the coin: the positive and the negative. On one end you have the hopefulness of the African American community in one person, while on the flip side you have elements of his life that grind that hopefulness to a saddening halt. That said, this chapter illuminates the gospel message of Tupac; there is more than enough negative press on Tupac on the internet and from his critics who saw him as a negative "black male." What I argue here is that Tupac creates an actual theological space for those who have been overlooked to connect with God. I am not asserting that we accept Tupac as a perfected person—he was human and had his errors. However,

This chapter focuses on ethnolifehistory and qualitative lyrical analysis methods[11] engaging the five major eras of Tupac's life, music, poetry, and theological themes. Those five eras are:[12]

1. Military Mind (1971–80)

2. Criminal Grind (1981–88)

3. The Ghetto is Destiny (1989–92)

4. Outlaw (1992–95)

5. Ghetto Saint (1996–Present)

Moreover, this chapter looks at the intersection between the sacred and the profane, a place where Tupac resided daily and where he found a lot of meaning in God. It was a space outside the traditional environment of "church" and a space for the "thugs," the "niggas," and the "'hood rats." I define the term *sacred* as social reality in religious structure, set apart and made "holy" (e.g. Eucharist, communion). In contrast, I use the term *profane* as social reality in societal living not set apart, which is commonplace and irreverent toward the religious structure set forth by established orthodoxies. This chapter will illuminate the neo-sacred theology[13] of Tupac toward a contextualized theology of and for the 'hood. It will demonstrate that there is much to engage with and learn from, theologically speaking, in the "dark matter" of life, within what seems apparently blasphemous.[14]

---

within those errors, we find God and Christ at a deeper level, a level many of us are not willing to go to because it involves elements of the blasphemous.

[11] Ethnolifehistory is a method which investigates significant life-changing eras in a person's life. This method also allows a researcher to investigate the significant changes in a particular ethnic culture. This method is a combination of life narrative and ethnographic study, but now the researcher can look at the significant eras in a single person's life and analyze their influence. See Hodge, *Heaven Has a Ghetto*, 28–39, for a detailed description of this method.

[12] For a detailed and comprehensive review of each life era and how I arrived at these eras, see my work on Tupac's missiological gospel, in which I discuss the major changes from era to era and how Tupac emerged and defined himself through each one.

[13] This term is used to define the intersection of the profane and the sacred, a space which has elements of both deity and sin while yet pointing to divine edification in the midst of chaos, pain, blasphemy, and irreverence.

[14] This chapter takes up the argument begun by Benjamín Valentín in regard to sketching cultural theology and the importance of relevant cultural figures within a theological space. While Valentín argues for a Latino cultural theology, I would argue

Tupac and The Post-Soul Context

To begin, we must define four terms. First is the post-soul context: this is the era which began in the late 1960s and early 1970s that rejected dominant structures, systems, and meta-narratives which tended to exclude ethnic minorities and particularly the 'hood. The post-soul era rejects linear functional mantras[15] and embraces communal approaches to life, love, and God. The post-soul context was formed in the cocoon of a social shift which broke open the dam to the questioning of authority, challenging the status quo, asserting one's self identity in the public sphere, and questioning group leaders.[16] The post-soul is similar to the "postmodern" but embodies a more urban, ethnic minority, hip-hop worldview. Postmodern philosophy and theology, while similar in position, tend to exclude ethnic minorities and focus on an upper-middle-class white male hegemonic perspective. Therefore, while still recognizing the societal shift that occurred during those years, the post-soul is a more multicultural/ethnic approach to postmodernity and the issues it brings.[17]

---

that Tupac is part of that process even though he was African American and that many young Latinos—in particular—saw Tupac as part of their own cultural geography. For instance, Valentín asserts that Latino youth realize that culture matters; there are more ways they are getting oppressed other than economic; cultural imperialism, racism, and sexism affect Latino lives—Tupac addressed these in his music, and many listeners felt connected to this type of critical cultural discourse from him. Benjamín Valentín, "Tracings: Sketching the Cultural Geographies of Laino/a Theology," in Pinn and Valentín, *Creating Ourselves*, 39–40.

[15] Sequential-based reasoning, linear worldviews (first this, then that, finally this, etc.), and simplistic answers.

[16] As discussed in Nelson George, *Hiphop America* (New York: Penguin Books, 1998); Hodge, *The Soul of Hip Hop*; Mark Anthony Neal, "Sold out on Soul: The Corporate Annexation of Black Popular Music," *Popular Music and Society* 21, no. 3 (1997); Mark Anthony Neal, *What the Music Said: Black Popular Music and Black Public Culture* (New York: Routledge, 1999); Mark Anthony Neal, *Soul Babies: Black Popular Culture and the Post-Soul Aesthetic* (New York: Routledge, 2002); Pinn, *The Black Church in the Post-Civil Rights Era*; Anthony Pinn, *Embodiment and the New Shape of Black Theological Thought*, Religion, Race, and Ethnicity (New York: New York University Press, 2010).

[17] For example, books such as Douglas Kellner and Steven Best's *Postmodern Theory: Critical Interrogations* (New York: Guilford Press, 1991) fall short of mentioning the social, religious, and cultural shift that the civil rights movement brought to the American public sphere. Moreover, Raymond Betts, *A History of Popular Culture: More of Everything, Faster, and Brighter* (New York: Routledge, 2004) does not mention—even briefly—the contributions of hip hop and rap moguls. Gil Scott Heron, Ray Charles, and even the television show *Fresh Prince of Bel-Air* were never mentioned in the

Second, post-soul theology is the theology of the post-soul context. Its vernacular prioritizes a connection with a God of the oppressed and disenfranchised. Post-soul theology seeks to better understand God in the profane, the blasphemous, and the irreverent; moreover, it makes God accessible to humans in a multi-ethnic and inclusive way while still recognizing the atrocities committed in the name of religion.

The third term is neo-secular. Many renowned evangelical theologians have argued that we live in a "secular" culture. However, within the post-soul context, spirituality makes its reemergence and seeks to discover God in the ordinary. This pathway is foreign to traditional methodologies of salvation. The neo-secular is a mixture of sacred and profane spiritual journeys pursuing God in a space outside traditional forms of worship.

Fourth, there is the neo-sacred: This is the new sacred, rooted in the post-soul theological context. This sacred space embodies city corners, alleyways, club rooms, cocktail lounges, and spaces/places which are extraneous to many who call themselves "Christian." The neo-sacred is Tupac's message to the pimps, the hookers, the thugs, the niggas, those overlooked by society, missionaries, and many church-goers. The neo-sacred is concerned with finding God in the post-soul socio-ecological landscape and making God accessible for all.

For Tupac, a new type of theological discourse was needed in the face of severe economic, social, and political disparities. For example, in one of his first songs, "Panther Power," Tupac bellows:

> As real as it seems the American Dream
> Ain't nothing but another calculated scheme
> To get us locked up shot up back in chains
> To deny us of the future rob our names
> Kept my history of mystery but now I see
> The American Dream wasn't meant for me
> Cause lady liberty is a hypocrite she lied to me[18]

---

literature. While each of these represents major changes and social shifts, they were not engaged. The post-soul is therefore a parallel conceptual framework including those excluded voices and creating space for artists like Tupac. Tupac asserted time after time that race played a role in the historical discourse of people, and the post-soul aids in filling that void.

[18] Tupac, "Panther Power," *The Lost Tapes* (1989/2000).

Tupac calls out the very fabric of the "American Dream" (home owner-ship, being educated, affordable health care, and day care)[19] and chal-lenges its apparent mythology for the ghetto poor. Where is God in all of this? Where is justice for those who do not live the commercialized embodiment of "the good life"? Tupac asserts the neo-sacred within this pain and disillusionment in a song titled "Lord Knows":

> I smoke a blunt to take the pain out
> And if I wasn't high, I'd probably try to blow my brains out
> I'm hopeless, they shoulda killed me as a baby
> And now they got me trapped in the storm, I'm goin crazy
> Forgive me; they wanna see me in my casket
> and if I don't blast I'll be the victim of them bastards
> I'm losin hope, they got me stressin, can the Lord forgive me
> Got the spirit of a thug in me[20]

At the same time, Tupac realizes that this is not the way life was sup-posed to be. He is fully aware that God has not intended people to behave in an inhumane fashion. He calls out to God in a post-soul style, decrying his lifestyle:

> Fuck the friendships, I ride alone
> Destination Death Row, finally found a home
> Plus all my homies wanna die, call it euthanasia
> Dear Lord, look how sick this ghetto made us, sincerely
> yours I'm a thug, the product of a broken home[21]

In these lyrics, Tupac "does what he has to" in order to survive within these types of injustices, while still asking the poignant theological ques-tions of God in the face of suffering. Tupac presents a voice to engage culture, deal with conflict, create connective narrative, generate com-munity, dispel the traditional powers, and call people to a different level

---

[19] These four "American Dream" taxonomies are what Fred Block, et al., "The Compassion Gap in American Poverty Policy," *Contexts* 5, no. 2 (2006), describe as the four main constructs of the "American Dream," and how the exponential increase in all four of those areas between 1973 and 2003 have almost eliminated the middle class. For Tupac, and many other black scholars, the poor, the ghetto, and African Americans are at the bottom of this avalanche of misery.

[20] Tupac, "Lord Knows," *Me against the World* (1995).

[21] Tupac, "Letter to the President," *Still I Rise* (1999).

of engagement with God. Cheryl Kirk-Duggan would say that "like James Baldwin, Shakur confronted black suffering with a moral ire."[22] For those who would argue that this type of approach to life is vile, immoral, and "sinful," Tupac would reply that only God can judge him:

> Oh my Lord, tell me what I'm livin for
> Everybody's droppin got me knockin on heaven's door
> And all my memories, of seein brothers bleed
> And everybody grieves, but still nobody sees
> Recollect your thoughts don't get caught up in the mix
> Cause the media is full of dirty tricks
> Only God can judge me[23]

Blues music had a similar sense. Contextual, relevant, gritty, and reflections of Southern ghetto life, many white conservatives and religious blacks dismissed the blues as evil, sinful, and altogether vile. Teresa Reed reminds us that "blues singing was associated with the brothel, the juke joint, and the dregs of black-American society."[24] Still, despite the stench of "sin," Reed argues that the "religious commentary is salient in the blues text. . . . [T]hese lyrics treat religion in a way that yields two important kinds of information: integration of secular thought with sacred and . . . the postbellum shift in black-American religious consciousness."[25] Tupac's music is merely a continuation of this postbellum shift, now with rap music.[26]

A great example of part of this shift came in the late 1960s and early 1970s, when a heated debate was brewing, stating that black theology had no relevance and merely reflected an "angry" and "hateful" message from blacks.[27] Black theologian Herbert Edwards, in response to claims from some white theologians that black theology was not a valid theological approach, argued that black theology provided contextualization, a voice, and a way for those who had previously been either dismissed

---

[22] Kirk-Duggan, "The Theo-poetic Theological Ethics of Lauryn Hill and Tupac Shakur," 219.

[23] Tupac, "Only God Can Judge Me," *All Eyez on Me* (1996).

[24] Reed, *The Holy Profane: Religion in Black Popular Music*, 39.

[25] Ibid., 39–40.

[26] See Hodge, *The Soul of Hip Hop*.

[27] See James H. Cone, *Black Theology and Black Power*, 5th ed. (Maryknoll, NY: Orbis Books, 1997).

by white evangelicals or forcibly assimilated to their tradition. Tupac begins to create such a black theological space.[28]

Tupac argues the inadequacy of the previous and existing theologies for the present Crisis—poverty, recidivism rates for young urban males, racism, and classism. Tupac never once questioned, blasphemed, or cursed the name of God or Jesus. What Tupac did do was to call out religious officials, traditionalized churches (churches practicing hyper-traditionalism and adherence to the "letter of the law"), conventional forms of religion, irrelevant theologies, and current methods of evangelism.

Tupac was not a trained theologian, pastor, or evangelist[29] in the way one would recognize from the rigor of the seminary. Tupac did not have the eloquence of a T.D. Jakes or the growl of a Baptist preacher. Still, Tupac was able to connect God to the streets and give those who had never heard of God a vision for what their life could be like. Lacking formal training never disqualified anyone from doing "God's work." Still, Tupac never really came to any solid conclusions about a theology of the 'hood. He began the discussion, but because of his early death, never finished the mantra of a ghetto gospel.

> We probably in Hell already, our dumb asses not knowin
> Everybody kissin ass to go to heaven ain't goin
> Put my soul on it, I'm fightin devil niggaz daily
> Plus the media be crucifying brothers severely.[30]

This aptly titled song, "Blasphemy," was a rejection of a form of black theology that places the pastor at the center of the church, creates a pious stature for him (and it typically is a *him*), and discourages honest questions and doubts from emerging within the congregation. Tupac not only challenges but shatters the status quo by placing context and reality into his message within this song. He further states:

---

[28] Edwards, while discussing black theology, argues that in order for theologies to have a concrete basis they must prove the inadequacy of the preceding theologies, establish and prove their own adequacy for the present, and establish continuity with the primordial, normative expressions of the faith. Herbert O. Edwards, "Black Theology: Retrospect and Prospect," *Journal of Religious Thought* 32, no. 2 (1975): 46–47.

[29] Nineteen of the twenty interviews stated that Tupac was their "pastor" and connection to theology. They told me that Tupac was a prophet because of the way he could interpret theological matters and make it "clear" for them. See Hodge, *The Soul of Hip Hop*.

[30] Tupac, "Blasphemy," *The Don Killuminati: The 7 Day Theory* (1996).

The preacher want me buried why? Cause I know he a liar
Have you ever seen a crackhead, that's eternal fire
Why you got these kids minds, thinkin that they evil
while the preacher bein richer you say honor God's people
Should we cry, when the Pope die, my request
We should cry if they cried when we buried Malcolm X
Mama tell me am I wrong, is God just another cop
waitin to beat my ass if I don't go pop?[31]

Tupac continues his shattering of the status quo of theological "nice answers" by offering up metaphorical comparisons:

They ask us why we mutilate each other like we do
They wonder why we hold such little worth for human life
Facing all this drama
To ask us why we turn from bad to worse is to ignore from which we came
You see, you wouldn't ask why the rose that grew from the concrete had damaged petals
On the contrary, we would all celebrate its tenacity
We would all love its will to reach the sun
Well, we are the roses
This is the concrete
And these are my damaged petals
Don't ask me why
Thank God, nigga
Ask me how[32]

In one of his greatest theological songs, "So Many Tears," Tupac pushes past the "milk" theology, described by Paul in 1 Corinthians 3:2, and into a mature theological stance on life:

Now that I'm strugglin in this business, by any means
Label me greedy gettin green, but seldom seen
And fuck the world cause I'm cursed, I'm havin visions
of leavin here in a hearse, God can you feel me?
Take me away from all the pressure, and all the pain
Show me some happiness again, I'm goin blind

[31] In this verse we can also see Tupac connecting with mainstream theological thought by asking the serious question of God. In other words, is God just another white conservative, wanting me to fit in and wear suits and ties like I've been told and have seen? Is there a place for the real nigga and thug in heaven?

[32] Tupac, "Mama Just a Little Girl," *Better Dayz* (2002).

I spend my time in this cell, ain't livin well
I know my destiny is Hell, where did I fail?
My life is in denial, and when I die,
baptized in eternal fire I'll shed so many tears
Lord, I suffered through the years, and shed so many tears.[33]

The post-soul context requires one to disembody and deconstruct current theological mantras which continually hold up tradition. Pain, injustice, and racism force the post-soulist to look beyond the "standard" and ask God for more. Simplistic answers are rejected and despised: it gets God off the hook too easily to say "just pray about it,"[34] and in times of pain and injustice, everything needs to be on the hook, including God. The procedure is quite simple: have a conversation with God, be real, and do not be afraid to use strong language to describe your pain:

Was it my fault papa didn't plan it out
Broke out left me to be the man of the house
I couldn't take it, had to make a profit
Down the block, got a glock, and I clock grip
Makin G's was my mission
Movin enough of this shit to get my mama out the kitchen and
why must I sock a fella, just to live large like Rockefeller
First you didn't give a fuck, but you're learnin now
If you don't respect the town then we'll burn you down
God damn it's a motherfuckin riot

I see no changes, all I see is racist faces
Misplaced hate makes disgrace to races
We under I wonder what it take to make this
one better place, let's erase the wait state
Take the evil out the people they'll be acting right
Cause both black and white are smokin crack tonight
And only time we deal is when we kill each other
It takes skill to be real, time to heal each other

Pull a trigger kill a nigger he's a hero
Mo' nigga mo' nigga mo' niggaz

---

[33] Tupac,"So Many Tears," *Me against the World* (1995).

[34] Anthony B. Pinn, *Why Lord? Suffering and Evil in Black Theology* (New York: Continuum, 1995), describes this type of theological process as nitty-gritty hermeneutics, pushing past the basics of theology and into the depths of life to ask God "tougher questions." Acceptance of pain is put into context and the hermeneutic moves into the "nitty gritty" of life.

I'd rather be dead than a po' nigga
Let the Lord judge the criminals
If I die, I wonder if heaven got a ghetto[35]

For Tupac, the goal was to create a contextualized way in a world that was forgotten (part of the post-soul deconstruction process): the 'hood. In his song "Searching for Black Jesuz," Tupac and the Outlawz search for a deity that can relate to them, one who "smokes like we smoke, drinks like we drink."[36] In the song "Picture Me Rolling," Tupac questions whether or not God can forgive him as he asks, "Will God forgive me for all the dirt a nigga did to feed his kids?"[37] In this neo-sacred element, Tupac begins to ask the longstanding theological question: what does forgiveness really look like for sinners?

For the post-soulist, this process of searching for God in the mystery, the hurt, the pain, and then finding God in that heinous mixture is a welcome breath of fresh air compared to the avoidance and three-point sermons that so much of evangelical theology has become. It is the heart of dialogue and the very place God is experienced. In fact, almost anyone who has experienced deep loss and pain in which God's hand felt far can relate. For example, "White Man's World" combines Tupac's request for heavenly favor and reprisal in a process similar to the psalms: "God bless me please. . . . Making my enemies bleed."[38] Within those statements much more is at work—a fundamental attempt to make God accessible in a social structure which has been forgotten and left for dead.

More of the neo-sacred and post-soul theology arises in songs such as "Hail Mary." The song suggests a liturgical prayer, beseeching listeners to follow God and to "follow me; eat my flesh."[39] While it might appear that Tupac is asking his listeners to see him as "God," in fact Tupac was acting as a type of pastoral go-between. Tupac, in several interviews from the early 1990s, made reference to people in the 'hood not always having a clear path to God, and that in that absence of such a path, if he was the only pathway, then so be it.[40] Tupac made it clear he was not

---

[35] Lyrics taken from throughout Tupac, "I Wonder If Heaven Got a Ghetto" (Original hip-hop version) *R U Still Down* (1997).

[36] 2Pac & The Outlawz,"Black Jesus," *Still I Rise* (Interscope Records, 1999).

[37] Tupac interview with *Vibe Magazine*, approximately 1995.

[38] Tupac, "White Man's World," *Makaveli-Don Killuminati: The 7-Day Theory* (Deathrow Records, 1996).

[39] Tupac Shakur, "Hail Mary," *Makaveli-Don Killuminati: The 7-Day Theory* (Deathrow Records, 1996).

[40] Tupac interview with *Vibe Magazine*, approximately 1995.

God or Jesus, but merely a conduit and a beacon to a contextualized Jesuz.[41]

Tupac fills part of the vacancy for those who doubt. In the song "Po Nigga Blues," Tupac poses a question to God which oozes with spiritual doubt: "I wonder if the Lord ever heard of me, huh, I need loot, so I'm doin' what I do."[42] In other words, will God really forgive me when I am practicing socially unapproved standards of living? Dyson reminds us that "Tupac's religious ideas were complex and unorthodox, perhaps even contradictory, though that would not make him unique among his believers." Part of that vacancy felt in the 'hood also comes with images of heaven: streets of gold, mansions, pearly gates, and a God who is "perfect"—these may be too much for the person living on streets riddled with potholes, in project housing, around broken gates, and with white racist images of God. Paulo Freire boldly states that within situations of oppression, the main goal of the oppressed should be to "liberate themselves from their oppressors."[43] Tupac was helping to create that pathway for liberation.[44]

Tupac had a post-soul gospel message for his fans, community, and society, embodying both the sacred and the profane. Tupac owned a lot of his own "sins" and shortcomings which, in post-soul contexts, creates

[41] Note the letter *S* has been dropped to demonstrate the contextualization of the Christ figure for the 'hood. And the letter *Z* at the end of Jesus' name was added to give a portrait of a Jesus who could sympathize and connect with a people that were downtrodden and broken. The letter *Z* is consistent with hip hop's vernacular to change words and phrases to fit the context and annunciate words for a hip-hop community. The *Z* also represented a Jesus who was not only "above" in theological discussions but also "below" in reachable form. The *Z* gives new dimensions to the portrait of Christ and validates the struggles, life, narrative, and spirituality for many hip hoppers. Hodge, *The Soul Of Hip Hop*, chap. 6.

[42] "Po Nigga Blues," *Loyal to the Game* (Amaru Interscope Records, 2004).

[43] Paulo Freire, *Pedagogy of the Oppressed*, trans. Myra Bergman Ramos (New York: Continuum, 1970), 28.

[44] It is interesting to note that within my interviews, a theme of liberation from traditional church arose from the interviewees. "To move away from," "get out from under," and "move out" were all phrases from respondents when asked, "How has Tupac's music, poetry, and spirituality affected you theologically?" These phrases were part of a larger discussion on how contemporary religion had become corrupted and lost its "edge" in life. Whether or not race was a factor in this response was not analyzed. This would be something for further study, but there is a clear implication here that the interviewees felt they needed to move out from their current theological situation and that Tupac helped them to do just that.

a kind of transparency and authenticity. His listeners could identity with a marred, scarred, profanity-ridden, and broken ghetto "preacher." Within that profanity, an attempt to create honest communication between God and humankind is at work. Tupac and E.D.I. contend, in the song "The Uppercut," that "I'm a product of the pimp, the pusher, and the reverend. . . .we all lost souls trying to find our way to heaven."[45]

Dyson asserts that "Tupac aimed to enhance awareness of the divine, of spiritual reality, by means of challenging orthodox beliefs and traditional religious practices."[46] Tupac's "gospel," in essence, was a mature one that sought to better apprehend God in the core of a world gone askew.

Locating Tupac's Gospel

Tupac's "good news" about life in the 'hood is a type of the "indecent theology" that Marcella Althaus-Reid discusses in *Indecent Theology: Theological Perversions in Sex, Gender, and Politics*,[47] as grand narratives of God have collapsed in the 'hood, creating parallel narratives that offend the dominant ones. Tupac's gospel, at its core, seeks to give marginalized urban dwellers (and poor whites as well) a voice to God and a place for meaning in unbearable conditions. Tupac is an indirect missiologist,[48] bringing a neo-secular message of God's love to the 'hood and contextualizing epistemological processes—in other words, constructing a new knowledge set of life in the 'hood—for a generation raised in the crack cocaine milieu. Jamal Joseph notes that Tupac had a huge heart for people to understand a better way of living, to know positive role models, and to be critical thinkers.[49]

There are three gospel messages within his music: The gospel of hold on, the gospel of keeping ya head up, and the gospel of heaven having a ghetto.

---

[45] Tupac,"The Uppercut," *Loyal to the Game* (Amaru Interscope Records, 2004).

[46] Michael Eric Dyson, *Holler If You Hear Me: Searching for Tupac Shakur* (New York: Basic Civitas, 2001), 204.

[47] Marcella Althaus-Reid, *Indecent Theology: Theological Perversions in Sex, Gender, and Politics* (New York: Routledge, 2000).

[48] While Tupac was not a trained "missiologist" in the orthodox sense, Tupac's heart was to reach out to those on whom society has given up. Tupac was also concerned with educating people in the ways of Jesus, connecting Tupac to the Great Commission in Matt 28:16-20.

[49] Jamal Jospeh, *Tupac Shakur: Legacy* (New York: Atria Books, 2006), 16–23.

First, the gospel of hold on encouraged those who have given up or are about to give up on life or other people.[50] Tupac encourages his listener to see that there is hope for a brighter tomorrow:

> God
> When I was alone, and had nothing
> I asked for a friend to help me bear the pain
> No one came, except God
> When I needed a breath to rise, from my sleep
> No one could help me . . . except God
> When all I saw was sadness, and I needed answers
> No one heard me, except God
> So when I'm asked . . . who I give my unconditional love to?
> I look for no other name, except God[51]

In this poem, titled "God," Tupac calls out to God and asks for a conduit. He finds it in the midst of hurt. James Cone calls this type of process "revelation" and argues, "For black theology, revelation is not just a past event or a contemporary event in which it is difficult to recognize the activity of God. Revelation is a black event."[52] In this poem, Tupac takes on the revelation and looks for no one else but God.

In the song "So Many Tears,"[53] Tupac begs God not to forget a nigga, "Lord I suffered through the years and shed so many tears. . . . Dear God please let me in."[54] There is a paradoxical optimism in the midst of extreme pain, hurt, despair, and violence.[55] Tupac calls the person to seek a better way and higher level of understanding.

---

[50] See Iverem, "The Politics of 'Fuck It' and the Passion to be a Free Black."

[51] Tupac read by Rev. Run, "God," *The Rose That Grew from Concrete*, vol. 1 (Interscope Records, 2000).

[52] James Cone, *A Black Theology of Liberation*, 20th ed. (Maryknoll, NY: Orbis Books, 1990), 30.

[53] Tupac, "So Many Tears," *Me against the World* (Amaru/ Interscope/ Jive Records, 1995).

[54] This mindset is no different from what slaves had to deal with and their vision that God would eventually help them. Luke Powery asserts that the spirit of lament is combined with celebration and that they go hand in hand. Luke A. Powery, *Spirit Speech: Lament and Celebration in Preaching* (Nashville, TN: Abington Press, 2009).

[55] See Rudolph Otto, *The Idea of the Holy*, 2nd ed. (London, England: Oxford University Press, 1950), 12–24. This ideology connects with a concept that Rudolf Otto calls "The Mysterium Tremendum," the mysteriousness of what God did in spite of an appalling situation. For Otto, this meant that "A God comprehended is no God" (25). In other words, holding on does not always mean it will make sense or will even

The gospel of keeping your head up was a frequent theme in Tupac's discourse. Howard Thurman stated that one of the ingenuities of black slave culture was the ability to not diminish hopes, dreams, or visions to immediate experience; the immediate experience may be hurtful, may be problematic, may be nefarious, may even be abusive, but one must foster, encourage, manifest, manage the future vision that allows one to escape the immediate consequences of despair. Hopelessness occurs when one has the inability to imagine a different future.[56] In this gospel Tupac is essentially making sense of immediate pain and suffering. Tupac would say, "Yes, I'm holding on, but where do I look?"

Tupac wanted his fans to know that the ideology of "keeping ya head up" was not done in vain. In the face of extreme opposition and hurt, there was still a way to move forward. Even when things seemed as though they could not get any better, Tupac would tell his fans that there was a better way. Life did not end on the experience of the immediate event; one's errors and successes were not necessarily their defining moment.

> If I upset you don't stress, never forget
> That God isn't finished with me yet
> I feel his hand on my brain
> When I write rhymes I go blind and let the Lord do his thang
> But am I less holy?
> Cause I chose to puff a blunt, and drink a beer with my homies
> Before we find world peace
> We gotta find peace and end the war in the streets, my ghetto gospel[57]

Tupac attempted to bring a pragmatic type of hope for the 'hood through his music instead of traditional hymns. Tupac replaced them with the Thug Life mantra and his message of encouragement in hard times.[58]

"feel right." This was an area for Tupac that helped him deal with the bigger picture of sin and the brokenness of humankind.

[56] Also see James H. Cone, *The Spirituals and the Blues: An Interpretation* (Maryknoll, NY: Orbis Books, 1991); Dyson, *Between God and Gangsta Rap: Bearing Witness to Black Culture*; R. Peters, "Examining the Economic Crisis as a Crisis of Values," *Interpretation* 65, no. 2 (2011); Powery, *Spirit Speech: Lament and Celebration in Preaching*. These works discuss the power behind vision, hope, and future-oriented mind-sets in the midst of pain, hurt, and despair.

[57] Tupac, "Ghetto Gospel," *Loyal to the Game* (2004).

[58] This was one of the reasons why Tupac was so calm, almost at peace, with the knowledge of his imminent death. Joseph, *Tupac Shakur: Legacy*. Tupac was fully aware

Regarding the authority of what is from God and what is not, Dyson writes:

> [C]ountless sacred narratives are hardly distinguishable from con-
> temporary rap. . . . The prophet Jeremiah belched despair from the
> belly of his relentless pessimism. And the Psalms are full of midnight
> and bad cheer. This is not to argue that the contrasting moral frame-
> works of rap and religion do not color our interpretation of their
> often-opposing creeds. But we must not forget that unpopular and
> unacceptable views are sometimes later regarded as prophetic. It is
> a central moral contention of Christianity that God may be disguised
> in the clothing—and maybe even the rap—of society's most despised
> members.[59]

Tupac was part of this long tradition of lament, praise, and life in the secular, or what James Cone calls the "secular spiritual."[60]

In the song "Hold Ya Head," Tupac encourages those who are in prison, in pain, and lost to hold on and keep that head up in times of trouble. Through weed, alcohol, and even illicit sex, a post-soul theology arises:[61]

> The weed got me tweakin in my mind, I'm thinkin.
> God bless the child that can hold his own
> Indeed, enemies bleed when I hold my chrome
> Let these words be the last to my unborn seeds
> Hope to raise my young nation in this world of greed
> Currency means nothin if you still ain't free
> Money breeds jealousy, take the game from me
> I hope for better days, trouble comes naturally
> Running from authorities 'til they capture me
> And my aim is to spread mo' smiles than tears
> Utilize lessons learned from my childhood years
> Maybe Mama had it all right, rest yo' head
> Tradin conversation all night, bless the dead
> To the homies that I used to have that no longer roll

---

that life did not end here. Even though he did not have it easy and his situation was nefarious, there was a better place in heaven set for him.

[59] Dyson, *Holler If You Hear Me*, 208–9.

[60] James Cone, "The Blues: A Secular Spiritual," in *Sacred Music of the Secular City: From Blues to Rap*, ed. Jon Michael Spencer (Durham, NC: Duke University Press, 1992), 68–97.

[61] Jesus himself was considered a heretic, a blasphemer, and a profane individual for his views on spiritual matters. See Miles, *Christ*.

Catch a brother at the crossroads . . .
Plus nobody knows my soul, watchin time pass
Through the glass of my drop-top Rolls, hold ya head![62]

In the song "Still I Rise," Tupac laments to the Lord that the struggle is almost too much to bear; pain and misery parade his life and the journey seems like it will never end. Yet, in the end, still I rise. "Tupac sounds out that in times of trouble, God is with you, so keep your head up. Even the words in that phrase, 'head up' is meant to persuade one to look unto the heavens from which our help comes."[63]

Finally, the gospel of heaven having a ghetto was a prolific thought in Tupac's worldview, contextualizing heaven and making it accessible for people who do not subscribe to Euro-Western theology. Tupac even calls himself the "ghetto missionary." In an interview on B.E.T. Tupac states:

> If I can't be free, if I can't live with the same respect as the next man, then I don't wanna be here. Because God has cursed me to see what life should be like. If God had wanted me to be this person, to be happy here, he wouldn't let me feel so oppressed. He wouldn't let me feel so trampled on; you know what I'm saying? He wouldn't let me think the things I think. So, I feel like I'm doing God's work, you know what I'm saying? Just because I don't have nothing to pass around for people to put in the bucket don't mean I'm not doing God's work; I feel like I'm doing God's work. Because, these ghetto kids ain't God's children? And I don't see no missionaries coming through there. So I'm doing God's work. While Reverend Jackson do his shit up in the middle class and he go to the White House and have dinner and pray over the president, I'm up in the 'hood doing my work with my folks.[64]

Here Tupac expresses not only the divisions of class within black society, but also within its theological walls.[65] Tupac knows it is his mission to

---

[62] Tupac, "Hold Ya Head," *The Don Killuminati: The 7 Day Theory* (1996).

[63] Hodge, *The Soul of Hip-Hop*, 150.

[64] Taken from an interview done on Black Entertainment Television (B.E.T.) by Ed Gordon in 1994.

[65] This is an ongoing debate and issue within black culture and the black church. For a further discussion, see Michael Eric Dyson, *Is Bill Cosby Right? Or Has the Black Middle Class Lost Its Mind?* (New York: Basic Civitas Books, 2005); Eric C. Lincoln and Lawrence H. Mamiya, *The Black Church in the African American Experience* (Durham & London: Duke University Press, 1990); Pinn, *The Black Church in the Post–Civil Rights Era.*

bring a gospel to those who have been left out and have not been invited to the anticipated heavenly party with its unspoiled clean streets. The thought then is this: if life continues according to plan, heaven will have cops waiting to "beat our ass" the minute we walk through the gates. Therefore, Tupac decided to ask the question: Does heaven have a ghetto? In other words, can I be accepted in this realm that has continually told me I am neither worthy nor acceptable? Can I be taken for my own worth as I am, or do I have to enter through the back so as not to disturb the residents nor mar the fine linen?

The great writer, mystic, and theologian Howard Thurman asks the relevant and almost irreligious question regarding religion and its message to the poor and disheveled, "What does our religion say to them?" Thurman's challenge says:

> I can count on the fingers of one hand the number of times that I have heard a sermon on the meaning of religion, on Christianity, to the man who stands with his back against the wall. It is urgent that my meaning be crystal clear. The masses of men live with their backs constantly against the wall. They are the poor, the disinherited, the dispossessed. What does our religion say to them?[66]

Tupac took the challenge and made an attempt to create a gospel message for those poor, disinherited, and dispossessed peoples living in the urban enclaves called the ghetto; Tupac created a transcendental space for the thug, the nigga, and the pimp to find God.[67]

Tupac's answer to his own question, "Does heaven got a ghetto?" is yes! But not in the literal sense. Tupac never said that there is poverty, crime, gentrification, and homelessness in God's kingdom. The term is

[66] Howard Thurman, *Jesus and the Disinherited* (Boston, MA: Beacon Press, 1976), 13.

[67] These types of questions create theological conundrums in contemporary evangelical theology, which echo vagueness and ambiguity regarding God's love to marginalized peoples. Therefore, the hip hopper, the ghetto person, and Tupac himself pose a new question: If social structures and systems have failed us, wouldn't the church and religion follow suit? Tupac could no longer sit by and accept a traditional view of Jesus or Christianity. Tupac needed a stronger theology than that, a Christ who could accept the thug and the marginalized person. This was the outcry in songs like "I Wonder If Heaven Got a Ghetto?" and "Black Jesuz." These were expressions of a deeper search for God and spirituality. These were also fundamental questions of who God really is, questions that many of us ask ourselves. Are we really "saved"? See Hodge, *Heaven Has a Ghetto*, 264–65.

used figuratively, symbolically, as if to ask, "Is the gospel big enough to fit everyone who wants to fit in, and can God handle me if he really created me?" Tupac resoundingly said yes. He encouraged his audience, as a pastor would his flock, to see that there was a different image of heaven and that there was room for those who did not fit in a traditional evangelical (at times white) theology.[68]

> Who's got the heart to stand beside me?
> I feel my enemies creepin up in silence
> Dark prayer, scream violence—demons all around me
> Can't even bend my knees just a lost cloud; Black Jesus
> give me a reason to survive, in this earthly hell
> Cause I swear, they tryin to break my well
> I'm on the edge lookin down at this volatile pit
> Will it matter if I cease to exist? Black Jesus[69]

Toward A Theology of Tupac the Post-Soul Prophet

Tupac was not perfect. He was baptized in the dirty waters of marketing, social representations of blackness, stereotypes of the gangsta, the tattooed thug, and the poor black child. He was not Jesus incarnate, nor was he the "perfect" role model for everyone. Before he left for prison, he told Jada Pinkett Smith that he wanted to quit thuggin' and give up on rap and solely do acting.[70] However, Tupac ended up embodying the same black male image he had fought so hard against for so long: the cyclical prison inmate, the nihilistic black male, the paranoid pessimistic urbanite.

It is within these conflicts that this paradox between the sacred and the profane arises—a post-soul theology with Tupac in the middle. Tupac embodied both sin and deity. Within this contradiction, there is both good and evil, sin and salvation, dirt and cleanliness all at work and having the ability to create a fuller religious person, one who is honest about both the "good" and the "bad." This is the human struggle. Tupac, in this sense, was no different from Paul. What Tupac knew to do right, he did not do, because the flesh was weak (Rom 7:7-24). Still, within that

---

[68] This is also something I discuss at length in my chapter on engaging the theology of the profane in *The Soul of Hip Hop: Rims, Timbs and a Cultural Theology*: 159–64.

[69] 2Pac & The Outlawz, "Black Jesus," *Still I Rise* (Interscope Records, 1999).

[70] Dyson, *Holler If You Hear Me*, 215–16.

weakness, he sought to find space to find God and Jesus. This is a large part of post-soul theology. Tupac gave us this gospel and let people know that he was not the way; he was only pointing the way to Jesuz.[71]

Bibliography

Althaus-Reid, Marcella. *Indecent Theology: Theological Perversions in Sex, Gender, and Politics*. New York, NY: Routledge, 2000.

Best Steven, Douglas Kellner. *Postmodern Theory: Critical Interrogations*. New York, NY: Guilford Press, 1991.

Betts, Raymond. *A History of Popular Culture*. New York, NY: Routledge, 2004.

Block, Fred, Anna C. Korteweg, Kerry Woodward, Zach Schiller, and Imrul Mazid. "The Compassion Gap in American Poverty Policy." *Contexts* 5, no. 2 (2006): 14–20.

Cone, James H. *A Black Theology of Liberation*. 20th ed. Maryknoll, NY: Orbis Books, 1990.

———. *Black Theology and Black Power*. 5th ed. Maryknoll, NY: Orbis Books, 1997.

———. "The Blues: A Secular Spiritual." In *Sacred Music of the Secular City: From Blues to Rap*, edited by Jon Michael Spencer, 68–97. Durham, NC: Duke University Press, 1992.

———. *God of the Oppressed*. Maryknoll, NY: Orbis Books, 1997.

———. *The Spirituals and the Blues: An Interpretation*. Maryknoll, New York: Orbis Books, 1991.

Covert, Tawnya Adkins. "Consumption and Citizenship during the Second World War." *Journal of Consumer Culture* 3 (2003): 315–42.

Dyson, Michael Eric. *Between God and Gangsta Rap: Bearing Witness to Black Culture*. New York: Oxford University Press, 1996.

———. *Holler If You Hear Me: Searching for Tupac Shakur*. New York, NY: Basic Civitas, 2001.

———. *Is Bill Cosby Right? Or Has the Black Middle Class Lost Its Mind?* New York, NY: Basic Civitas Books, 2005.

Edwards, Herbert O. "Black Theology: Retrospect and Prospect." *Journal of Religious Thought*, no. 32 (1975): 46–59.

---

[71] This connects back to John the Baptist in John 1:19-32, where he denies that he is the One and that the one who comes after him is Jesus, who gives life eternally.

Freire, Paulo. *Pedagogy of the Oppressed*. Translated by Myra Bergman Ramos. New York, NY: Continuum, 1970.

George, Nelson. *Hiphop America*. New York: Penguin Books, 1998.

Hodge, Daniel White. *Heaven Has a Ghetto: The Missiological Gospel & Theology of Tupac Amaru Shakur*. Saarbrucken, Germany: VDM Verlag Dr. Muller Academic, 2009.

———. *The Soul of Hip Hop: Rims, Timbs and a Cultural Theology*. Downers Grove, IL: InterVarsity Press, 2010.

Iverem, Esther. "The Politics of 'Fuck It' and the Passion to Be a Free Black." In *Tough Love: The Life and Death of Tupac Shakur*, edited by Michael Datcher and Kwame Alexander, 41–47. Alexandria, VA: Black Words Books, 1997.

Joseph, Jamal. *Tupac Shakur: Legacy*. New York, NY: Atria Books, 2006.

Kain & Abel, & Master P. "Black Jesus," *The 7 Sins*. Priority Records, 1996.

Kirk-Duggan, Cheryl A. "The Theo-Poetic Theological Ethics of Lauryn Hill and Tupac Shakur." In *Creating Ourselves: African Americans and Hispanic Americans on Popular Culture and Religious Expression*, edited by Anthony B. Pinn and Benjamín Valentín, 204–23. Durham, NC: Duke University Press, 2009.

Lash, Scott. "Postmodernism as Humanism? Urban Space and Social Theory." In *Theories of Modernity and Postmodernity*, edited by Bryan S. Turner, 45–61. Thousand Oaks, CA: Sage Publications, 1990.

———. *Sociology of Posmodernism*. New York, NY: Routledge, 1990.

Lincoln, Eric C., and Lawrence H. Mamiya. *The Black Church in the African American Experience*. Durham & London: Duke University Press, 1990.

Miles, Jack. *Christ: A Crisis in the Life of God*. New York: Alfred A. Knopf, 2001.

Neal, Mark Anthony. "Sold out on Soul: The Corporate Annexation of Black Popular Music." *Popular Music and Society* 21, no. 3 (1997): 117.

———. *Soul Babies: Black Popular Culture and the Post-Soul Aesthetic*. New York, NY: Routledge, 2002.

———. *What the Music Said: Black Popular Music and Black Public Culture*. New York, NY: Routledge, 1999.

Otto, Rudolph. *The Idea of the Holy*. 2nd ed. London, England: Oxford University Press, 1950.

Peters, R. "Examining the Economic Crisis as a Crisis of Values." *Interpretation* 65, no. 2 (2011): 154.

Pinn, Anthony. *The Black Church in the Post-Civil Rights Era*. Maryknoll, NY: Orbis Books, 2002.

————. *Embodiment and the New Shape of Black Theology: Religion, Race, and Ethnicity*. New York: New York University Press, 2010.

Pinn, Anthony B. *Why Lord? Suffering and Evil in Black Theology*. New York: Continuum, 1995.

Powery, Luke A. *Spirit Speech: Lament and Celebration in Preaching*. Nashville, TN: Abingdon Press, 2009.

Reed, Teresa L. *The Holy Profane: Religion in Black Popular Music*. Lexington, KY: The University Press of Kentucky, 2003.

Thurman, Howard. *Jesus and the Disinherited*. Boston, MA: Beacon Press, 1976.

Valentín, Benjamín. "Tracings: Sketching the Cultural Geographies of Laino/a Theology." In *Creating Ourselves: African Americans and Hispanic Americans on Popular Culture and Religious Expression*, edited by Anthony B. Pinn and Benjamín Valentín, 38–61. Durham, NC: Duke University Press, 2009.

Watkins, Ralph Basui. *Hip-Hop Redemption: Finding God in the Rhythm and the Rhyme*, Engaging Culture. Grand Rapids, MI: Baker Academic, 2011.

Chapter 9

Tom Waits, Nick Cave, and Martin Heidegger: On Singing of the God Who Will Not Be Named

Jeffrey F. Keuss

You went to the museum
You climbed a spiral stair
You searched for me all among
The knowledgeable air
I was hidden, babe, hiding all away
I was hidden, dear, hiding all away

You entered the cathedral
When you heard the solemn knell
I was not sitting with the gargoyles
I was not swinging from the bell
I was hiding, dear, I was hiding all away
I was hiding, dear, I was hiding all away

Nick Cave & The Bad Seeds, *Hiding All Away*[1]

If there are fundamental questions that haunt and drive human culture throughout the centuries, one of the most important is "Where is God?" As artists and theologians seek to locate God, whether through metaphor or creedal affirmation, God seems to show up all-too-briefly—and then seems to elude our gaze, our voice, our penitent prayers, as if God has disappeared. As Old Testament scholar Walter Brueggemann notes in his *Theology of the Old Testament*:

---

[1] Nick Cave & The Bad Seeds, "Hiding All Away," *Abattoir Blues/ Lyre of Orpheus* (Anti/Epigraph, 2004).

The primal subject of an Old Testament theology is of course God. But because the Old Testament does not (and never intends to) provide a coherent and comprehensive offer of God, this subject matter is more difficult, complex and problematic than we might expect. For the most part, the Old Testament text gives only hints, traces, fragments, and vignettes, with no suggestion of how all these elements might fit together, if indeed they do. What does emerge, in any case, is an awareness that the elusive but dominating Subject of the Old Testament cannot be comprehended in any preconceived categories. The God of the Old Testament does not easily conform to the expectations of Christian dogmatic theology, nor to the categories of any Hellenistic perennial philosophy. . . . The Character who will emerge from such a patient study at the end will still be elusive and more than a little surprising.[2]

L. William Countryman wrote in *The Poetic Imagination* that "the dynamic created by the alternation of absence and presence is simply a defining fact of human existence. . . . [T]his dialectic of absence and presence" is where "the life force that gives energy and movement to the rest [of life resides]."[3] In the works of Christian mystics, the created world serves as a sensible symbol displaying the unlikely relation between the transcendent God and the world that manifests this hidden transcendence. As Bernard McGinn notes in regard to the mystical tradition, early Christians were called to hold the tension of God as both revealed and elusive, and the work of the faithful was to accept that "all things both reveal and conceal God. The 'dissimilar similarity' that constitutes every created

---

[2] Walter Brueggemann, *Theology of the Old Testament: Testimony, Dispute, Advocacy* (Minneapolis, MN: Augsburg Fortress, 1997), 117. This is echoed by Samuel Terrien in his book *The Elusive Presence*, where he describes the single thread that unifies the Hebrew and Christian Scriptures as being a long game of "hide and seek," with God perpetually elusive. Terrien argues that what it means to experience faith is the experience of God's elusive presence, which is the sweeping narrative that ultimately joins together the disparate stories through the Scriptures, as well as the claims that humans have made for centuries in relation to God. Of course, abstractions, such as "covenant relationship" arise, but they are grounded in and refer to the experience of absence and presence, or else they become only words about words. See Samuel Terrien, *The Elusive Presence: Toward a New Biblical Theology* (San Francisco, CA: Harper and Row, 1978).

[3] L. William Countryman, *The Poetic Imagination: An Anglican Spiritual Tradition* (New York: Orbis, 1999), 92.

manifestation of God is both a similarity to be affirmed and a dissimilarity to be denied."[4]

The analogy between God and the created cosmos takes a special form, as noted by Hans Urs von Balthasar: "Things are both like God and unlike him, but God is not like things."[5] The poet Wallace Stevens in "An Ordinary Evening in New Haven" has summed up the role of the artist as an eternal chasing after some medium by which humans can capture this God who is "both like and unlike" that which we create, and to ultimately "fling ourselves, constantly longing" after an authentic form that can acknowledge both the presence and absence of the Sacred who is the "intricate evasion of 'as.'"[6] This "intricate evasion" that Stevens speaks of in the whisper of a poem points to the never-ending struggle artists have in relying solely upon analogies and metaphors as being sufficient in representing and acknowledging the Divine. True, the power of words, according to Stevens, can change our perception of the world, as seen at the end of his poem: "an alteration / Of words that was a change of nature, more / Than the difference that clouds make over a town. / The countrymen were changed and each constant thing. / Their dark-colored words had redescribed the citrons."[7] Yet although the citrons are "redescribed," they ultimately remain unchanged, and we are left wondering if there is anything beyond our capacity to taste and touch and see, to animate and sustain our life. This is similar to Maurice Blanchot's theory of poetry and the limits of language. As Blanchot notes in his collection of essays entitled *The Work of Fire*, conventional language leaves no space or possibility for revelation due to its essentialist drive to fully describe and capture meaning. In discussing Kafka's *The Castle*, he states "the value and dignity of everyday words is to be as close as possible to nothing. Invisible, not letting anything be seen, always beyond themselves, always on this side of things, a pure awareness crosses them, so discreetly that it itself can sometimes be lacking."[8] Blanchot goes on to state that true art is that which pushes us beyond grasping

---

[4] Bernard McGinn, *The Foundations of Mysticism* (New York: Crossroad, 1992), 174.

[5] Hans Urs von Balthasar, *The Glory of the Lord: A Theological Aesthetics*, vol. 2 (New York: Crossroad, 1982), 168.

[6] Wallace Stevens, "An Ordinary Evening in New Haven," in *The Collected Poems* (New York: Vintage Books, 1990), 486.

[7] Ibid.

[8] Maurice Blanchot, "The Language of Fiction," in *The Work of Fire*, trans. Charlotte Mandell (Stanford, CA: Stanford University Press, 1995), 75–76.

for meaning in the word itself where "everything then is nullity. And yet, understanding does not stop occurring."

What is offered in the music of Nick Cave and Tom Waits is a releasing of meaning that does not "take refuge in simple invisibility,"[9] as Blanchot states, by simply becoming a passive window to merely look through, or dismissive and banal to the point of triviality. No, language that is at once particular and solid, yet transcendently rises and falls when entwined with music, can truly subvert, challenge, strain against restriction, and ultimately embody both the presence and absence of the Sacred in all the power and the glory, all the beauty and terror, all the shouting and silence of the truly poetic. The early twentieth-century philosopher Martin Heidegger marks the search for God as an eternally elusive task, which is why theology as mere rhetoric and reasoned strategy always fails. For Heidegger, seeking after God only leaves a trail of theological tomes that feed broken, battered institutions strewn through the ages with little to no evidence of having touched the hem of the Divine, let alone authenticating the Sacred with any kerygmatic assurance. As Heidegger stated during a lecture to students during a course he was teaching in Freiburg: *Das Heilige läßt sich überhaupt nicht "theologisch" ausmachen, denn [. . .] immer dort, wo die Theologie aufkommt, [hat] der Gott schon die Flucht begonnen* ("Wherever theology comes up, the god has been on the run for quite a while").[10] For the Christian faith, this "running after God" has for over two millennia made tracks in the soil of the intellectual, aesthetic, sociological and political strata and we are still, to quote U2, "running to stand still."[11] Yet what has become obvious to many is that theologians and church people are not the only ones chasing. God is showing up in places many theologians might overlook, like rock music. Can rock music help us make contact with the elusive Divine in ways that traditional theological, biblical, and doctrinal scholarship perhaps cannot on its own? Most certainly. As seen in artists like Tom Waits and Nick Cave, artists are attentive to a concern central to the question of God, and from which academic theologians and church-goers could learn a thing or two.

---

[9] Maurice Blanchot, *The Infinite Conversation*, trans. Susan Hanson (Minneapolis: University of Minnesota Press, 1993), 29.

[10] Martin Heidegger, *Vom Wesen der Wahrheit. Zur Platons Höhlengleichnis und Theätet, Gesamtausgabe*, vol. 52, 132, cited in Damir Barbaric, ed., *Das Spatwerk Heidegger: Ereignis—Sage—Geviert* (Verlag Königshausen & Neumann, 2007), 188.

[11] U2, "Running to Stand Still," *The Joshua Tree* (Island, 1987).

What has become evident, with the growing trend of fans and artists in rock music making deeply intentional choices to dialogue about the nature of the Divine in everyday life, is that popular music offers a necessary counterpoint to academic and ecclesial theology. In Dietrich Bonhoeffer's final writings prior to his martyrdom, published as *Letters and Papers from Prison*, he notes that to love God fully, we must seek other voices or melodies (to use Bonhoeffer's musical analogy) that are distinct from our own ways of knowing, akin to musical counterpoint. He describes a deep *cantus firmus*—the enduring melodic baseline (both as the standard for reasoned calculation and the rhythmic series of notes that support and push the melody) that permeates all of life—and how listening and providing counterpoints to this *cantus firmus* in our life reminds us of a deep melody that is beyond us:

> God wants us to love him eternally with our whole hearts—not in such a way as to injure or weaken our earthly love, but to provide a kind of *cantus firmus* to which the other melodies of life provide the counterpoint . . . Where the *cantus firmus* is clear and plain, the counterpoint can be developed to its limits. The two are 'undivided and yet distinct,' in the words of the Chalcedonian definition, like Christ in his divine and human natures. May not the attraction and importance of polyphony in music consist in its being a musical reflection of this Christological fact and therefore of our *vita christiana*? . . . Only a polyphony of this kind can give life a wholeness and at the same time assure us that nothing calamitous can happen as long as the *cantus firmus* is kept going. Please, Eberhard, do not fear and hate the separation, if it should come again with all its dangers, but rely on the *cantus firmus*—I don't know whether I have made myself clear now, but one so seldom speaks of such things.[12]

To this end, academic and ecclesial theology will be deficient without the correlational counterpoint of other voices. The voice of popular culture speaking a distinctly different language is a critical and necessary voice that needs to be taken seriously in order for theology to fulfill its mandate. Many of the musicians discussed throughout this volume sing in a minor key in relation to the major key of the Church institutions and its theological formulations. But as Bonhoeffer reminds us, the *cantus firmus* of God is known to bring together the language of these seemingly

---

[12] Dietrich Bonhoeffer, *Letters and Papers from Prison* (New York: Touchstone, 1953, 1997), 162–63.

dissonant counterpoints—voices like rock music—and through this necessary critical correlation, the language of theology together in counterpoint with rock music will find moments of harmony previously unrealized.

Another way of asserting this is acknowledging that the modes of knowing God through the centuries have spoken in both *kataphatic* and *apophatic* modes. Kataphatic or positive language would correspond with the procession of the divine out of itself into its manifestation in and as the cosmos, while apophatic or negative language would articulate the path of the created soul's return to the unmanifest divine transcendence. When affirmative statements traditionally germane to academic and ecclesial theology (*kataphatic*) join with modes of knowing that are at times dissonant and elusive, such as the art created by musicians such as Cave and Waits (*apophatic*), then the way of authentic and intimate union with the God that cannot be named, yet cannot be denied, is approached and even embraced.

This approach is drawn theologically from a classic text from the mystic Pseudo-Dionysius' *Mystical Theology*:[13]

> Since it is the Cause of all beings we should posit and ascribe to it all the affirmations we make in regard to beings (*kataphasis*), and more appropriately, we should negate all these affirmations since it surpasses all being (*apophasis*). Now we should not conclude that the negations are simply the opposites of the affirmations, but rather that the cause of all is considerably prior to this; as it is beyond privations, it is also beyond every denial, beyond every assertion.[14]

Since God remains transcendently above creation as Cause, not being a being among beings, the second, negative mode of language is called for: the apophatic. In the music of artists such as Tom Waits and Nick Cave, the elusiveness of God is potently acknowledged and sung with such power as to not only be heard but felt.

Tom Waits

Tom Waits is one of the unsung heroes of paradoxical theological insights that seek after God yet at the same time acknowledge the elusive character of the Divine. At times more of a carnival barker than a theo-

---

[13] *Pseudo-Dionysius: The Complete Works* (New York: Paulist Press, 1987).

[14] Dionysius, *The Mystical Theology* in *Pseudo-Dionysius: The Complete Works* (New York: Paulist Press, 1987), 1000.

logian *per se*, Waits surprises, shocks, and stuns the listener with images of God and the church wrapped in seemingly profane situations. Take some of these quotes from lyrics from his back catalogue:

> "The Lord is a very busy man. . . . Jesus is always looking for the big picture."[15]

> "Don't you know there ain't no devil, there's just God when he's drunk."[16]

> "Even Jesus wanted just a little more time, when he was walkin' Spanish down the hall"

> "You can tell me that it's gospel / but I know that it's only church."[17]

> "If you've lost all hope, if you've lost all your faith / I know you can be cared for, I know you can be safe / And all of the shamefuls, and all of the whores. And even the soldier who pierced the side of the Lord / Is down there by the train."[18]

As Tom sang in *Black Market Baby*, "There's no prayer like desire,"[19] and central to much of his work is the role that desire plays and provokes in humans seeking after meaning amid their brokenness. The characters that populate his music are reminiscent of Jacob, who, upon wrestling with the angel, not only is renamed Israel but will perpetually limp the remainder of his days. To meet God is to be disfigured in the ways that culture might offer images of the beatific. No Fra Angelico gold leaf, no Botticelli pudgy angels in Waits' carnival of freaks and broken-down losers. For Waits, the God behind all things is only experienced at the true end of our humanity, the limit-nature of meaning and the apocalyptic totality of existence. Take the opening track from his album *Bone Machine* titled "Earth Died Screaming."

It is a song that erupts with all the redemptive horror of falling face-first into Flannery O'Connor's *Wise Blood*. While "Earth Died Screaming" is a song for the end of the world—"What does it matter, a dream of love or a dream of lies / We're all going to be in the same place when we die"—"Jesus Gonna Be Here" is a song of sorrowful hope beyond hope amid a miserable world:

---

[15] Tom Waits, "Way Down In The Hole," *Big Time* (Island, 1988).

[16] Tom Waits, "Heartattack and Vine," *Heartattack and Vine* (Elektra/WEA, 1990).

[17] Tom Waits, "That Feel," *Bone Machine* (Island, 1992).

[18] Tom Waits, "Down There By The Train," *Orphans* (Anti, 2006).

[19] Tom Waits, "Black Market Baby," *Mule Variations* (Anti, 1999).

Well, Jesus gonna be here
He gonna be here soon, yeah
He gonna cover us up with leaves
With a blanket from the moon, yeah
With a promise and a vow
And a lullaby for my brow
Jesus gonna be here
He gonna be here soon, yeah.[20]

The song has the whiskey-stained tremor of a preacher pushed beyond reason—perhaps beyond theology—akin to the honest laments and heartbreak found in the musings of Asaph in Psalm 73. There is sorrow, there is cynicism, but there is also hope, like flowers in the dirt. As Mark Rowland says about Waits, his music has "a religious quality. And a love of mystery. The music brings that together: The search for mystery implicit in the sound of the music, and it takes on the aura of a spiritual quest. Not to solve the mystery, but to find it."[21]

In the hands of some singer-songwriters, these lyrics would come off as camp or, at worst, painfully unaware of conditions. But somehow Tom Waits can do this, and I listen to him scratching out a plea for unity and peace, like in "Day after Tomorrow" from his album *Real Gone*:

You can't deny, the other side
Don't want to die anymore then we do
What I'm trying to say is don't they pray
to the same god that we do?
And tell me how does god choose
whose prayers does he refuse?
Who turns the wheel
Who throws the dice
on the day after tomorrow
I'm not fighting, for justice
I am not fighting, for freedom
I am fighting, for my life
and another day in the world here[22]

[20] Tom Waits, "Jesus Gonna Be Here," *Bone Machine* (Island, 1992).

[21] Mark Rowland, "Tom Waits Is Flying Upside Down (On Purpose)," in *Innocent When You Dream: Tom Waits—The Collected Interviews*, ed. Mac Montandon (London: Orion Books, 2005), 103.

[22] Tom Waits, "Day after Tomorrow," *Real Gone* (Anti, 2004).

The God that Tom Waits offers is shocking, full of surprises, at times volatile with purpose, and offering a darkness that is darker than my own. Waits' world is all too clear and very hard to ignore. Yet just when we think we have this God locked down, Waits offers another encounter that subverts and yet confirms that this is the same God we met before, but nothing like what we anticipated. As Robert Lloyd recounts in an interview with him, Waits responds to questions of ultimate concern with statements like "I usually have a hard time talking about things directly, you know?"[23] In so doing, he generates irony by returning a question with a question, leaving the reader/listener with a question mark and not a period. Rather than being evasive and difficult (although there is that, too), this demonstrates both a playfulness and openness to possibility rather than foreclosure and a call for certainty. That seems to be the earthiness of Jesus' ministry as well: a groundedness that demands faith to apprehend its ultimate concern. In Waits' theological reading of Scripture, the Sacred is so vivid, so tangible and so painfully attuned to our wavelengths as people who live and breathe and bleed in this world of laughter and pain, that Divinity is not merely transcendent but fully incarnate, both beautiful and flawed simultaneously.

As I look back upon my past reflections on Tom Waits' work, I come back to the world he sees and the now-and-not-yet kingdom he is singing into existence. As I have argued elsewhere about him, "Tom Waits' kingdom of God is filled with one-legged dwarves, blind dogs, drunk preachers, forgotten children, and all humanity in between. Amidst this 'audio *noir*,' no one is marginalized other than those who find solace in drawing the margins in the first place."[24] Listening and experiencing Waits' world again and again continues to prove this well, such as in the challenge found in the first line of "Sins of My Father," in which Waits sings an insightful charge to the congregation: "God said: don't give me your tin horn prayers."[25] He zeros in on those seeking religion over and against experiencing God with reckless abandon in "Come On Up To The House": "Come down off the cross / we can use the wood."[26] Only by walking away from that to which we cling for certainty and solidity can we enter into a life of faith and transcendence. In this call to come

[23] Tom Waits in Robert Lloyd, "Gone North: Tom Waits, Upcountry," in Montandon, *Innocent When You Dream*, 225.

[24] See Jeffrey F. Keuss, *Your Neighbor's Hymnal* (Eugene, OR: Cascade Books, 2011).

[25] Tom Waits, "Sins of My Father," *Real Gone* (Anti, 2004).

[26] Tom Waits, "Come On Up To The House," *Mule Variations* (Anti, 1999).

down, in leaving behind the forms that you have grown so accustomed to as the border and foundation of faith, and embracing the totality of abandon into the arms of a God who is both near yet far, can an utterance of prayer that is authentic be found. This is a vision of the apocalypse shared by Nick Cave, as well.

Nick Cave

In an interview, artist Nick Cave responded to the question of whether he thought of himself as a religious artist in this way:

> No. As a person sitting here now, no I'm not, but I do write songs and I have, over the years, I have a kind of community that I look over, which are the characters that come crawl out of my largely narrative songs. And within that environment, I think some kind of god exists and sometimes it's malevolent and sometimes it's kind and sometimes it's just there by its absence in some kind of way. But do I personally believe in a personal god? No, I don't.[27]

For Nick Cave, knowing "some kind of God" exists in his music in ways that are different from the lack of a God he experiences personally is not a hat tip to atheism. For Cave, the elusiveness of God is very real, and only in the exercise of artistic creation is this God to be found. Searching and finding this elusive God will cost us more than a proverbial pound of flesh, however. To embrace this God will cost everything, and then some. As seen and heard through Nick Cave's work, to seek and embrace God is a work of authentic praxis that is rarely private and ultimately very public, working out with fear and trembling before believers, or in the case of a rock performer, his audience. Chris Bilton, in his reflections on Nick Cave's unique form of pop celebrity, observes that "authenticity (real or perceived) is what gives power to the pop music celebrity. Cave seems to embody both aspects—conscious of his elevated state, but also intent on authenticity. . . . [P]op music is the one art form closest to a living audience, and exerts considerable personal influence simply by proximity of a live concert setting. Challenging their audiences to engage directly with the performance, and essentially becoming performers

---

[27] Nick Cave, "Nick Cave on the Death of Bunny Munro," *The Guardian* (11 September 2009), http://www.guardian.co.uk/books/audio/2009/sep/10/nick-cave-bunny-munro.

themselves. . . . [Cave] uncompromisingly challenged the very definition of performer, audience, singer, frontman, and even rock music."[28]
The very act of performance for Cave is akin to Jesus' sacramental mandate found in Luke's gospel, where the Son of God offers a beguiling
and ever-deconstructing locus for the disciples to attend to in their
devotion:

> After taking the cup, he gave thanks and said, "Take this and divide
> it among you, for I tell you I will not drink again from the fruit of
> the vine until the kingdom of God comes." And He took the bread,
> gave thanks and broke it, and gave it to them, saying, "This is my
> body given for you; do this in remembrance of me."[29]

In setting before the disciples the iconoclastic play of images that form
and rupture as the body and blood, both as the presence and absence of
the Divine, Jesus challenges the essentialist repose for those seeking to
remember the biblical Jesus as a dynamic, not static, reality only appre-
hended through imagination. This directive of Christ framed in Luke
22:19, "do this in remembrance of me," renders its meaning from the
Greek τοῦτο ποιεῖτε εἰς τὴν ἐμὴν ἀνάμνησιν, where "do this" is
etymologically based on ποιεῖτε (*poieite*) from which the word "poetry"
is derived.[30] "Make poetry in remembrance of me" is the mandate of the
soon-to-be deconstructed and risen Lord of the meal. This call for the
listener to locate the elusive God in the ever-forming and-rupturing
poetry of the sacramental meal is a call that Cave readily embraces in
his art. In his lecture entitled "The Flesh Made Word," recorded for the
BBC in 1996, Cave makes the following statement about the nature of
God as tied to the creative imagination:

> God is a product of a creative imagination and God is that imagina-
> tion taken flight. . . . Christ, who calls himself both the Son of Man
> and the Son of God as the occasion warranted, was exactly that: a
> man of flesh and blood, so in touch with the creative forces inside
> himself, so open to his brilliant flame-like imagination, that he be-
> came the physical embodiment of that force: God. . . . What Christ

---

[28] Chris Bilton, "An Audience for Antagonism," in *Cultural Seeds: Essays on the Work of Nick Cave*, ed. Karen Welberry and Tanya Dalziell (London: Ashgate, 2009), 83.

[29] Luke 22:17-19 (New International Version)

[30] For a longer exegesis of my use of *poieite*, see Jeffrey F. Keuss, *Freedom of the Self: Kenosis, Cultural Identity and Mission at the Crossroads* (Eugene, OR: Pickwick, 2010).

shows us here is that the creative imagination has the power to combat all enemies, that we are protected by the flow of our own inspiration. . . . Just as we are divine creations, so must we in turn create. Divinity must be given its freedom to flow through us, through language, through communication, through imagination. I believe this is our spiritual duty, made clear to us through the example of Christ. . . . Through us, God finds his voice, for just as we need God, he in turn needs us.[31]

For Nick Cave and Tom Waits, there is an overturning of traditional modes of apprehending the "Where is God?" question by announcing a profound reversal: to locate God is to acknowledge both the elusive presence and the absence of the Divine. In order to embrace this tension we must see and hear *through* the lens of poetic naming and unnaming, rather than the certainty of discourse. This is a tradition that Cave and Waits share with many of the mystics of the Christian tradition, as well as phenomenological theorists such as Martin Heidegger.

As noted by Martin Schäfer,[32] Martin Heidegger's discussion of art and the sacred appear together in his lectures in the winter of 1934/35, which are a close reading of the poet Friedrich Hölderlin, published as *What is Called Thinking?*[33] For Heidegger, reading Hölderlin means experiencing something completely "other" in relation to the then-modern traditions of Western thought. In his view, Hölderlin takes the risk of journeying beyond the domain of Western systematic thought and, as Heidegger puts it, to ask through his act of writing "the question that has yet to be asked." This is the famous Heideggerian notion of *Dasein* as opposed to beings, which (although indicated in pre-Socratic thinking) begins to disappear in Plato's philosophy and ultimately throughout the history of Western philosophy. According to Heidegger, this loss of the question of *Dasein* prevents humanity from *being* in the world *as being-in-the-world*; the "being there," that is *Dasein*. As a consequence, humanity not only merely inhabits "world," but views "world" as a thing which can be used and controlled, a "tool." Instead of viewing the world as tool only for prescribed purposes akin to propaganda, the crea-

---

[31] Nick Cave, "The Flesh Made Word" (BBC Radio 3 Religious Services, 1996).

[32] Martin Schäfer, "The Sacred: A Figureless Figure; On Heidegger," paper presented at the Conference on Theology and Criticism at Johns Hopkins University, March 4–7, 1999.

[33] Martin Heidegger, *What Is Called Thinking?*, trans. J. Glenn Gray (New York: Harper and Row, 1968).

tion of art in and through poetic imagination provides for Heidegger a means through which we may once again recover truth. This is what Paul Ricoeur termed "the internal relations of dependence,"[34] whereby art releases us into a truth without the screen of theories and arguments that cloud out and distract us from a depth and height of our true nature as created in the *Imago Dei*, allowing a recasting of the world into a transformed "possible" world worth living into. This is the "true fiction" of art and the "worlding of worlds" that both Waits and Cave compel the listener to enter into, a world that at times is freakish and disturbing, where God is unbridled and absolutely free and where there is no hiding place from grace, beauty, sorrows, or love in all its various forms and content.

This, in a nutshell, is the priestly act of the rock artist, propelling the listener into an unselfish, forgetful repose that is free from the synthetic and the constrained and to the place where the Sacred resides and is posited beyond one's own control. Here the possibility of *Dasein*'s authenticity can be experienced: the positing of the simple fact that there is *something* rather than *nothing* allows for the possibility of *being*. The sacred is then the realm where things have come wholly back into their truest self in a form of deep authenticity and abandon. Ultimately, the artist presents art and the song, the painting, the poem will become for us the foundry for transformation, a workshop within which purpose and meaning can and does reside, and the writer/poet/rock singer, in naming the space, is the founder and framer of meaning.

This is also true for both Nick Cave and Tom Waits as they wrestle with their role as poets who are responsible for having faith in the presence and absence of the Divine. Tom Waits performs this priestly act in his song "Down in the Hole."[35] Here, Waits takes on the role of the fire and brimstone preacher affirming the clear demarcation between salvation resting in the presence and providence of Jesus and the damnation that comes with Satan:

> When you walk through the garden
> you gotta watch your back
> well I beg your pardon
> walk the straight and narrow track

---

[34] See Paul Ricoeur, *Hermeneutics and the Human Sciences* (Cambridge: Cambridge University Press, 1981), 182ff.

[35] Tom Waits, "Down in the Hole," *Frank's Wild Years* (Island, 1990).

> if you walk with Jesus
> he's gonna save your soul
> you gotta keep the devil
> way down in the hole
> he's got the fire and the fury
> at his command
> well you don't have to worry
> if you hold on to Jesus' hand
> we'll all be safe from Satan
> when the thunder rolls
> just gotta help me keep the devil
> way down in the hole
> All the angels sing about Jesus' mighty sword
> and they'll shield you with their wings
> and keep you close to the lord
> don't pay heed to temptation
> for his hands are so cold
> you gotta help me keep the devil
> way down in the hole.

As the preacher, Waits acknowledges the palpable reality of God and figures this God within classic language from Christian tradition that has resonance with both theological understandings and poetic imaginations of angelic struggle from Dante to John Milton to Frank Peretti to the *Left Behind* series. Yet Waits also sings of the reality we see around us of the elusive absence of God, as he does poignantly in "God's Away on Business":[36]

> The ship is sinking
> The ship is sinking
> The ship is sinking
> There's leak, there's leak,
> In the boiler room
> The poor, the lame, the blind
> Who are the ones that we kept in charge?
> Killers, thieves, and lawyers
>
> God's away, God's away,
> God's away on Business. Business.
> God's away, God's away,
> God's away on Business. Business.

---

[36] Tom Waits, "God's Away On Business," *Blood Money* (Anti, 2002).

Where is God in Tom Waits' universe? He is both present and "away on business" at the same time. God is both at work finding evil to defeat and seemingly indifferent to the very same suffering. This both/and of God's elusive nature as here and not here draws the listener into a deep and necessary dissonance whereby locating God in Waits' conception is never predictable or convenient.

As noted in the collection titled *Nick Cave Stories*,[37] there is a description of "The Exhibition" which was created and installed by the Arts Centre in Melbourne, Australia from 2007 to 2009. Part of the travelling exhibition includes an open Bible where Nick Cave has written "why is faith essential to eternal life, why the need to believe?" over chapter 17 in the Gospel of John, which is the last of the four chapters where Jesus teaches the disciples after the institution of the Last Supper. The importance of faith for Cave is evident throughout his work, an ever-seeking, finding and losing again of the one that is "hiding all away." Yet this elusiveness means that faith as a poetry-making praxis is the only mode by which we can apprehend the Sacred.

Another example comes from not merely alluding to how God is framed by culture, but by subverting and subsequently enlivening sacred texts themselves. Nick Cave was commissioned to offer an introduction to the Gospel of Mark for a series that the Glasgow-based publisher Canongate released in 1998. In his introduction, Cave notes the role that creativity plays in understanding and apprehending the Christ portrayed by the gospel writers as one who calls humanity to an imaginative repose that frees the God found in scripture "to fly" rather than merely laying down to die:

> The Christ that emerges from Mark, tramping through the haphazard events of His life, had a ringing intensity about him that I could not resist. Christ spoke to me through His isolation, through the burden of His death, through His rage at the mundane, through His sorrow. Christ, it seemed to me was the victim of humanity's lack of imagination, was hammered to the cross with the nails of creative vapidity. . . . Christ understood that we as humans were forever held to the ground by the pull of gravity—our ordinariness, our mediocrity—and it was through His example that He gave our imaginations the freedom to fly.[38]

[37] Nick Cave, "The Exhibition," as noted in *Nick Cave Stories* (Melbourne, Australia: Victorian Arts Centre Trust, 2007).

[38] Nick Cave, "Introduction to the Gospel according to Mark," in *The Gospel of Mark* (London: Canongate, 1998), xi.

Moreover, he makes the point in his lecture "The Flesh Made Word" that what Christ embodies is the purity of imagination itself, and this is what humanity has lost and it is imagination that ultimately would cost Christ his life:

> He came with the gift of language, or love, of imagination. Said Jesus, in the Gospel of John, "The words that I speak unto you, they are spirit and they are life" [John 6:63], and it is these words, His language, the logos, that sings so eloquently and mysteriously from the Gospels. Christ is the imagination, at times terrible, irrational, incendiary and beautiful.[39]

Cave and Waits share this vision whereby God is ultimately acknowledged and embraced in a collapsing of seemingly opposing descriptors—terrible, irrational, incendiary, beautiful— into a singular yet multivalent Holy God that offers an apocalyptic totality and surplus of meaning that only imaginative performativity can begin to see, touch, taste, and hear.

For Cave and Waits, like Heidegger, form itself dissolves in their compositions into both a positivity and negativity where that which was embodied is dispersed into and throughout the conceptual in ways that draws the listener into the presence of the transcendent. Here one can think of the second chapter of Luke's gospel where Zechariah, standing before the angel Gabriel, is stunned into silence for months, his form of religious knowing dissolved in a theophany, the in-breaking of the Divine into mundane life. Zechariah's tradition mandated that the son to be born must be named after the father, yet the messenger of God has given him a (w)hol(l)y other name that breaks with every expectation—John— and is announced not in discursive apologetics *per se* but in exaltation akin to the opening anthem of a rock show, where Zechariah the priest becomes the lead singer for the theophany at hand, announcing both the end of his legacy—not naming his son after himself—and the future that will unname him in the act of naming. By naming John, Zechariah loses his silence and begins to speak again, yet in speaking the name instructed by the Divine, his name is forever silenced so that the future may happen through the ministry of John.

Like Zechariah's stunned silence, Heidegger finds in this silence of the sacred (or rather "sacred silence") a *mourning* of language, which is

---

[39] Nick Cave, "The Flesh Made Word," in *King Ink II* (London: Black Spring, 1997), 140–41.

also the mourning "of" the Sacred (in the double sense of the genitive case) through Hölderlin's mourning for the vanished gods of ancient Greece and Christianity. According to Heidegger, this act of mourning will never be accomplished as a Freudian work of mourning which overcomes its lost object. Neither will this mourning lose itself by clinging to this object in a melancholic fashion. As with Nick Cave shouting a triumphant "I've been hiding all away," and Tom Waits declaring like a Southern carnival barker that "God's away on business," Heidegger presents the act of sacred mourning as the act of letting the vanished gods become what they always have been: vanished. True and authentic art like Cave and Waits' music keeps a sacred space open in which God could indeed show up and for many fans often does. It is ironic that Waits is much more reticent to acknowledge the place of God in his work than Cave is, especially in the commentary provided by Cave noting his troubling relationship with figuring and experiencing the Sacred, and yet Waits offers the stronger evidence of faith in this God that cannot be fully named. For Heidegger, the Sacred is the transcendental spacing in which epiphany could happen without being produced by human will. The Sacred therefore signifies the absence of religion without offering a new one. The elusive God is the known in absence or failure of the name, never a metaphor or a trope, which a writer would be able to create, let alone master.

In this way, Heidegger allows for and provokes gaps and fracture that are readily exposed. But where is wholeness then to come from? For Heidegger, this is the space that awaits the coming of the Sacred and the call to the subject to come alive in the Divine presence that is both near and far. This is what I believe Tom Waits and Nick Cave allude to in their music by "repentance" within the context of music. Repentance is the return to authentic being (*metanoia*) through a waiting amid the fissure opened for and through the sacred. It is a place destabilizing of context and character and ultimately a turning toward the "possible." It is a place where language fails to fix certainty and its power to name is lost. Yet this is not something to be named, only marked by "unalterable longings." It is the true artist who stands in this troubling gap of meaning that is both found and lost, never to be fixed or locked down but always on the move. Rather than close this fissure by trying to dominate or control meaning by naming God into certitude and therefore away from the active repose of faith, the musician's true vocation is to prevent such closure upon meaning and truth by continually reopening this sacred space through the making of art anew that always points over the next horizon and calls after God again and again and again as if it is the first time and the last time. In *The Origin of the Work of Art*, written at the same time as his lectures on Hölderlin, Heidegger uses a word for this openness of sacred space that is opened up by the shock of *Dichtung* or "Truth" as being a *Gestalt* or "figuring." The *Gestalt* of the sacred is never there but always a trace to withdraw and at the same time a shock to come. It is *the gift of form* rather than the Nietzschean *power to form*. The Heideggerian figuring of the sacred, though hidden, is an imprint or type that draws the line separating that which remains whole before the holy from that which becomes scattered in everyday life which is the profane. A withdrawal and retreat of the figurative in language, of its metaphors and tropes, is a sign of the sacred, and at the same time this withdrawal retraces the original figure as the *Gestalt—the opening beyond naming for the Sacred to arise*. Heidegger uses a poetic term to describe this—the call of a *sanfter Wahnsinn* or a "gentle madness."[40] This madness is madness because it sweeps language away by its own destructive power of naming and unnaming in order to free meaning from sign and symbol alike.

When both Waits and Cave throw themselves on the fires of their performance, setting aflame the language and intention of naming, it is a madness *par excellence*. And yet this madness is gentle because in sweeping language away, it also affects the gathering of language in poetic naming. It acknowledges that our feeble attempts to approach and embrace that which is beyond our grasp is not the folly of fools, but the humble call of the broken-hearted drunk, the lame and groping failure, the lost lover, and the ecstatic prince alike who are willing to leave control and certainty behind in the face of grace beyond grace, love beyond love. Perhaps this is the character not only of madness but of devotion and faith in God as well. The gentle madness that both Cave and Waits exhibit throughout their art in the performativity of their over-the-top personas, which hush and scream after God with banging chains, pounding guitars and images of saints and sinners alike, is a call to not merely listen, but to believe such a world and such a God is awaiting us although perhaps "hiding all away." To this gentle madness both Cave and Waits await any and all who wish to sing, dance, stomp their feet, and shed a tear before the God they both cannot name and yet cannot deny.

---

[40] Schäfer, "The Sacred: A Figureless Figure; On Heidegger." See also lecture IX in Martin Heidegger, *What is Called Thinking?*, 88ff.

Contributors

Tom Beaudoin is associate professor of theology in the Graduate School of Religion at Fordham University in New York City, and his research focuses on spiritual and secular practices in the contemporary world. He is the author of three books, including *Witness to Dispossession: The Vocation of a Postmodern Theologian*, and also directs the Rock and Theology project for Liturgical Press, where theologians who are also practicing musicians and fans write about the relationship between religion and popular music. He is president-elect of the Association of Practical Theology and plays bass guitar for two New York rock bands.

David Dault is the host of the radio show *Things Not Seen: Conversations about Culture and Faith*. From 1993 to 2004 he was a touring musician and songwriter. His scholarly work focuses on the cultural history of Bible publication, and he has been part of the faculty of religion departments at American Baptist College in Nashville and Christian Brothers University in Memphis. He currently lives with his family in Chicago.

Michael Iafrate is a theologian and songwriter from West Virginia and a doctoral candidate in theology at the University of St. Michael's College at the University of Toronto. His theological interests include liberation theologies, ecclesiologies, theology and popular music, religion and social movements, and Appalachian studies. He has been active in independent music circles for about twenty years in such bands as The Minus Tide and M Iafrate & The Priesthood, and he will release two new records, *Christian Burial* and *Nonsubstantiation*, in 2013. His website is www.michaeliafrate.com.

Maeve Louise Heaney is from Dublin, Ireland, and is a consecrated member of a Catholic institute of consecrated life, the Verbum Dei Missionary Fraternity. A musician and composer, she also teaches systematic theology, with a particular focus on the areas of theological aesthetics and music. She is visiting adjunct professor at the San Pablo Instituto de Teología, Madrid, and will be taking a position on the faculty of theology at the Banyo Campus of Australian Catholic University in Brisbane.

167

Jeff Keuss is a professor and director of the University Scholars program at Seattle Pacific University. Prior to coming to SPU, he served as a professor and director for the Centre of Literature, Theology and the Arts in the School of Divinity at University of Glasgow, Scotland. He has published articles, chapters, and reviews on the interdisciplinary engagement of theology, literature, and contemporary culture and is the North American general editor for the journal *Literature and Theology* and on the advisory board for *The Other Journal*. He is the author of *A Poetics of Jesus: The Search for Christ through Writing in the Nineteenth Century*; *The Sacred and the Profane: Contemporary Issues in Hermeneutics*; *Freedom of the Self: Kenosis, Cultural Identity and Mission at the Crossroads*, and *Your Neighbor's Hymnal: What Popular Music Can Teach Us about Faith, Hope and Love*. He is a regular blogger on his personal web site, jeffkeuss.com.

Mary McDonough has a law degree and worked as a Legal Aid lawyer. She returned to school to study theology, earning her PhD in ethics from the Graduate Theological Union where she was affiliated with the Jesuit School. She has been a visiting scholar at The Hastings Center, has taught ethics as an adjunct professor, and is the author of *Can a Health Care Market Be Moral? A Catholic Vision*. Her research interests include bioethics and the relationship between ethics, law, and the arts. She is also an avid guitar player.

Gina Messina-Dysert is dean of the School of Graduate and Professional Studies at Ursuline College and cofounder of Feminism and Religion. She has authored multiple articles and the forthcoming book *Rape Culture and Spiritual Violence*. Messina-Dysert is also coeditor (with Rosemary Radford Ruether) of the forthcoming anthology *Feminism and Religion in the 21st Century*. Her research interests are theologically and ethically driven, involve a feminist and interdisciplinary approach, and are influenced by her activist roots and experience working with survivors of rape and domestic violence.

Christian Scharen teaches worship and practical theology at Luther Seminary in Saint Paul, Minnesota, having previously taught at Yale University Divinity School. Trained in theological ethics, ethnography, and social theory, Scharen brings a lively Christian imagination to critical engagement with culture. His writings have appeared in *The Cresset, Books & Culture, The Christian Century, Dialog, Generate*, and other publications. He is married to Sonja, a nurse-midwife, and has two children, Isaiah and Grace. He loves old churches, *A Prairie Home Companion* (a must for Lutherans in diaspora), and dark beer.

Myles Werntz is postdoctoral fellow in theology and ethics at Baylor University. He is the coeditor of two volumes of posthumous work of John Howard Yoder— *Nonviolence: A Brief History* and *Revolutionary Christianity*—as well as essays on Yoder, Dorothy Day, and twentieth-century ecclesiology. He is the coeditor of *Corners in the City of God: Theology, Philosophy and* The Wire.

Daniel White Hodge is the director of the Center for Youth Ministry Studies and assistant professor of youth ministry at North Park University. He teaches classes around the world on subjects such as black popular culture, personality and the self, hip-hop discourse, and race/ethnicity within religion. He is the author of *Heaven Has a Ghetto: The Missiological Gospel and Theology of Tupac Amaru Shakur* and *The Soul of Hip Hop: Rims, Timbs, and a Cultural Theology.* He is currently working on a book titled *The Hostile Gospel: Finding Religion in the Post-Soul Theology of Hip Hop.*